DATE DUE

BRODART, CO.

Cat. No. 23-221

Twilight of the Republic

TWILIGHT
OF THE
REPUBLIC

*Empire and Exceptionalism
in the American Political Tradition*

JUSTIN B. LITKE

UNIVERSITY PRESS OF KENTUCKY

Scholarly publisher for the Commonwealth,
serving Bellarmine University, Berea College, Centre College of Kentucky,
Eastern Kentucky University, The Filson Historical Society, Georgetown College,
Kentucky Historical Society, Kentucky State University, Morehead State University,
Murray State University, Northern Kentucky University, Transylvania University,
University of Kentucky, University of Louisville, and Western Kentucky
University.
All rights reserved.

Editorial and Sales Offices: The University Press of Kentucky
663 South Limestone Street, Lexington, Kentucky 40508-4008
www.kentuckypress.com

17 16 15 14 13   5 4 3 2 1

Library of Congress Cataloging-in-Publication Data

Litke, Justin B., 1984-
  Twilight of the republic : empire and exceptionalism in the American political
tradition / Justin B. Litke.
      pages cm
  Includes bibliographical references and index.
  ISBN 978-0-8131-4220-3 (hardcover : alk. paper) — ISBN 978-0-8131-4222-7 (epub) —
  ISBN 978-0-8131-4221-0 (pdf)
  1. Exceptionalism—United States—History. 2. National characteristics,
American—History. 3. Political culture—United States—History. I. Title.
  E169.1.L56 2013
  306.20973—dc23   2013010407

This book is printed on acid-free paper meeting the requirements of the American
National Standard for Permanence in Paper for Printed Library Materials.

Manufactured in the United States of America.

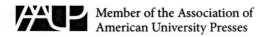 Member of the Association of
American University Presses

To Sarah

He hath not dealt so with every nation, neither have they known his judgments.

—Psalm 147:20

No more can I think of Port William and the United States in the same thought. A nation is an idea, and Port William is not. Maybe there is no live connection between a little place and a big idea. I think there is not.

—Jayber Crow

What you have as heritage,
Take now as task;
For thus you will make it your own!

—Johann Wolfgang von Goethe

CONTENTS

Introduction   1

1. The Problem of American Exceptionalism   5

2. John Winthrop: A Divinely Sanctioned, Practically Circumscribed Colony   23

3. The Founders: A Providentially Guided, Temporally Bound Country   53

4. Abraham Lincoln: An Ideally United, Potentially Unbound Union   85

5. Albert Beveridge: A Racially Defined, Imperially Aimed Nation   115

Conclusion: The Possibility of a New and Traditional American Political Order   145

Acknowledgments   155

Notes   157

Bibliography   195

Index   207

INTRODUCTION

What happens if a country's worldview is radically changed? If the particular priorities and traditions that informed the life of a people are laid aside, something has to fill the void. New ones are taken up and a new worldview is formed. But what if the changes happen slowly and subtly? What if the changes, once in place, are no longer recognized as changes? The traditions, priorities, actions, and words that formerly characterized that country and that people will live on in documents and monuments, but not in the lives of citizens. In other words, the vital elements of the people's self-conception will be all but lost. The now-changed state of things will be taken for granted. A new self-conception will be arrayed against the original one. This people will act differently but will still try to speak the same. The old, traditional words are spoken, but they are accompanied by new behaviors. Because the same words are used, the new worldview continues be shaped by the old one, but it will be as new wine in old wineskins. The new ways of acting and being will eventually burst the old wineskins and both the wine and the skins will be lost. The people will no longer be who they are and will have forgotten who they were.

This is America today. From colonial times up to the turn of the twentieth century, the country's particular way of acting both domestically and in foreign affairs was fairly circumscribed and inwardly focused. It was a robust, lived political tradition. But over the same period, new self-conceptions and ways of acting entered into American political life, and these gradually changed the meaning of the principal words and symbols used to articulate, interpret, and understand the American political tradition. The words that formerly led Americans to think of themselves in one way now lead them to think and act in thoroughly different ways. The same words from the Constitution, the Declaration of Independence, and seminal colonial documents have come to mean things very different from before. What is more, most citizens today cannot see the change *as* a change because they are unaware of the tradition as it previously existed. The result has been a great confusion about what constitutes the American political tradition and a consequently decreasing coherence in debates on the role of America in the world and the role of the government in Americans' lives at home. We are at odds with ourselves and we do not know why.

Today America is highly assertive in foreign affairs and highly centralized in its domestic life. American domestic politics is increasingly characterized by populist appeals for solutions from the center—Washington —and it takes only a passing familiarity with the ideals of the framers of the Constitution to realize how far we have fallen from their republican aspirations. A change has happened, yet some think this change justified.

Perhaps, so goes the argument, today's geopolitical situation demands a political theory and self-understanding that go beyond the scope of republicanism. Republicanism and an older style of representative government may not meet the challenges we face today. Perhaps the world cannot long remain stable without America's ubiquity in commercial, political, and military affairs. Perhaps a retrenchment into the more circumscribed mode of American politics would mean that today's American way of life—relatively dominant and powerful abroad, relatively affluent and peaceful at home— would end. Political problems today are Big Problems. We cannot go back or become more naïve, it might be said.

Adopting this view is tempting, but it should by no means be our final word. The persistent principles of American politics have a long and rich history, born of centuries of self-government and reflection. Mere expediency should not overshadow these principles. Who are we as a people? What does it mean to be an American? What is the particularly American understanding of politics? These questions and answers are given by the symbols and myths of our tradition, fashioned out of materials inherited from Western civilization. But today these symbols are unfamiliar to many. If we are currently at odds with ourselves, if we currently lack a coherent account of politics, and if we wish to see with fresh eyes the nature of the American political tradition, a reassessment of those symbols is in order.

In studying the foundations of the American political tradition and in measuring the figurative distance between today's America and yesterday's, we gain an even better perspective on the republican crisis confronting us. This crisis is manifest in a decreased ability of Americans to participate in their own governance and an increased perception of the need for top-down solutions both at home and abroad. The "mass politics" warned against in the wake of the Second World War has largely come to pass.[1]

We stand at a fork in the road. Whether we remain on our current path—which leads farther and farther away from the American political tradition *as it was* even as we pay lip service to that tradition and its founders—will be known only in time. If we are to resist the inertia of the present moment and actively choose a better way ahead, the best first step is a reflective inquiry into the nature of the American political tradition. We must have a ready and plausible answer to the more theoretical and reflective question, Who are we as a people, as Americans? before we can have an answer to the practical question, Where do we go from here? This inquiry can only begin to answer the former question and, properly, seeks to leave the latter one to all citizens. Madison, among others, feared the consequences of imperialism abroad on self-government at home. Tocqueville, among others, foresaw the possible future temptation of Americans to prefer an "equality in servitude to inequality in liberty." But if republicanism is still the aim of American politics, we need to take a long look into the mirror of our own political tradition, to regain a sense of who we are as a country and as a people, and to begin living up to the high examples of our past.

Upon such an examination and reflection, we are able to see that a great shift occurred around the turn of the twentieth century. America began to behave differently from before, evincing a new way Americans thought of themselves. It was a shift of paramount significance because of the way it fundamentally changed domestic policy, foreign policy, the way federal agencies and state governments work, and even the way individual citizens interact with each other and with all levels of government. This change, decades and centuries in the making, came to fruition in the invasion and annexation of the Philippines, Hawaii, and Cuba. Whether or not you believe that the advent of imperial politics is a problem, the shift took place. Explaining why and how that shift occurred is part of the work of this book. While full isolation of its exact causes is not possible, the principal elements of the change—largely in Americans' self-conception—can be discerned.

When we act, we usually speak and give context, justification, and shape to those actions. Our contextualizations and justifications suggest—sometimes inchoately, sometimes more systematically and explicitly—something about our own nature and character. It is just so with American laws, constitutions, and other government action. The way Americans think and act politically today and the way we have thought and acted throughout our history, from the early colonists onward, is linked with the picture we have of ourselves as a people. This is where the term *American exceptionalism* usually enters into discussions of policy, law, and history, often confusing rather than clarifying any controversies. It need not be this way.

The idea of American exceptionalism, in one version or another, is almost always employed in arguments advocating or rejecting a particular course of political action. Because of this, the meaning of the term has immediate practical significance. What you say about American exceptionalism governs what can rightly be said about the propriety of a certain political act. Yet the theoretical significance of the term is also great, closely linked as it is to the definition and meaning of Americans' self-conception. In this one term, then, practical, theoretical, and historical significance converge. Identifying the principal elements of this term as an idea and as a phenomenon will explain the shift to a decidedly imperial politics in American thought and action. Doing so will give a fresh view of the colonial, founding, Civil War, and Progressive periods in American history, but it will also have a more than scholarly significance. Republicans of every age have recognized that a people cut off from their history will not long persist in self-government. In this regard America is in dire straits. The country stands at a twilight point in its history, a moment when not all light has left the land but that possibility is heavily felt.

At the present moment (as ever), the fate of the republic relies on the reappropriation of the American political tradition through the review and renewal of the citizenry's understanding of it. Those who agree that it is unbecoming of a free people to assume direct political power over another people will find that their views are supported by a long, lived political tradition in America. This is one way Americans have traditionally thought of themselves—and it enjoyed a long and lengthy period as their operative self-conception. This tradition is not, however, very widely held today; this book is aimed at arresting the current moment's momentum and reinvigorating the tradition that once led people the world over to envy the American political order. Even those who see this imperial shift as unproblematic will benefit from a deeper understanding of the manner in which it came about. Whether or not the shift in American political thought and action from a largely decentralized and republican polity to a highly centralized, imperial one is permanent will be known only in time. But it is my hope that this study can help to turn the tide by renewing our acquaintance with who we are, who we have been, and who we might be. The present moment of twilight precedes either a new dawn or the final dusk of republicanism in America. Which one follows depends on us.

1

THE PROBLEM OF AMERICAN EXCEPTIONALISM

Wide and seemingly interminable disagreements are prominently on display nearly any time the words *American exceptionalism* are uttered. They are today a shorthand for the popular view that America is not subject to criticism or constraint—at least not beyond any very minimal level. Those who "support" American exceptionalism often critique the idea's opponents as unpatriotic and un-American. Yet those who oppose American exceptionalism in this way are difficult to identify.[1] Chief among current opponents of American exceptionalism is, it is said, President Barack Obama, who in his first trip abroad as president espoused a number of equivocal senses of the term simultaneously.[2] If he is genuinely confused about the precise meaning of the term, the president is far from alone.

The question of American exceptionalism has perplexed historians and social scientists for over a century. Part of the confusion arises from the various meanings of the term, though even when there is agreement on the term's meaning this has not assured similar conclusions about its underlying causes. For a hundred years the scholarship on the topic has mainly focused on finding what lies at the root of America's uniqueness.[3] Some have argued that it is America's lack of a feudal past that sets it apart—along with the Lockean liberal consensus that follows from this.[4] Others have said it is America's unique foundation in, or aversion to, philosophical politics.[5] Some have argued that it is America's unique cultural heritage of liberty, egalitarianism, individualism, populism, and laissez-faire that explains the difference.[6] American uniqueness has been attributed to its unique political system, particularly its federal structure.[7] Still others have claimed American exceptionalism is due to the place of the frontier in American life, or America's unique economic circumstances— whether it is the character and history of organized labor, the early advent of universal white manhood suffrage, the degree of upward mobility, or the abundance of job and business opportunities and American natural resources.[8] But uniqueness can be taken in a number of different ways, a point I will amplify later. There is, to say the least, little consensus on either the nature or the causes of American exceptionalism. Many social scientists argue that America is indeed an exceptional country, though the notion is not held universally in academe; numerous historians have come to deny the claim.[9] Many of these authors silently suggest that the idea of American exceptionalism is uncomplicated, since very few discuss their particular meaning in using the term. That the numerous articles and monographs on the subject do not seem to engage one another, however, suggests a reason that the use of the term, and the ensuing debate, is largely uncritical.

Nearly all this scholarship to date contains an important common thread. On core methodological considerations, even critics of American exceptionalism seem to agree with exceptionalist proponents. All of these scholars understand the term *American exceptionalism* to be a claim in the idiom of comparative political science or comparative history. At the core of the term, it is thought, American exceptionalism means that there is either some standard from which America deviates—perhaps one provided by a historical ideology such as Marxism—or that America deviates from an empirical pattern set by similar countries—as with America's high rates of imprisonment, and so on. These scholars' primarily comparative tack means that the question of American exceptionalism is usually taken to be an empirical one, answerable by survey analysis and the cataloging of various other measurable phenomena. Though the scholarship is fairly unified on this point, scholars' resulting accounts intersect little or not at all. Their methodological unity appears to be their only point of unity. Their conclusions are as diverse as the data they use. Some have tried to account for and move beyond these impasses, though with little success. Because of this, a new way of moving forward is needed. The new way forward should not partake of the same basic assumptions as these accounts, because a similar inconclusiveness is likely to be the result. Rather than social science or comparative history, there can be a new way forward through political theory. But, for reasons of both ideology and scholarly interest, other ways and methods have predominated.

Werner Sombart and Marxist Theories of History

The term *American exceptionalism* is a relatively recent one, born out of the twentieth-century confrontation of communist thought with American persistence in capitalism.[10] Growing adherence to Marxist theories of history led many observers to look forward to the day when America, at the forefront of capitalism on the eve of the twentieth century, would lead the world into the age of global socialism and communism. It was a matter of time only, so the theory went, until America's highly advanced capitalist economy would foment the revolution of the proletariat and take the first steps toward a worldwide communist order. Yet in the early years of the twentieth century, impatience began to build, leading to inquiry. In 1906 the German academic Werner Sombart published *Why Is There No Socialism in the United States?*, a short book that essentially answers its title as a trick question. At the end of the work Sombart says, in effect, "Be patient. There will be soon."[11] If Sombart was not convinced of the radical difference between the American case and others, his book nonetheless became the touchstone for a long (and ongoing) exploration of the topic. Much of the scholarly literature on American exceptionalism is centered on the question of America's unique economic history, mechanisms, and policies. The permeability of economic classes, or the lack of economic classes at all, the causes for failure of the various socialist activists, and even the famous theoretical arguments of Louis Hartz all have their origins in thoughts similar to those Sombart penned at the dawn of the twentieth century.[12]

The orientation toward Marxist-style history has been one of the most enduring features of the scholarship on American exceptionalism. By this I mean precisely the manner in which Hartz uses Europe as a touchstone in studying America. The approach is comparative at the deepest level, and the heart of it is a presumption that history follows a particular, determined course that may be discerned by examining Europe. Cognizance of this fact about the scholarship brings out important questions of methodology that should be addressed: what has been the relationship between Marxist theories of history and the questions asked, methods used, and answers found in the social sciences regarding American exceptionalism? If Marxist-style theories of history have indeed provided guidance to the social sciences, then might there be certain phenomena or factors that have been overlooked because they lie outside Marxism's criteria of relevance?[13] If Marxist theories of history have indeed provided guidance to the social sciences, then what might fill the void now that they are increasingly displaced? Because most scholars seem to take for granted that their own use of the term *American exceptionalism* is, unproblematically, the same as others' usage, there have been only a few accounts of the possible range of meanings of the term. To begin an answer to these questions, those accounts need to be considered.

The Two Main Senses of *American Exceptionalism*

There are today two main senses of *American exceptionalism* as the term is usually used; they divide according to the degree to which each includes a comparative aspect. The sense of the term that is primarily and mainly comparative is the sense in which social scientists most often use it. The other main sense of the term is only secondarily comparative and can be called the sense of American uniqueness, or "unique" American exceptionalism.[14]

The "comparative" sense of American exceptionalism is found primarily in social science, though some historians and political theorists can also be placed in this camp. Often, the use of this comparative sense means that a normal pattern has been established in some way—whether through scientific research and induction or through ideology—and that a particularly notable case, that is, America, deviates from this normal pattern. This sense is primarily comparative because its meaning derives from a comparison with other, similar things; a sense of uniqueness is only secondarily comparative because setting something out as unique, though still having reference to other things, requires comparison in only a secondary or derivative way.

The comparative sense is illustrated well in many of the essays found in Peter H. Schuck and James Q. Wilson's *Understanding America: The Anatomy of an Exceptional Nation*. In essay after essay, one particular American institution, aspect of culture, or public policy is established as the exception from a dominant, usually international, pattern. But the sense employed by social and political scientists is not the only "comparative" sense of *American exceptionalism*. Historians and political theorists can also understand the term in this way: the Marxist ideological interpretation of history sets a "normal" pattern from which the U.S. case deviates. The normal pattern is the historical progression described by Marx: from simple society through feudalism and capitalism to socialism and communism. In comparing this pattern with the American case, a deep contradiction was felt. This is a comparison of the United States against an established pattern, but the pattern is established here by ideology rather than scientific induction. As a rule, authors hewing to the comparative sense are seeking predictive power, whether because they are trying to support their own social scientific theory or findings or because they wish to marshal support for an existing theory or ideology.[15] Thus the comparative sense of American exceptionalism need not be methodologically empirical, though it is often so.

The other main sense of the term *American exceptionalism* I will call the "unique" sense. This sense, too, has a comparative aspect, but it is only secondary. Usually employed by political actors or more humanistic scholars, this sense of the term often has connotations of idiosyncrasy or praise or has roots in religious thought. And though the comparative sense of the term is not wholly without policy implications, it is usually this second "unique" sense that is employed to persuade others to a particular course of political action.

There are three main "subsenses" under this unique sense. The first is epitomized by John Winthrop. The first resident governor of the Massachusetts Bay Colony is often associated with the idea of American exceptionalism. Though much more will be said to evaluate such claims in chapter 2, here we can anticipate the findings of that chapter by categorizing his claim—and any others like it—as the "exemplary" sense of American exceptionalism. Rather than primarily generating an exception to a pattern, Winthrop calls on the colonists to set a pattern by responding to God's call to live lives of high Christian virtue. This sense is somewhat comparative because it is defined with a limited and secondary reference to other peoples. But the meaning of the term is mainly to pick out America—or in this case, the colony at Massachusetts Bay—as unique. God, after all, has chosen the colonists "from among the nations."

Uniqueness is also the focus and primary meaning when Alexis de Tocqueville—said to be the one to coin the term—speaks of the "exceptional" position of the Americans. He makes the claim throughout his 1835 masterpiece, *Democracy in America*, often when discussing the unique origins of American institutions and cultural patterns. This is also the sense in which the authors of the *Federalist* can be called American exceptionalists, which will be discussed more fully in chapter 3. Together, Tocqueville and the *Federalist* could be called institutional or cultural exceptionalists.

With Tocqueville and Winthrop we see that the "unique" sense of American exceptionalism is closely tied to religion, unlike the "comparative" sense. This is true, too, of the main sense in which unique American exceptionalism is most often employed in contemporary political arguments. Under a third subsense of unique American exceptionalism, America is supposed to have a mission to civilize, educate, or otherwise dominate the world politically or economically. This sense—"imperial" American exceptionalism—surfaces recognizably for the first time at the turn of the twentieth century when the United States attacked, annexed, or took possession of Cuba, the Philippines, Hawaii, and other territories. This is the main sense in which the idea of American exceptionalism is politically operative and the sense that is of the greatest practical consequence.[16]

In sum, for the purposes of this project there are two main senses of the term *American exceptionalism*: "comparative" and "unique." The comparative sense includes both empirical and ideological meanings of the term; the unique sense includes exemplary exceptionalism, cultural exceptionalism, and imperial exceptionalism. The last sense, imperial exceptionalism, is my primary focus.[17]

THE COMPARATIVE SENSE OF THE TERM AMERICAN EXCEPTIONALISM

Though he is far from alone, Seymour Martin Lipset is perhaps the best known of the authors claiming that the oldest use of the term *American exceptionalism* is found in Tocqueville's *Democracy in America*. Lipset argues the point explicitly at the outset of his book *American Exceptionalism: A Double-Edged Sword*.[18] In short, Lipset says explicitly that Tocqueville pioneered the claim in one particular sentence in *Democracy in America*. Lipset's argument is problematic, perhaps most fundamentally because Lipset assumes that Tocqueville's claim is the first in a scholarly field that was yet to be fully developed in Tocqueville's day: contemporary political science. Because of this, Lipset does not defend the propriety of his own comparative sense of the term *American exceptionalism* or his comparative approach; he simply takes it for granted.[19] This reading of Tocqueville serves as the foundation of Lipset's entire book, which contains chapters that compare the United States, in turns, with Canada and Japan; the analysis of the other chapters involves more cursory comparisons, though maintaining the deeply comparative approach. There is much at stake, however, in his glancing interpretation of Tocqueville. If he is mistaken, then his method and findings are open to doubt, along with those of numerous other authors who have written on the topic from the same comparative, scientific perspective.[20]

A short examination of the passage Lipset uses to justify his approach, in fact, belies the claim as he has made it. Neither in the edition to which Lipset refers nor in any of the other major English editions of *Democracy in America* is the particular term *American exceptionalism* used to translate Tocqueville's words.[21] The point seems a small one when it is noted that the original French does not lend itself to translation with that two-word term: "La situation des Américains est donc entièrement exceptionelle, et il est à croire qu'aucun peuple démocratique n'y sera jamais place."[22] Because of this, any critique of Lipset should perhaps be moderate. It might be asked, however, why Lipset so explicitly asserts that Tocqueville coined the term, and in that particular passage. The ambiguity of Lipset's writing and citation suggest, perhaps, that he did not have in mind the attribution to Tocqueville of the strict invention and definition of the two-word term *American exceptionalism*. Rather, Lipset may have only been suggesting that Tocqueville's work as a whole stands for the claim that America is an exception to the general state of world democracies; perhaps, he would say in his defense, the particular passage points this up in a particularly direct manner. Lipset would, then, not be citing Tocqueville's particular passage as the one needful piece of evidence but citing, by way of an example, a passage that is representative of the whole text. Certainly the English edition used by Lipset suggests this much: "The position of the Americans is therefore quite exceptional, and it may be believed that no democratic people will ever be placed in a similar one." Tocqueville goes on to list several major traits of American life and history that seem highly unlikely ever to occur again:

> Their strictly Puritanical origin, their exclusively commercial habits, even the country they inhabit, which seems to divert their minds from the pursuit of science, literature, and the arts, the proximity of Europe, which allows them to neglect these pursuits without relapsing into barbarism, a thousand special causes, of which I have only been able to point out the most important, have singularly concurred to fix the mind of the American upon purely practical objects. . . . Let us cease, then, to view all democratic nations under the example of the American people, and attempt to survey them at length with their own features.[23]

The last sentence in the passage suggests the inaccuracy of Lipset's interpretation. Rather than a claim in the idiom of comparative political science, Tocqueville argues for the idiosyncrasy of American politics. If he can be said to embrace the term *American exceptionalism* at all, it would be instead the "unique" sense of American exceptionalism, not the comparative sense preferred by social scientists like Lipset. Democratic politics in one land, Tocqueville argues, will not necessarily tell you much about democratic politics in another.[24] This idiosyncrasy should caution one against the very comparative method that Lipset pursues.

To be sure, Tocqueville makes numerous comparisons in the book, frequently recalling the character of the French, English, and American peoples side by side. But Tocqueville's comparisons are not, as Lipset believes, made in the idiom of comparative political science. He is not extracting a general principle of democracy from a number of parallel cases. References to English or French experiences are made in the interest of throwing differences into sharper relief so that they are easier to see, not in order to prove a scientific claim through the isolation of variables, as Lipset seeks to do.[25] Perhaps one would go too far to suggest that Lipset interprets Tocqueville in this way only to save himself the trouble of formulating a full-fledged methodology. Yet even backing away from that claim, his reading of Tocqueville is inaccurate. As it stands, his *American Exceptionalism: A Double-Edged Sword* is yet another study like those he had published for the previous four decades, marshaling data from several countries and sifting through the results looking for both patterns and outliers.[26] It is unsurprising that such a method actually finds what it is looking for: a dominant pattern and at least one exception to it. The comparative, scientific method of analysis actually tends toward results like this.

SOCIAL SCIENCE'S AMERICAN EXCEPTIONALISM

In the editor's introduction to *Is America Different?: A New Look at American Exceptionalism*, Byron Shafer notes three possible ways to understand the term; in the course of laying them out, Shafer exhibits some consciousness of the problems associated with treating the idea, though he fails to overcome these problems. Each of the three senses he perceives requires a different method; keeping those methods and senses straight will, he thinks, help answer his title question clearly. The first main sense of American exceptionalism he calls "simple distinctiveness," by which he means the "dictionary sense of being clearly and recognizably different from elsewhere." But for the purposes of social science, Shafer notes, this sense is problematic because all societies, "observed closely enough, are distinct, while all societies, observed with sufficient distance, are simultaneously similar." The claim to American exceptionalism may be, Shafer notes, entirely dependent on the scale of one's inquiry.[27] But if the term is truly a claim to American uniqueness in only a minimally comparative way, then the scientific method may not be appropriate for studying this sense of American exceptionalism at all.[28] This is what I have called "unique" American exceptionalism. The need for comparison, then, means the claim to "simple distinctiveness" must be abandoned by social scientists because there can be no deep investigation using their preferred tools. The social scientist will have to employ a different sense of the term.

Shafer proposes a second main sense of the term *American exceptionalism* that "revolves around the assertion that there is a general model of societal progression for developed nations in the world—and the United States does not fit this model." This is what I have called simply "comparative" American exceptionalism. Shafer thinks this second sense has two branches, one self-congratulatory and one more pejorative; John Winthrop's 1630 sermon "A Model of Christian Charity" belongs to the first, Shafer says, and has to do with the unique opportunities available in America and nowhere else; various American theorists of Marxism belong to the second subbranch, which is said to have saved Marxist history from being proven wrong by America's persistent capitalism.[29] The initial problem posed by the first sense of the term above (a lack of context or grounds for induction) may be solved by Marxist theories of history, since there is for the convinced Marxist a standard progression of history; the basic Marxist account of history can serve as the normal pattern from which the United States seems to vary. This seems to be the connection between Marxist theories of history and the methods of the social sciences.[30] Put otherwise, a thoroughgoing Marxist cannot be a thoroughgoing scientist, and vice versa—though milder versions of each could, and certainly do, coexist. Shafer thinks the "Winthrop branch" of this second sense is just as untenable as the Marxist branch because, over time, the United States has been shown to be ultimately very similar to other developing nations. Since many nations in the contemporary world seem to exhibit the "unique" characteristics of eighteenth-century America, and since Europe no longer seems destined for radical communism, the credibility of both branches of Shafer's second sense of *American exceptionalism* has declined.[31] This, too, is a dead end for social scientists, he thinks.[32]

In introducing a third main sense of the term, Shafer offers a defense of the route taken by the authors in his book. This third sense is an examination of "peculiarly American approaches to major social sectors—to government, to the economy, to culture, to religion, to education, and to public policy, as we have isolated them in this volume—and to their interaction in the larger society around them."[33] That is, Shafer's third main sense of the term is a specific example in the social science scholarly literature that seeks to avoid the problems of the first two senses. It looks to keep its scope neither too large nor too small (in order to avoid the fault of Shafer's first main sense of American exceptionalism) and to focus on the empirical realities of American life (to avoid the fault of Shafer's second main sense). Scholars will avoid ideological history by avoiding history altogether, seeking rather to measure American life and evaluate the claim to American exceptionalism by examining empirical data.[34] While his approach seems to answer the objections some have raised, it is framed throughout as a question of social science, and so is prone to the weaknesses that that approach contains.

Shafer assumes that the methodology of empirical social science is adequate to the task of exploring the phenomenon of American exceptionalism. Yet Shafer's new method does not succeed. Though it is aimed at advancing the scholarly debate through agreement with certain baseline assumptions, even the eight authors in the volume do not all agree that America is exceptional.[35] It could be argued, however, that methodological consensus and not agreement on findings was Shafer's main goal. If this is so, then Shafer's victory is real but small. A methodological consensus among a group of social scientists amounts to an agreement on the merits of the scientific method—hardly a monumental achievement. As long as this method is used, similar conclusions are bound to follow.

A common set of meanings and assumptions is, however, a worthy goal. Such a framework would necessarily be broader than the social sciences, since as Lipset has pointed out, social scientists are not the only ones taking up American exceptionalism as a theme.[36]

The main problem with the social scientists' accounts of American exceptionalism to date is that they are not capable of accounting for the phenomenon as it shows up. A great deal of ink spilled and words exchanged on "American exceptionalism" has little to do with comparative social science. To understand American exceptionalism, however, perhaps it is not a change within the method of social science that is needed, but a move away from scientific analysis.

Political Theory and American Exceptionalism

Understanding the accounts of the origin of a people is important for understanding that particular people's self-conception, and in the American case doing so is particularly illuminating. No matter how they are interpreted, the documents and symbols that constitute the heart of the American political tradition can be named in a fairly short list even by those least informed about public affairs. These provide a baseline of understanding from which we can better evaluate the nature of the tradition and the changes it has undergone through the centuries.

Following Eric Voegelin, Willmoore Kendall and George Carey note that it is through "symbols" that "a people becomes a people, that is, gets itself politically organized for action in history." These "symbols" crop up, then, when a people *does* something and are above all most indicative of the thing done. In part, Voegelin and Kendall and Carey draw a contrast between this approach and one focusing on more well-known thinkers in the history of political philosophy. "Political philosophy," Kendall and Carey write, " . . . is a tardy development in the history of a people, and, moreover, a development precisely out of the stuff of symbols and myths."[37] It is myopic to consider only a people's political philosophy when trying to understand their political theory, history, and behavior. When theorists seek to plumb the depths of a people's thinking on politics only in comparison with the writings of Locke, Montesquieu, and other philosophers, they obtain only a narrow, late, and reified account of a people's self-conception. Such has been the case with the American political tradition for some time; only the Declaration of Independence, the Constitution, and the *Federalist* are thought to be relevant—if even all of these—and only in terms of various ideas and movements in eighteenth-century philosophy. The difference between symbols and myths, on the one hand, and political philosophy, on the other, might be likened to the distinction between the video of an entire sporting event and the snapshots of its pivotal moments. The moments are important, but absent the context of the rules of the game and the flow of events in the match, a snapshot is unintelligible. A purely philosophical method is limited to analysis of particular moments in the life of a people— and late moments at that. A method that can better account for the history of a people and their ideas will understand those ideas as they have actually existed. This is why it is sometimes said that Voegelin's method may be more empirical than the empiricists'.

Rather than an analysis of philosophical treatises, Kendall and Carey begin with what most consider to be the most basic symbol in the American political tradition, the Mayflower Compact. They continue with documents exhibiting political actions from the middle and later colonial periods as the people of the colonies find their own political footing. Such an approach avoids some of the pitfalls of the more dominant approaches to American political thought; the antinomy often perceived between the Declaration and the Constitution, for example, is shown to be false if both documents are understood in the light of the whole tradition that preceded them. The presence of clauses in the Constitution that protect slavery, for example, are taken to contradict the equality clause in the Declaration of Independence. But understanding these documents as political acts and not as rarified treatises of political thought helps to ameliorate the sense of contradiction. The tradition makes more sense as a whole if these documents are interpreted not as philosophical treatises or statements but as the concrete political acts they were intended to be. Finding the "basic symbols" of the tradition involves, then, a second judgment: whether the basic symbols, once identified, have remained vital, lived out, and operative in the life of the American people; in short, whether the tradition as it was once lived out either remains intact (even if changed) or has become "derailed."[38]

Derailment is a Voegelinian term that suggests a certain tradition may run off its rails, that is, change the course that it previously followed. The word has connotations of real disaster and this is intentional. Voegelin's "symbols" are historical by nature, and this is the chief advantage of his insight. The antecedent symbols, which contain the possibilities of the consequents, are "compact"; these compact symbols undergo a process of "differentiation" over time, a process that is mostly opaque until it has happened. Note that, in order to perceive a tradition's derailment, one must first possess the data of both previous and subsequent history. The judgment in question is a *historical* judgment and cannot be made immediately after an event occurs or a symbol is articulated. This is another way of stating the obvious: the history of the present moment cannot yet be written. But the judgments of history are vitally important for both the way we conceive of ourselves as a people and the way we act.

Accurate analysis along these lines requires the ability to distinguish "derailments" from "differentiations." In order to determine the difference, we should "show some kind of historical continuity between the beginning we seize upon and that much later moment at which the people is in fact constituted as a people for action in history."[39] Thus, not just any document will do. Some are more important than others and common consent lists the most important ones relatively easily: formative colonial documents, the Declaration of Independence, the Articles of Confederation, and the Constitution, to name only the most central ones. But because the list is historical, it cannot stop there. Later generations formulate their own symbols, which add to, subtract from, and refract the original arc of these symbols in both meaning and political operation.

It is readily seen that, under this method, the determination of which symbols are most basic is vitally important for understanding a people as they are.[40] Taking a late symbol as the basic one would give the whole analysis a false color, while picking one that is too early would mean that the "people" in question is not yet really one people. The "people" of the Mayflower Compact does not seem to be the same "people" as the one indicated in the Declaration of Independence. The "people" of the Declaration, however, is the same as that of the Constitution and today. Yet the later people, the American people, owes much to the people of the Massachusetts Bay Colony, such that the later Americans represent a differentiation in the life of the American political tradition, of which the Mayflower Compact is the chief and primary antecedent.[41]

Among the insights that this method allows, a particularly illustrative one concerns the way the early Puritan colonists conceived of society: for them state, society, and church were not differentiated. Their thoughts on church governance as compared to social norms or laws and regulations were not as distinct to them as they are for us today. For the Puritans, to consider one of these categories was to consider them all; this means that a category mistake often committed in the scholarship can be avoided when using this method.

Another advantage of this conceptualization of history is that one can, looking backward, see the various lines of development through history without claiming that development was strictly necessary.[42] In the case of the United States, this means that one can probe the various compact symbols of the colonies without also arguing that either the manner or the fact of their eventual emergence as the United States was inevitable.[43]

This sort of detailed methodological consideration is important because understanding the phenomenon of American exceptionalism requires a nuanced understanding of history and the role of a people's self-conception in formulating and appropriating that history. Here, then, is the method that will be able to supply a fuller understanding of the idea of American exceptionalism. Political theory, over and against social science or comparative history, can see the phenomenon for what it is because implicit in the idea and in its articulation is a deep historical and theoretical engagement with a people's myths and symbols—items that fall outside the criteria of relevance in these other disciplines. This approach to the idea of American exceptionalism will open it up to examination as a claim to uniqueness, with serious consequences for evaluating and understanding political action. This approach allows us to see that, rather than a claim in the idiom of contemporary social science, something like American exceptionalism was, in the beginning, a claim made in the idiom of political and religious thought.[44]

The Elements of the Idea of American Exceptionalism: A Roadmap

If we are to look for the "basic symbol" in regard to American exceptionalism—that first, foundational articulation of the notion—we need look no further than John Winthrop's sermon "A Model of Christian Charity."[45] The worldview of the New England Puritans, especially as it bears on history, is the earliest recognizable instance of a thought like *American exceptionalism* on these shores. It should be noted at the outset that Winthrop's sermon, which contains the famous phrase calling the Massachusetts Bay Colony a "city on a hill," is not about America at all. Though it has been construed as such in recent years, it must be recalled that, when he spoke those words in 1630, an autonomous and independent country on the western shores of the Atlantic could scarcely have been thinkable. Conditions in New England were hard, and even if they had not been, many conceived of the project at Massachusetts Bay as a kind of pilot program. The community and way of life were to be developed and practiced with a view to returning to England; they would be welcomed as rulers and lawgivers to remake English and all Christian society in New England's image. The colonists were to serve as an exemplar to the world, but their failure in the task would be equally exemplary of what God does to those who disobey him and squander his graces and friendship. Winthrop's "city on a hill," far from offering a license to do as they pleased, was a deeply held covenant that each individual in society was party to, with God as its executor.

The central Puritan idea that lends itself to being the precursor to later conceptions of American exceptionalism is not, then, Winthrop's famous passage. It is rather his views on history and politics as a whole that demonstrate the Puritan confidence in being God's chosen people, the New Jerusalem from the Book of Revelation. One can see, at a glance, the surface resemblance between contemporary conceptions of American exceptionalism, mostly having to do with America's right to vast influence on the international stage, and the pride of place in salvation history claimed by the Puritans. The contemporary conception bears the impression of the original, even if, as with an old coin, some of the originally sharp features have worn away. One of the most conspicuous features of New England Puritan society was its imitation of the societal order of the Pentateuch in the Old Testament, especially the conception of the order itself as a covenant with God. As with all covenants of that type, rich rewards were associated with its fulfillment and bitter punishments with its breach.[46] Yet if one side of the two-pronged conception is worn away, a kind of simple chosenness only remains. Without forbearance to God, without his being a party to the operation of society, chosenness is mere specialness and specialness becomes license. If the goal of the original covenant was the perfection of the community but a possible chastisement from God no longer reins in the desires of a "chosen people," it is little wonder that a line can be drawn from the "exemplary" politics of the Puritans to the imperial actions of some figures from the Progressive Era.[47]

The line, however, is not direct and causal. There were two major modifications in American history that were necessary for the evolution to take place as it did. First, a subtle change had to be made in the purpose of government. Society had to be reoriented, on the one hand, away from temporal perfection as evidence for eternal salvation and, on the other, toward seeing government as encouraging virtue and good order only here and now. Concretely, this meant a transition was effected from conceiving of God as pilot of the ship of state to conceiving of God as granting humanity the ability to build and pilot the ship themselves. One still believes, in both cases, that God is in control of history. But his approach to governance, by the time of the framing of the Constitution, came to be thought of as indirect, achieved through the arrangement of American circumstances in a particularly advantageous way. Rather than interrupting history to achieve his ends, God—often referred to merely as "Providence" during the constitutional period—comes to be thought of as working through history. This leads, however, to the second main step between the Puritans and the Progressives.

It is a short step from seeing God as using history to achieve his plans to scouring history to reveal what God's plans are, have been, and will be. It is an even shorter step from merely discerning God's plan for history to see-ing history itself as having its own plan, logic, and direction. But all sorts of ungodly things happen without interruption or decrease. Doubt may thus be raised as to whether or not God is in charge of history. This removal of God from any active role in history was partly achieved when the constitutional generation relegated God to a powerful but passive role. To go from passive to absent is the more decisive move, but it is hardly surprising given the first.

By the time, and in the figure, of Abraham Lincoln, we begin to see the removal of God from the conception of America's place in the world, though the change was started in the constitutional period and a kind of balance was sustained for a time between the new humanistic focus and the older conception of a Christian- and virtue-based political order.[48] Just like the conception of a covenant before it, the conception of government as the "deliberate rule of a virtuous people" would not last.[49] In Lincoln's reinterpretation of the framers' tradition we have a prominent view of America as an idea, as a proposition. A proposition, it will be noted, is a human creation; hence we have the implicit excision of God from the American political order. With the recasting of the framers as philosophers advocating abstract propositions, there is the consequent casting aside of God and the limits he placed formerly on the political realm. This does not mean that Lincoln ceases to speak of God and his importance to and involvement with America. Far from it: Lincoln has been called the "first and best civil theologian in American history."[50] But the God Lincoln describes is, ultimately, one who may be deleted from the story without its losing conceptual coherence.[51]

Once God has been removed from the public life of the American political order, an interesting thing happens. In the Progressive Era God sneaks back into American politics through the private back door. Because God is no longer guiding the everyday course of events, nor even arranging American circumstances beneficently, it comes to be thought that he has inspired the propositions and ideas on which the country was founded and that this divine sanction gives special license to the few who truly understand it. Here surfaces the idea of imperial American exceptionalism. Rather than a passive beneficence or an active choosing and binding into a covenant, and rather even than a pure "uniqueness" based on America's founding principles, America comes to be thought of as God's right arm on earth. Such a sanction amounts to a severing, once and for all, of the ties that previously reined in Americans' ambition. So ends the course from the "exemplary" exceptionalism of Massachusetts Bay to the imperial exceptionalism of the Progressives, though the course does not follow smooth lines of ascent or decline. Over the intervening years, various aspects of

Americans' self-conception are posited, abandoned, recovered, and recombined in new ways. Those new combinations have served to confuse and divide us politically—the very opposite of the work myths and symbols are to perform. One particular combination, the imperial one, partakes of the earlier ones but was not inevitable. The new wine burst the old wineskins and has left us adrift in history, largely unaware of who we are and who we were. It is little surprising that, without the knowledge of who we are, there is no consensus on what we should be doing, either at home or abroad. This confusion, paralysis, and ignorance might be reversed, however, if an adequate acquaintance with the American political tradition becomes widely held. A new, lived account of the American political tradition can become such only if the tradition itself is reappropriated with each new generation and renewed in the lives of the citizens.

2

JOHN WINTHROP

A Divinely Sanctioned, Practically Circumscribed Colony

Though many have held John Winthrop up as the first American exceptionalist, particularly for his now-famous simile that the colony at Massachusetts Bay will be as a "city on a hill," a few reflections are sufficient to initially draw that claim into question.

First and foremost, the idea of American exceptionalism is, strictly speaking, concerned with the exceptional nature of the United States of America. Yet Winthrop had never heard of the United States. The fledgling colonies on these shores—even if most of them could be grouped together by their common English origin—had very different aims. These dots of civilization punctuated only the slightest part of the vast continent, and the future political order of the Constitution was still 150 years away. Even the 1620 founding of the Pilgrim colony at Plymouth was quite different in character from that of the colony at Massachusetts Bay.

When it is asserted that Winthrop was the first American exceptionalist, the claim almost invariably rests on the self-evidently exceptionalist quality of his use of the phrase "city on a hill."[1] An examination of the whole discourse from which it is drawn and the context of that particular phrase will dispel the careless anachronism of these arguments. In an extended analysis, I will show that the phrase "city on a hill," far from making a claim to exceptionalism, makes the opposite claim: that the new colony—if it lives according to its initial mandate, or if it transgresses that mandate—will yield foreseeable, not exceptional, results. Winthrop's exceptionalism is exemplary, not imperial. The work the colonists undertake is not private; yet it does exclusively belong to them, at least at this early stage. This is tied to the Massachusetts Bay Puritan theory of history, which is tied to Winthrop's articulation of the covenant and its function in history. As Bercovitch notes, that pattern of thought is later subsumed into the general consciousness of most Americans and plays a central role in their self-understanding. Thus the claim that Winthrop's "city on a hill" phrase has *something* to do with American exceptionalism is right, but usually for the wrong reasons. Upon examination, however, it is clear that Winthrop is no imperialist and that if he can be called an American exceptionalist at all, it is of the sort I called exemplary exceptionalism.[2]

To establish this, two documents will be taken up: "Reasons to Be Considered, and Objections with Answers" and "A Model of Christian Charity"; they constitute the seed of the idea of American exceptionalism. The first contains an extremely explicit and clear statement of the aims of the Massachusetts Bay Colony. In understanding the arguments of this document, Winthrop's vision for the future of the colony may be glimpsed. The second document, far more famous than the first, is a sermon or discourse given on the occasion of the Winthrop fleet's departure for New England and is said to be the key link between Winthrop and American exceptionalism. These documents contain the same basic elements or symbols found in the Mayflower Compact and give the "sense" of the community on the question of political order.[3] Close examination of the meaning of Winthrop's words will help dispel the usual confusion between what the Puritans thought and the role they come to play later in American history. The distinction is stark. The uses to which they are put differ widely from the plain sense of the words and their context.

In examining these documents according to the modified Voegelinian interpretive method of Kendall and Carey, I am committed to examining whatever symbols can be found that articulate how, at each period I will take up, the American people (or the people of the colony) saw themselves. What were they doing? Why? What significance did it have? With this approach, the real political theory of a people is examined, rather than merely one person's political thought. I am looking for language symbols that were operative for each group—the language symbols that are not dead letters but that sprang forth as active principles of the life of the community. These symbols need not fit exactly with the standard to which Kendall and Carey adhere in their work, because the kind of representation they detail has not always been the operative mode of representation at each stage of American history (or, for that matter, human history).

Though Kendall and Carey are right to point out that the rule of a "deliberate assembly" is a crucial symbol in the American political tradition, this point need not mean that this is the only kind of symbol in the tradition.

Now, there could be many different layers of representation in any society, with different ones dominating at particular moments. It is interesting in this regard to ponder the representativeness of the president of the United States. Here is an individual man who, in some sense, represents all Americans. Yet his representativeness is not the same as the representativeness of each U.S. congressman or senator (see chapters 3 and 4). I do not mean that only a single mode of representation is operative or accepted at any one time. In the case of the generations after the founding period, the representation *of* the people is thought most appropriately to be achieved *by* the people.[4] And though it seems that there are intimations of this form of representation even early on in the life of the colonists at Massachusetts Bay, it is Winthrop himself who articulates the aims and direction and purpose of the new community at its earliest stages.[5]

Voegelin writes, "In order to come into existence, a society must articulate itself by producing a representative that will act for it."[6] Recall that Voegelin is inquiring into "the nature of representation as the form by which a political society gains existence for action in history."[7] In articulating itself as a society, then, a given people unites for action in history. If the Puritans of Massachusetts Bay are a distinct people, then a symbol that articulates who they are must exist. Kendall and Carey dwell at length on the Fundamental Orders of Connecticut (1639) and the Massachusetts Body of Liberties (1641). But following their method and words of caution, it ought to be asked whether or not there are earlier symbols in the political life of the colony.[8] Because of the importance assigned to Winthrop by many scholars, it ought to be asked why Kendall and Carey do not consider him. The answer is readily found.

Kendall and Carey have already established a frame through which to view their data: namely, those documents that no one could dispute were foundational, from the Mayflower Compact onward. The Fundamental Orders and the Body of Liberties are the next chronological symbols that fit that bill. Yet in narrowing their frame, something important has been left out, namely, the documents I consider in this chapter. What is missed has to do with Voegelin's words quoted above; in the course of *The New Science of Politics*, Voegelin makes it clear that, although Western societies *tend* toward the full articulation of the people as their own representative, a people does not always represent itself in history.[9] It is frequently an individual leader or king who represents the people to themselves, to others, and to God. This is why sacrifices to the gods must, often in human history, be offered by the king. It is only in *his* person that the task can truly be completed on behalf of the whole people. Just so, John Winthrop—though no king—stands with the other leaders of the *Arbella* fleet as the representative of the whole people to themselves and to God. He, who would shortly be extolled as a new Nehemiah and who invites comparisons to Moses, articulates who the Massachusetts Bay colonists are as a people, what they aim to do, and where they fit in the sweep of history. In performing especially this last task, he interprets his people "as representatives of a transcendent truth."[10] Thus an examination of Winthrop's writings may stand in for the truth of the way of life at Massachusetts Bay. It serves as an operative account of their life, especially, because Winthrop is not only their mouthpiece but also the head of the colony's body politic, along with the other magistrates. And though he does not occupy the position wholly by himself, his primacy goes un-challenged at the earliest stages of his time as governor. At this moment in his people's history, his representativeness has the authority of acclamation, and that is the moment under examination here.

Before examining Winthrop's account, however, several points about the difference between the colonies of Plymouth and Massachusetts Bay should be brought out in order to make clearer the nature of the Massachusetts Bay project. The key difference between the Pilgrims of Plymouth and the Puritans of Massachusetts Bay is in their different practical approach to a problem perceived in common. Though both groups saw the Anglican church as increasingly corrupt, the Pilgrims (also appropriately called Sepa-rating Puritans) argued that only separation from that body would allow for a truly Christian life, while the Puritans were decidedly and emphatically Nonseparatist.[11] The groups' own experiences help account for this differ-ence in character. The Pilgrims fled to Holland and then New England in search of a space in which to worship as they saw fit; they viewed the old political and religious order of England as corrupt beyond regeneration and, therefore, saw only the most drastic of remedies as adequate to addressing the illness. They would amputate themselves from the rest of the body and form their own pure, distinct, and separate society; thus the corruption of the rest of the body, from which they were figuratively cut off upon their emigration, would be unable to spread to them. This meant that the Pilgrims viewed the interaction of religion and politics very differently from the Pu-ritans at Massachusetts Bay.[12] The Puritans, too, saw corruption in England but thought it not beyond cure. Though they also left English shores, their aim in leaving was the regeneration of a more ancient and pure Christian mode of living. They would seek refuge in the wilderness from the coming "calamity." When this happened, the Puritan colonists would be waiting to welcome their Christian brothers and sisters, already having made the wilderness more hospitable for them.[13]

The key difference in religion led to a key difference in political thought and practice. Though the Mayflower Compact is said to be "in some sense" the articulation of a religious society, it should be said, too, that the Pilgrims' aims are somewhat amorphous.[14] This lies in stark contrast to the explicit aims of the Massachusetts Bay Puritans. God, for the Pilgrims, seems to be a *witness* to their political founding. But as Perry Miller has noted, the Puritans of Massachusetts Bay saw themselves not as *imitating* the covenant God first made with Abraham but as *renewing* and *recasting* that same covenant according to the will of God *today*, just as Moses and others recast the initial Abrahamic covenant.[15] The Pilgrims, in contrast, viewed their work as significant mainly, and perhaps exclusively, for themselves. The Puritans, however, viewed their work as significant for *all* Christians, even if it practically consisted of an intense *inward* focus. Keeping in mind these differences, we turn to the Puritans' own account in the "Reasons."

For several reasons it might be said that this first document under consideration is by no means an *American* symbol. First, it was written by Englishmen, in England, for an English audience. Second, in no way does the document constitute a political act, unlike the Mayflower Compact, the Fundamental Orders of Connecticut, or the Massachusetts Body of Liberties. In answer to these objections, I submit, first, that the men of the colonies at Plymouth and Massachusetts Bay were Englishmen, too. Though in a strange land, they came to it with their English thoughts, habits, expectations, and goals. They saw themselves as Englishmen, as would many in the colonies for the next century and a half. Yet just as much, or perhaps even more so, the colonists at Massachusetts Bay saw themselves as Christians; they embarked upon a Christian mission, not an English one.[16]

The Puritan project has always been a staple in the American imagination, generally; understanding it is indispensable for understanding the idea of American exceptionalism. And though it might not look like a political act, the "Reasons" is indeed a document that seeks to persuade peers to undertake a common task. It is an argument both justifying a venture and recruiting others to join in it. If it is not itself a political document, one can say it is at least a document of prepolitical action, and it would seem that the same kinds of Voegelinian arguments about symbols apply to it, too, in this way. Further buttressing such an understanding is the development of the "Reasons" through several changing drafts—a sign of at least limited deliberation and concert.[17] Third, as Perry Miller has noted, "as for the Fundamental Orders themselves, we should observe that they were not invoked *in vacuo*, but only after the colony had been in existence almost three years; they were not dictated by an a priori philosophy, but were rather the legalizing of existing practice."[18] This means that to understand the Fundamental Orders more adequately, we must first understand the early *practices* of the colony. But these practices can be understood only by understanding contemporary accounts, of which the "Reasons" and the "Model" discourse are two prominent and authoritative examples.

The "Reasons" Considered

First among the reasons given to "justify" the settling of the colony at Massachusetts Bay is the benefit of carrying the "Gospel into those parts of the world, to help the coming of the fullness of the Gentiles."[19] Their mission is missionary. Such a provision is curiously missing from Winthrop's "Model," however, and it is puzzling that that later document—so clearly intended as the setting out of their new way of life—does not focus on the propagation of Christian truth. When the rest of this first major reason is given, however, it becomes clearer why the first two clauses do not make another appearance in "Model."

This missionary first reason is rounded out by saying that this spreading of the Gospel will have the effect, also, of raising "a bulwark against the kingdom of Antichrist which the Jesuits labor to rear up in those parts." The phrase connotes a Puritan participation in the ongoing global contest between Catholics and Protestants, marking out New England as a new front in the conflict. Loren Baritz notes the similarity to the Jesuits' commission. The Puritans' emigration was no retreat; this was not possible: "The Puritan could not separate himself from sin because he had a commission similar to the Jesuits' to fight the good fight. According to the English Puritan preachers, the business of the Christian was relentless war against the forces of evil."[20] Eager to dispel the appearance of retreat from sin, the Puritans of Massachusetts Bay argued that they would outflank it by establishing an extremely strong foothold in the new world.[21]

For the colonists, the ongoing fight against the forces of the Antichrist (i.e., the Catholic Church) had reached a turning point with the emigration of the *Arbella* fleet. Here was the latest episode in both the Reformation and in salvation history.[22] Just as Luther, Calvin, and the other Reformers began the process of freeing the Christian world of the pernicious influence of "popery," so also would the Puritan colonists' efforts redound to that goal. Just as the Reformers called for a rededication to the central principles of the faith, so also did the Reformers' movement itself—Winthrop and many others thought—stand in need of reinvigoration. At the moment, the English church seemed to be edging toward rapprochement with Catholicism. Although the 1630 Massachusetts Bay colonists did not go so far as to believe that separation from the English church was the only way to reform—in contradistinction to the 1620 emigrants, they were decidedly against this—their strategy did involve a retreat from its midst. It was thought that a new land, isolated from the pernicious tendencies of the Arminian powers in London and Canterbury, could provide shelter from the coming "general calamity" portended by the ascendancy of these forces.

Despite the military metaphors, however, the Puritans were not sailing to New England to engage in armed conflict with the Catholic missionaries there. Neither were they emigrating only for the purpose of conversion and the spread of the Gospel. They were setting up a bulwark, a point of resistance that is stationary by nature. They were setting up a colony that would run according to a new way of life, which would *in turn* serve as a bulwark. The spread of the Gospel would be one with the maintenance of their community and the preservation of their main mission there—fulfilling the covenant with God upon which they were about to enter—and it is important to note this here because it sheds light on the cognate passages in the "Model" discourse, which I will examine later.[23] Early on, then, the chief purpose of the new colony is the setting up of a new way of life. This new way of life has significance for all Christians, but it is an inwardly focused project, both individually and corporately: the only avenue for its achievement is the living out of Christian virtues by every colonist; in this, the community will become an example to all.

The corruption of the churches of Europe and the consequent "coming calamity" is the second of the Puritans' nine major reasons for emigration.[24] To worship God in a purer church would be easier in the New England wilderness because of both the greater distance from insidious forces and the superior membership of the new church as a whole. This particular church founding and advancement into the wilderness will be of service to the church universal, since the church in New England will prepare a place to which future numbers might flee. Even in what they saw as a unique role for themselves in salvation history, then, the Puritans did not consider themselves a wholly independent church setting out on its own; here again they are emphatically Nonseparatist.

The third reason justifying emigration is the material situation in England. The presence of too many people on too little land, Winthrop says, has caused a degradation of respect for human life and a decrease in the ability to care for the poor. At first it is surprising that such an apparently mundane reason for emigration ranks third in importance on a list otherwise preoccupied with more transcendent reasons. Yet in this mundane impetus we see what has been called the Puritans' "typological" view of history.[25] It is often said that Christians in general have two sources of revelation: nature and the Bible. The former is constituted by all the wisdom man can obtain through sound deliberation on his observations; it is the source of natural law. Not all Christians, however, affirm the pair; some hew exclusively to the Bible.[26] Such Christians view the book of nature as unreliable because correctly reading it requires belief in the reliability of human reason, about which there are many views.[27] Nevertheless, here Winthrop evinces his belief in what could be called a "third book": the book of history.

God sometimes arranges circumstances in such a way as to goad men in one direction or another. Winthrop believed *just this* was happening in the clearing out and opening up of the New England wilderness. This, combined with the relative exhaustion of the English soil, the crowding of English land, and the relative poverty of worthy citizens in England, was taken as a clue to the will of God. It was only in reading *this* book (and confirming it in scripture) that such insights could be gained.[28] Though it does not seem that John Winthrop turned biblical exegesis "inside out" by transferring the "source of meaning from scripture to secular history," as Bercovitch has written of Cotton Mather, it could be said that Winthrop opened the door to Mather's more extreme move.[29] This seems to have been a fairly unique view even in Protestantism, as Bercovitch has noted:

> In this vision of the Theopolis Americana the idea of national election takes on a literalness undreamed of by Luther or Foxe. It is the kind of literalness, in fact, assumed by the colonists about themselves. Luther believed that the Germans might help create the first truly Christian kingdom; Foxe and Milton hoped that England would lead the world in the destruction of the Antichrist. The New

England Puritans gave America the status of visible sainthood. The subsequent impact of their concept cannot be overestimated. Whatever the extent of its influence, it contributes significantly to the link between the New England and the American Way, to the usurpation of American identity by the United States, and to the anthropomorphic nationalism that characterizes our literature—not the secular anthropomorphism of parenthood (British homeland, German fatherland), but the eschatological anthropomorphism of spiritual biography: American dream, manifest destiny, redeemer nation, and, fundamentally, the American self as representative of universal truth.[30]

Though Bercovitch's assertion might suggest otherwise, the notion that America is a "redeemer nation" need not mean that either the Massachusetts Bay Colony or the United States of America becomes an imperial power. That requires a corruption of the original Puritan understanding under discussion here.[31] Yet the charge of imperialism is one Puritan scholarship has had to deal with, not least because of Winthrop's ideas about justice toward the Indians.

In order to head off objections about the ownership of New England's land, Winthrop recalls God's injunction in Genesis that man should "increase and multiply, replenish the earth and subdue it." The cultivation of the earth, he argues, redounds both to man's material benefit and God's glory. Furthermore, the land in New England lies uncultivated while England's land groans under the pressure to feed its inhabitants. It would only be right to move westward and improve New England's unenclosed—and, therefore, free and unclaimed—land; doing so is the act of a good steward of God's gifts in Creation.[32]

This argument is first among the "objections" considered.[33] Winthrop repeats emphatically the fact that the lands in New England lie uncultivated and unenclosed; this means they belong to no one person and may be taken if, first, they are improved and, second, enough common land is left for the others' subsistence. After giving several biblical examples to support his argument, Winthrop notes that the "natives" possess the primitive right to the open land but argues that if they are left with enough open territory on which they can hunt and live, then their rights have not been violated. He adds, further, that the "natives" will benefit from the new colony's presence because they can be taught English agricultural techniques whereby to improve the land and that the number of "natives" in the land has drastically decreased of late because of a plague sent by God—indicating there is more room for a new population. Note again the reading of history as a book of revelation: "God hath consumed the natives with a great plague in those parts [New England], so as there be few inhabitants left."[34]

Winthrop's fifth "reason" concerns the extent to which church members have grown "intemperate" in England. Luxuries have become near necessities, but this means that there are fewer resources with which a man might be generous toward his family and the local poor. Further, because of the availability of luxuries, there is a greater temptation to cheat and deceive one's partners in business. All of this could be remedied, Winthrop implies, in the rougher environs of the New England wilderness; luxuries, not being present, would not be such a problem, and the membership of a close-knit Christian community would be less likely to cheat and deceive one another.

Sixth, Winthrop laments the corruption of the seminaries and schools, which give only "evil examples" to the students, who become, in turn, "perverted" and "corrupted." Reiterating his point about the high cost of living, Winthrop complains not only about the schools' corruption but also about the heavy burden of their cost. Winthrop implies again that opening new schools in another location, with different personnel and greater ease of oversight, could solve such a problem.

Winthrop argues, seventh, that it is an "honorable" and "worthy" thing for any Christian to help in the building up of a new local church.[35] Eighth, Winthrop exhorts any "godly" Englishmen of "wealth and prosperity" to join the colonists and, in so doing, to set an example of trust in God. Since it would mean emigration into a very uncertain territory and life, the prominent citizens would be hazarding much greater risks than if they remained in England. All the more, then, Winthrop argues, will their example be noted, applauded, and effective. Winthrop also argues that the whole venture might be redeemed if more prominent Puritan citizens join him. The low character of the "adventurers" who usually populate such colonies is often a reason given for their wretchedness. If more prominent ministers and citizens do not go, the colony in Massachusetts would more resemble Virginia than Winthrop believes wise, in both perception and fact—a point he repeats in the objections below.

Ninth, and very important, Winthrop implies that this venture is itself a part of God's plan for the Christian church, giving the early commitment of so many prominent Puritans as evidence. Here again we see on display his reading of the vicissitudes of history as a clear signpost for the will of God.

Winthrop's nine main reasons in favor of the founding of the colony are followed by ten objections to the venture, with answers for each. I have already traced the first objection concerning the ownership of the land in New England; I will briefly consider the other nine.

The second objection noted was widespread at the time: if things are bad in England, then should not its best citizens stay and try to forestall the coming "calamity"? Winthrop answers that their leaving is yet another *sign* that the calamity is coming; their departure is not its *cause*. Staying would not necessarily prevent the events that their exodus portends. Perhaps, Winthrop argues, such an exodus will give pause to those in England not living lives of Christian virtue at present; they might reconsider their ways and reform their lives, which might ultimately benefit England. Moreover, the good of the church redounds to the good of all, and the success of this new local church in New England is certainly good for the church in general. Further, Winthrop argues that the opportunity to preach to New England's "natives" constitutes part of the Christian vocation and should not be overlooked. A third objection notes that even if the situation in England is bad, perhaps it is too early yet to flee into the wilderness. Winthrop answers that it is only prudent to go ahead and leave when safety is more assured, rather than await the calamity and risk the inability to escape.

Winthrop's fourth noted objection is perhaps the most interesting, especially near the end, where he makes a point sometimes denied in the scholarly literature about the self-conscious differences between the Massachusetts Bay Colony and other colonies.[36] The other colonies have been mediocre and suffered on account of "their own sloth," as in the case of Virginia. Moreover, Winthrop notes, the argument that some particular colonies have not succeeded says nothing of the impossibility of success for a new one. Winthrop also cautions against the possibility of putting too much stock in a limited human perspective; even the apparently degraded colonies—for example, Virginia—might ultimately be brought to "good use."

Winthrop notes three reasons that colonies like Virginia have failed and why, to the contrary, the Massachusetts Bay Colony will not. First, "their main end was carnal [i.e., commercial] and not religious."[37] Winthrop is clear here that the main end of the Massachusetts Bay Colony was religious. We have already seen that even the colony's commercial considerations were viewed in terms of Providence and salvation history. But up to this point Winthrop has not been so explicit in both marking out the colony as primarily a religious venture and in rejecting the commercial benefits as the "main end." Here he does so, eliminating any ambiguity. Another reason the Virginia colonists failed was that "they did not establish a right form of government." The new colony's form of government would be a mixture of the institutions of religion and politics. The particular balance effected will, Winthrop thinks, prevent Massachusetts Bay from succumbing to Virginia's pitfalls.[38]

The fifth through ninth objections deal with the potential difficulty encountered in the new colony. Were not these, too, signs that the venture was not currently the right course of action? Though the objections strategically concede Winthrop's peculiar view on the intelligibility of history, Winthrop carefully rejects each one. The fifth objection mentions the difficulty of the settlement, to which Winthrop replies in stereotypically Puritan fashion: yes, it will be difficult; "so is every good action." Similarly, the sixth objection holds that the magnitude of the task is above the capability of those undertaking it. Winthrop answers that weaker and smaller groups have done greater things than this. The seventh objection continues the theme and notes the absence of "natural fortifications" in New England. After mentioning the greater distance between the new colony and its enemies in Europe, Winthrop exhorts the reader to faith: those who are skeptical should "trust in [God] and not in outward means of safety"; they should know that they would not be sent to such a land without God also providing for their needs. Again, eighth, Winthrop's objector observes the possibility—recalling the fifth reason—that the colonists have grown too soft and comfortable in England to undertake the hazard of the wilderness. Yet Winthrop replies that God may be sending them out in order to purify them, just as he sent the Israelites into the desert to wander. Moreover, plentiful though the land will be, there is not yet enough excess for luxury. The difference will help the colonists live lives of simple virtue and require them to work hard for what they do obtain. Ninth, Winthrop notes the possible objection that the whole venture is so difficult that, in setting out to do it, they are presuming upon a miracle by God for their very survival. Winthrop answers that they are making sufficient provision—in planning and in procurement—for their defenses and other needs.

Last, Winthrop moves away from the theme of difficulty and hardship and addresses the objection that the colony's failure to do well will bring scandal upon all Puritan ministers, who have invested so much in it. Without denying the possibility of failure—even implying that it is a distinct possibility—Winthrop rejects this point by arguing that no entire profession is judged a failure on account of a single particular failing. Concerns about the difficulty of the task or the possible shame that accompanies the failure to complete it are unfounded.

Reformation, History, and Religion

After such a detailed analysis, and before moving on to the "Model" discourse, I want to take stock of the main points of the document, especially looking ahead to the points of analysis to come. First, recall that Winthrop has placed his colony in direct line with the aims and trajectory of the entire Reformation. The way of life they will pursue and cultivate is a direct consequence and crowning achievement of the Reformation, and though there is no guarantee of success, still their work is good and right. Second, Winthrop's peculiar reading of history means that the concrete circumstances of politics, economics, and other mundane events are taken to be signposts for God's will here and now, just like some parts of the scriptures.[39] Third, it is important to notice that the project, even from its conception in the time before Winthrop was governor, was intended as a religious and *not* a commercial venture. The primarily religious character of the new colony is confirmed by extended examination of Winthrop's most famous writing, his 1630 lay sermon "A Model of Christian Charity," which should now be taken up.

The "Model" Discourse

Many busy months intervened between the composition of the "Reasons" and "A Model of Christian Charity." Soon after the "Reasons" were apparently submitted to the governing board of the Massachusetts Bay Company, Matthew Craddock—who had until then been the company's governor—resigned and Winthrop was elected in his place.[40] Upon election Winthrop had thrust upon him both the spiritual and material preparation of the fleet to make the journey and to found the colony. In the spring of 1630 the momentous day arrived and hundreds of colonists set sail for New England.[41]

Recall that we are looking for the operative symbols in regard to the notion of American exceptionalism. We are very near to their initial discovery. Though one can find remarkable continuity between the 1620 Mayflower Compact, the 1639 Fundamental Orders of Connecticut, the 1641 Massachusetts Body of Liberties, and up through the 1789 Constitution—another set of symbols is missed by jumping from 1620 to 1639.[42] Winthrop's 1630 writings follow the same pattern as the other documents, though perhaps not as cleanly as the rest.

One of the most noticeable things about "Model" is its rigorous reasoning. In a series of objections and answers, Winthrop argues forcefully for the vital importance of mercy in the new community and the degree to which love must be its animating principle. Some have said that such arguments for unity are far from unique in the period; vast records of similar speeches by ships' captains are readily found.[43] Yet this begs the question of this particular sermon's current renown all the more, especially given its suppositions about society—so different in many respects from America's contemporary consensus (or lack thereof). Voegelin's method seems to imply the destruction of consensus through fragmentation over time. While the broad consensus agreeing with Winthrop's vision for society is certainly gone, it is difficult to imagine even a single fragment of society seeking to live today according to his vision. Thus arises the question of the necessary scale of a consensus and the degree of breadth required for it to become a true symbol.

Can a small remnant or splinter group constitute a core from which a society's symbols can be gleaned? Is broad consensus possible today? Or is it anachronistic to believe this kind of consensus was ever achievable? These interesting questions must be left unanswered at this point. But it should be noted that the renown of Winthrop today has much to do with Ronald Reagan's evocation of Winthrop's words as the paradigmatic proto-American, which he discussed in many speeches while president. Yet Winthrop and the Massachusetts Bay Colony occupied a prominent place in the American imagination in the early days of the Constitution and during Tocqueville's time. Their central place has never quite shifted, even if their contributions have only rarely been adequately recognized. One aspect of the sermon's uniqueness lies in the notion of the covenant and the role "Model" plays as a foundational document for the idea of a Christian political order in America.[44] Whether or not it owes its renown to the covenant discussed here, the strand of the American political tradition that begins with Winthrop develops ultimately into the imperial American exceptionalism found in the Progressive Era. Contemporary aggressive forms of American exceptionalism as a foreign policy stand at the very end of this strand.

The sermon, or "discourse" as Winthrop calls it, is divisible into three main sections. Though the first two are important for both understanding

Winthrop's vision for the new society and understanding the sermon as a whole, the third section dwarfs them in significance and density. Thus the third section will be treated at length; but in order to give context to the third section some reflection on the first two parts is also necessary. The first section proceeds from the sermon's opening point about the inequality of men, quoted below, to a discussion of the consequent need for mercy in society. As the discourse goes on, it is clear that mercy, the real lasting source of which is love, ultimately finds its importance in the unity of the new community. Unity will be possible, ultimately, only if the members of the community are merciful toward one another. All the arguments about that outward manifestation of love, that is, mercy, and the inward love granted only by Christ's possessing the soul are aimed at the radical unity of the people of God at Massachusetts Bay.[45]

The second part of the discourse is a necessary consequent of the first: in considering the vital importance of mercy in society, Winthrop reasons to the insufficiency of mercy alone. Mercy needs to spring from love if real unity and harmony are to be achieved in society. The third section similarly follows on the second, putting Winthrop's skill as an orator on full display. After setting out the importance of mercy and love to society, Winthrop speaks on behalf of the people in covenanting themselves to God in preparation for the founding of the colony. The last section, it will be seen, much resembles the form of the other "basic symbols of the American political tradition." It is an explicit reenactment of the ongoing covenant between God and man.[46] But before that third section is detailed, some key points about the first two sections should be noted.

In a discourse primarily about unity, it is perhaps surprising to begin with the presupposition of the unchangeability of diversity and inequality. Yet that is Winthrop's famous and clever beginning: "God Almighty in his most holy and wise Providence hath so disposed of the condition of mankind, as in all times some must be rich, some poor, some high and eminent in power and dignity; others mean and in subjection."[47] Immediately after these opening lines, Winthrop makes the decisive move (and in this we see, again, his skill as an orator): just as he did in the "Reasons" and just as he will do again in the body of the "Model" discourse, Winthrop raises a strong objection to his main concern.

Without explicitly framing the discourse as another sequence of question-answer-objection, he follows that form nonetheless. The implicit *question* is how the colonists before him will live together in harmony and serve as a "model of Christian charity." His *answer* is an account that links love and mercy to unity. The former two needed no justification to a crowd of Christian believers; using these as firm premises, Winthrop makes the case that mercy and love ought to guide the colonists into unity as a people, thus turning Christian virtues toward a mundane political good. It is in this context that he raises what could be a devastating *objection*: how can any community truly be unified if all in it are destined to diversity of station, some rich and some poor? How, in other words, might we reconcile the natural divisions among men with the natural need men have for each other, for living together, for unity? We have already seen his answer: we must live in mercy and love, as made possible by grace; grace, made possible by God's love for us and our covenant with him.

Mercy stands at the heart of Winthrop's treatment of several very practical questions, answers, and objections about lending, giving generously, and forgiving debts. Mercy, which he elsewhere calls the outward manifestation of love, means for the Christian a generous spirit, especially in regard to the need of his neighbor.[48] If anyone asks us to lend to him, we should do it regardless of his ability to pay. If he cannot pay, we must give him whatever he needs as a gift.[49] If it seems he can pay but ultimately he cannot, we must take it as a loss. Any property we have is ultimately God's to take and use for his own purposes, and so we must not jealously try to hold onto it as if it were our own.[50] Winthrop cites two scripture passages in support of his point.

The "primitive church" had "all things in common"; the Puritans, so often imitators of the ways of the Old Testament, also sought frequently to imitate those early Christian communities who shared all they had.[51] In seeking to live like the earliest Christians, the Puritans were, again, following the lead of the Reformation, which was premised in part on the idea that the contemporary church had strayed too far from the ancient example. Generations of tradition had accreted onto the precious relic of the church, it was thought, and the way to return to its origins was to chip off the extraneous layers. In some sense, then, reforming the church meant turning back the clock on church practice, and Winthrop calls his hearers to accomplish this in their own community. They would strive as much as possible to have "all in common," according to the scriptural model. Winthrop knows, however, that living this way is no easy task, and so he immediately cites a second passage.

This time Winthrop recalls the Old Testament example of Nehemiah and the gargantuan task laid on his shoulders: to lead Israel out of captivity in Babylon and back to the Promised Land to rebuild God's temple. The task required vast resources and each Israelite was called upon to hand over anything that could be of use. Just so, Winthrop suggests, the task ahead for the Massachusetts Bay Colony was indeed seemingly greater than they could accomplish. But it was God's command and he does not command in vain. This does not mean that God accomplishes it for them: they may be required to undergo significant hardship.[52] But the work is good work, just as Nehemiah's was, though similarly extremely difficult.

Winthrop had an answer, too, for those difficulties: God will come into the souls of the colonists and infuse in them his own spirit of love, which is the real foundation from which springs forth all these outward manifestations of love. Though in Adam we have all been "rent" from our Creator, Christ comes "and takes possession of the soul, and infuseth another principle[,] love to God and our brother."[53] It is in taking up the theme of love that Winthrop's central theme of unity begins to become apparent.

Love, Winthrop quotes from scripture, is the "bond of perfection." First, he writes, "it is a bond, or ligament. 21y it makes the work perfect."[54] Already in setting *ligament* as synonymous with *bond*, Winthrop introduces into the discourse the analogy of the body. Here we see, finally, how he will reconcile the contradiction with which he began. Though man is always prevented from natural unity with his fellows because of natural distinctions, their distinctions and differences are meant to work together for the harmony of the whole, not against each other in disharmony and division.[55] Winthrop argues there, at the head of the sermon, that God is glorified more in having men achieve his ends for him, rather than accomplishing them directly through his own power. Just as earthly "princes" are more glorious if they have many servants, so much greater is God's glory because his plan requires the working together of all men. The diversity of the people, further, means that God's diverse gifts and man's diverse virtues—also God's creation—are reduced to a unity of purpose. And though it is often man's partiality that renders possible the full flowering of Christian charity, man's gifts and virtues may also show God's glory. Yet even here, Winthrop argues, God's glory and not the individual good of *any one* man is the purpose. Thus, if Christian charity, that is, love, is the principle that knits together the community, it can overcome the natural divisions of rich and poor, high and low. Love must be the animating principle of the community if it is to accomplish and fulfill the covenant it is making with God in the course of this journey. Love, as the bond of perfection, will bridge the gaps between members and reduce all their individual gifts, virtues, vices, and privations to the unity of God's plan for man.

After reasserting the importance of an inward infusion of love in each colonist and its necessity for unity and the success of the colony, Winthrop undertakes the enactment of the covenant on behalf of the people in the third and final part of the discourse. In detailing what will be the dominant structure of documents in the American political tradition, Kendall and Carey identify four main parts: "(*a*) a part in which the signers identify themselves, say who they are; (*b*) a part in which they state the *purposes* for which they undertake the business in hand; (*c*) a part that contains an oath creating the body politic; and (*d*) an addendum to the oath, in which the signers clarify their obligations under the oath, letting us know what kind of thing the new body politic is to be."[56] Winthrop begins the third major section of the discourse by noting the necessity of making "some application" of its principles and arguments. This application will be "propounded" in four parts: "first the persons, 2ly, the work, 3ly, the end, 4ly, the means."[57] The similarity is striking. The structure first perceived in the Mayflower Compact and subsequently found in the other major documents of the American political tradition is also found here in what amounts to the true founding document for the people of Massachusetts Bay.[58]

First, Winthrop identifies the parties to the covenant: "[W]e are a company professing ourselves fellow members of Christ."[59] Even if they become strangers somehow in the new land or if some members come and go, they are hereby included in this unifying covenant of love and life in common.

Kendall and Carey's second "part" can be found in Winthrop's "2ly" and "3ly." The Massachusetts Bay Colony is setting out "by a mutual consent through a special overruling Providence, and a more than an ordinary approbation of the churches of Christ to seek out a place of cohabitation and consortship under a due form of government both civil and ecclesiastical."[60] This is what they will do in the New England wilderness. Their government will necessarily be animated by the spirit of love Winthrop has already discussed in the first two parts of the discourse. But this has a consequence not yet explicitly stated in the discourse. In the main, Winthrop has focused on the relation of mercy, love, and unity. But in bringing up the matter of government, a new possibility rears its head: what if the people do not in every instance live up to the model he has set before them? What if they fail to follow these guidelines to the letter? "In such cases as this," writes Winthrop, "the care of the public must oversway all private respects, by which not only conscience, but mere civil policy doth bind us; for it is a true rule that particular estates cannot subsist in the ruin of the public."[61] The presence of government suggests the need to correct sometimes the mistakes of the colonists. Winthrop here reserves this right to government and places the colony's authority over personal, private judgments into the covenant itself.[62] After identifying the parties to the covenant, Winthrop moves on to articulating its purpose.

"The end" of the colony at Massachusetts Bay, Winthrop says, "is to improve our lives to do more service to the Lord[,] the comfort and increase of the Body of Christ whereof we are members[,] that our selves and posterity may be the better preserved from the common corruptions of this evil world[,] to serve the Lord and work out our salvation under the power and purity of his holy ordinances."[63] This is a dense and deliberate statement. It should be examined carefully.

First, the colony is a project to "improve our lives." They are, first and foremost, leaving England in order to better achieve the salvation of their own souls. As has already been seen in the "Reasons," this is not the sole purpose of the new community: the first of the reasons had to do with evangelization of the "natives" in order to head off the progress of the Catholic missionaries, thereby taking a place on the front lines of the Reformation. But the articulation here begins with the "improve[ment of] our lives," and this is not for themselves alone but "to do more service to the Lord." This will result in the "comfort and increase of the Body of Christ whereof we are members," and the community will serve as a refuge from "the common corruptions of this evil world." Their task is the foundation of a place, set apart, for growth in holiness. The image is reminiscent of the "bulwark" Winthrop discussed several months before in the "Reasons." The colonists want to establish a safe haven of Christian living. The aim is to fortify their new home *against* the "evil world" and *for* themselves and their posterity, a place made secure in, and with the help of, living "under the power and purity of his holy ordinances." Participation in just this kind of community will allow them to "serve the Lord and work out our salvation." It was the opportunity to live in such a place that led them to hazard the dangerous journey and to weather the rough conditions of the frontier.

Though the Puritans' project has sometimes been thought of as utopian, it was not. They were seeking not so much to reenter the Garden of Eden as to leave behind the City of Cain and thereby to be more assured of passage into the New Jerusalem. Though their crass conception of Indian property rights has sometimes been thought to justify the label *imperialist*, it does not. We see here that the aim of their mission was pointed directly at their own hearts, homes, and neighbors. Their task was self-improvement and the setting up of a bulwark, as much for the working out of their own salvation as for combating the spread of "Antichrist." Lest the means be called into question, Winthrop specifies them immediately upon explicating the "work" and "end" of the covenant, clarifying an important point about the Puritans' inward focus.

The *means* to becoming this ideal Christian community in which they can live out their lives and work out their own salvation is, in short, the unity so prominently discussed in the rest of the discourse. "For the means whereby this must be effected," Winthrop writes, "they are 2fold, a *conformity* with the work and end we aim at."[64] In other words, the task will be accomplished, the covenant will be fulfilled, if the new community is *one* in support of the covenanted government and the covenanted vision of its purpose. Only in the double *conformity* of the "work" and "end" can the colony succeed. The colonists will have to be radically one on matters of government and on matters of the ultimate grounding of the colony. They will have to be one as a body is one, and the animating principle of this body, its soul, must be love. This means actually practicing the virtues that most Christian churches only profess:

> [W]e must not content ourselves with usual[,] ordinary means whatsoever we did or ought to have done when we lived in England, [but] the same must we do[,] and more also[,] where we go: that which the most in their churches maintain as a truth in profession only, we must bring into familiar and constant practice, as in this duty of love[,] we must love brotherly[,] without dissimulation, we must love one another with a pure heart[,] fervently we must bear one another's burdens, we must not look only on our own things, but also on the things of our brethren.[65]

This will not be easy, but it is necessary—all the more necessary, first, on account of the "more near bond of marriage" the colony is about to undertake in this covenant; second, because of the observed consequences of failure for even those who have strayed from God in good faith; third, the many blessings God has already granted them mean that he deserves some measure of grateful obedience.[66]

After all these considerations, Winthrop finally comes to what Kendall and Carey call the "part that contains an oath creating the body politic": "Thus stands the cause between God and us, we are entered into a covenant with him for this work, we have taken out a commission, the Lord hath given us leave to draw our own articles[,] we have professed to enterprise these actions upon these and these ends, we have hereupon besought him of favor and blessing."[67] The "articles" that will need to be "strictly observed" have been laid out in the discourse.[68] The colonists must do nothing less than live perfect Christian lives. Yet to them this did not, perhaps, seem as impossible a task as it may sound. The love of Christ, which is "infused" into the soul of every regenerate believer, is the "bond of perfection" and can produce the ability to live lives in perfect community, because it dissolves natural differences into the unity of mercy and love.

Immediately after the moment of covenanting, Winthrop explains how God's approval will be ascertained: he says, "[N]ow if the Lord shall please to hear us, and bring us in peace to the place we desire, then hath he ratified this covenant and sealed our commission." Here Winthrop again glimpses into the mind of God by reading the book of history: if the colonists make it across the Atlantic, they will know God has "ratified this covenant." If they do not make it, they will know they have come to some disfavor with God and he has not sealed their covenant. Either way, the events of visible history are taken as evidence of the will of God. In this, it could be said that Winthrop is following the custom of calling natural forces as "witnesses" to the covenant.[69]

After the enactment and ratification have been achieved, Winthrop follows with another traditional element of Old Testament covenants: a statement of blessings and curses that will attend the parties to the covenant upon, respectively, its fulfillment or breach. There are three rounds of blessing and cursing, though the first is incomplete. In stereotypically Puritan fashion, Winthrop begins with a dour statement: "But if we shall neglect the observation of these articles which are the ends we have propounded, and dissembling with our God, shall fall to embrace this present world and prosecute our carnal intentions, seeking great things for ourselves and our posterity, the Lord will surely break out in wrath against us[,] be revenged of such a perjured people[,] and make us know the price of the breach of such a covenant."[70] There is no mention here of the blessings of the covenant's fulfillment but instead a summary of the articles that will require "strict observance," beginning with a quotation from Micah:

Now the only way to avoid this shipwreck and to provide for our posterity is to follow the counsel of Micah, to do justly, to love mercy, and to walk humbly with our God, for this end, [1] we must be knit together in this work as one man, [2] we must entertain each other in brotherly affection, [3] we must be willing to abridge our selves of our superfluities, for the supply of others' necessities, [4] we must uphold a familiar commerce together in all meekness, gentleness, patience and liberality, [5] we must delight in each other, make others' conditions our own[,] rejoice together, mourn together, labour and suffer together, [6] always having before our eyes our commission and community in the work, our community as members of the same body, so shall we keep the unity of the spirit in the bond of peace.[71]

These articles, each of which has been alluded to and mentioned previously either in the body of the discourse or in the "Reasons," stand in for the fourth part that Kendall and Carey identify as constitutive of symbols in the American political tradition: "an addendum to the oath, in which the signers clarify their obligations under the oath, letting us know what kind of thing the new body politic is to be." First and last Winthrop calls for the whole people to be "knit together in this work as one man" and to be "members of the same body." In this way they will "keep the *unity* of the spirit in the bond of peace." In the last clause of this passage, the principal symbol of the whole discourse is laid bare. But being a unified community—note that here and elsewhere, even the specific word *community* connotes the *oneness* he seeks—can be achieved only in the manner he has laid out in the discourse and in the covenant just given them. But covenants have consequences, and the second round of praising and blessing, which follows on this summary of the covenant's articles, illustrates these consequences fully for the first time.

If these articles are met and the covenant fulfilled, then the colonists will reap the benefits of a truly chosen people: "[T]he Lord will be our God and delight to dwell among us, as his own people[,] and will command a blessing upon us in all our ways, so that we shall see much more of his wisdom[,] power[,] goodness[,] and truth than formerly we have been acquainted with, we shall find that the God of Israel is among us, when ten of us shall be able to resist a thousand of our enemies, when he shall make us a praise and glory, that men shall say of succeeding plantations: the Lord make it like that of New England."[72] That the God of Israel would dwell among them puts the new Puritan covenant in line with the Old Testament covenants, each of which the Puritans conceived as a renewal or reenactment of the one covenant that God first made with Abraham. Notice, then, that the covenant itself is a historical endeavor—it seeks blessings and stipulates curses that are alike manifest in history, not in the atemporal and ahistorical hereafter. God's dwelling among them, his blessing them in "all our ways," his revealing of himself to them in a newly intimate fashion, even the Old Testament–style metaphor of infused military might: in some sense all of these things are spiritual or atemporal blessings (with the possible exception of the incredibly inclusive blessing "in all our ways"). The last blessing listed here cannot *but* be temporal and historical: "when he shall make us a praise and glory, that men shall say of succeeding plantations: the Lord make it like that of New England." The praise of other men can occur only in the context of history. What is perhaps the key blessing, however, is shown to be decidedly ambiguous. The ambition to be admired and set up as an example is tied up with the round of "cursing" immediately following this last blessing. It contains the most famous line of the entire discourse, which is also historical in nature.

In midsentence Winthrop switches from the coming praise of the nations to their cursing of the new community:

> [F]or we must consider that we shall be as a city upon a hill, the eyes of all people are upon us; so that if we shall deal falsely with our God in this work we have undertaken and so cause him to withdraw his present help from us, we shall be made a story and a byword through the world, we shall open the mouths of enemies to speak evil of the ways of God and all professors for God's sake; we shall shame the faces of many of God's worthy servants, and cause their prayers to be turned into curses upon us 'til we be consumed out of the good land whither we are going.[73]

Far from a statement of imperial superiority or design, the most famous words John Winthrop ever spoke are a warning against the failure to be a good *example* to the world. Winthrop wants to sear into the minds of his hearers the dire consequences of failure, the terrible blame that will be assigned to them if they do not meet the high bar God has set for their community. If they fail, they would be responsible for others cursing the "ways of God." This, too, then, is a historical consequence. In the first round of cursing Winthrop has mentioned that their failure would mean incurring God's wrath. Near the end of this second round he says that forsaking the covenant would also mean being "consumed out of the good land whither we are going." But here we see in very sharp relief that the project at Massachusetts Bay is not one only for the members of the colony. Upon their success depends God's favor among men. Though they are to focus only on their community—on being unified in work and end and action—it will redound to the benefit of the world and accrue either to God's glory or shame.

It is true that the phrase *city on a hill* could just as easily be included in the blessing passage immediately before it. Yet this ambiguity may be deliberate. To be party to this covenant, to be a chosen people, to be set up on a hill by God, is to enter a profoundly ambiguous state. Here is the full meaning of what Robert Bellah calls the "ambiguity of chosenness": blessings attend our satisfaction of God's demands; the worst curses and his wrath attend our failure. Here is the symbol that Bellah believes persists through American history, albeit rent in two and only selectively preserved beyond its inception here in the early Puritan period.[74]

The ambiguity is reiterated with a third round of blessing and cursing. If we keep the covenant, we will "live and be multiplied, and that the Lord our God may bless us in the land whither we go to possess it." "But," Winthrop counters, "if our hearts shall turn away so that we will not obey, but shall be seduced and worship . . . other gods[,] our pleasures, and profits, and serve them; it is propounded unto us this day, we shall surely perish out of the good land whither we pass over this vast sea to possess it."[75] Here, too, in a document and people ostensibly centered on more transcendent things, we see the surprising historicity of the blessings and curses. The implication of comfortable and fruitful living in New England is the third blessing; another threat of "perishing" in the foreign land is the third curse.

History, Politics, and American Exceptionalism

The relationship between claims to American exceptionalism and theories of history was partially explored in the discussion of Marxism in chapter 1. Winthrop's peculiar theory of history has been pointed out in passing in the course of examining the documents above. The relation of these, however, has yet to be made fully explicit. To do so at this stage is to risk introducing a suggestive tone of historical inexorability into the discussion of American history. I do not intend this and will try to avoid it. Nevertheless, there is great value in looking beyond the Puritan period in order to make the points of interest here more intelligible.

In many instances, the claim to American exceptionalism today involves positing a theory of world history, or Western history, from which American history deviates. Marxism is the easy and appropriate example. It claims that the economic classes throughout the world are locked in a struggle for ascendancy and, at the end of the capitalist stage, the underclass will overthrow the overclass and install itself as a dictator, enacting socialist policies designed to hasten the onset of communist society. Two aspects of the theory bear striking similarity to Winthrop. First, the possibility of the theory relies on the intelligibility of history, on the idea that the vicissitudes of history actually have an order and logic that may be discerned. We have seen this in Winthrop's discussion of the economic situations in England and New England and in his comments on the illnesses that beset the "natives" of New England: Winthrop believes these portend the unfolding plan of divine Providence: England is about to succumb to a great calamity.[76] He believes, just like Marxist theory, that history has an intelligible purpose. As Bercovitch has put it, the Puritans saw themselves as representatives of all humanity: "The local emphasis was by no means parochial. The destiny of Christ's people in America was the destiny of mankind."[77] Winthrop also believes, like many a convinced Marxist, that history can be helped along if it is read correctly. Winthrop's exodus makes possible the establishment of a bulwark in the wilderness, which serves as the latest episode in salvation history. Some have seen in this, and in his talk of a "commission" distinct from the covenant, a capitulation to Arminianism. While Winthrop would have vehemently denied it, that his theory of history is open to that charge is fairly clear.[78] In his defense, however, it could be said that his theory does not claim to *sway* history but only to read it and, thus, provide the opportunity to act in accord with it.

American Exceptionalism and Winthrop's "City on a Hill"

A plausible first-blush reading of Winthrop's phrase *city on a hill* has been enough to make plausible the claim that he is the first American exceptionalist. After an in-depth examination of the context of the term—both in the document and in the context of Winthrop's larger vision for the colony at Massachusetts Bay—it is clearer than ever that such a claim is misguided. Winthrop could not possibly be an American exceptionalist as such: the United States of America—doubtless the referent in discussions of American exceptionalism—does not yet exist when Winthrop founds the Massachusetts Bay Colony. Yet it could perhaps be argued that he is a "Massachusetts Bay Colony exceptionalist," seeing his own colony as special in the world and in human history, and therefore, deserving of special prerogatives. This is also not the case.

The context of the phrase *city on a hill* makes Winthrop's meaning fairly clear. It falls in the middle of his three rounds of blessing and cursing at the end of the enactment and divine ratification of the covenant. Rather than a statement, then, that some set of rules applies to some nations or churches but not to Massachusetts Bay—rather than, that is, a "comparative" sense of exceptionalism—it states something very different: the world is watching us and waiting to evaluate our work until we succeed or fail. It is a statement not of any radical freedom from the rules and constraints that apply to other peoples but of the radical boundedness and circumscription of the colonists' lives that was just effected by the covenant. The phrase, rather than a license for the colony to command the world how to live, is a dire warning of the terrible consequences that the *colonists* will face if they fail to live lives of complete Christian virtue. The Massachusetts Bay Colony was above all "the errand within," to use Samuel Danforth's 1670 phrase.[79] Winthrop's key passage is also inwardly focused, an admonition for the Puritans to live up to their agreement with God, not an outwardly focused justification either for double standards or imperialism.

The phrase is an allusion to scripture and its context there sheds more light on Winthrop's meaning. The reference is to Matthew 5:14, which is a verse from Jesus's Sermon on the Mount. In preaching to those present Christ says,

> Blessed are ye when men revile you, and persecute *you*, and say all manner of evil against you for my sake, falsely. Rejoice and be glad, for great is your reward in heaven; for so persecuted they the Prophets which were before you. Ye are the salt of the earth; but if the salt have lost his savor, wherewith shall it be salted? It is thenceforth good for nothing, but to be cast out, and to be trodden under foot of men. Ye are the light of the world. A city that is set on a hill, cannot be hid. Neither do men light a candle, and put it under a bushel, but on a candlestick, and it giveth light unto all that are in the house. Let your light so shine before men, that they may see your good works, and glorify your Father which is in heaven.[80]

The Christian tradition has long interpreted this passage as speaking to preachers—and the Geneva Bible commentary, which Winthrop and most Puritans would have known well, does not depart from that tradition. Those who are reviled and persecuted on Jesus's account are those who, by the nature of their office, would be constantly out in plain view. The words here are a recognition of that and an exhortation not to shrink from their public ministry in the face of being reviled and persecuted. "A city that is set on a hill cannot be hid"; just so, a preacher is by definition a public person. His witness is out in the open, necessarily, and it is not incongruous with the role that Winthrop foresaw for the new colony. Massachusetts Bay would be a light to the world. It was going to show the world, in the flesh, the perfect Christian commonwealth. But this community "cannot be hid," and *this* is why the phrase is found at the end of the discourse and as part of the covenant section on blessing and cursing. The failure of so public a venture, of so ambitious an effort, would be as widely noticed as it would be disastrous. It would bring scandal to Puritans and ministers everywhere.[81] A city on a hill cannot be hid, so their very public mission will meet with either a very public success or a very public failure.[82]

The full context of the phrase thus makes clear that the Puritan project at Massachusetts Bay was not a design on worldly power. It was also not viewed as an easy task either vouchsafed or wholly accomplished by a generous God. Winthrop is keenly aware of the cost and very real possibility of failure. But these do not convince him to refrain from entering into the effort. If this *phrase's* direct connection to the idea of American exceptionalism is denied, then the connection between the idea of the Puritans and American exceptionalism might be called into question. Despite this, a deeper connection may be affirmed.

Exemplary Exceptionalism and the "End" of the Massachusetts Bay Colony

John Winthrop argues forcefully that the chief end of the Massachusetts Bay Colony was religious. The new community would embody a perfectly Christian way of life through its ordinances and "strict performance" of the articles of their covenant with God. This embodiment would, if successful, mean the new community was a light to the world; if unsuccessful, they would be a watchword to the nations. Either way, the particular work in Massachusetts has broad, even universal significance. Here, then, we are faced with the very center of the idea of American exceptionalism: the claims to universality that lie at the heart of Christianity.

Though meant to be focused on the beam in one's own eye, it is easy for us to see, and be tempted to dislodge, the speck in another's.[83] To know and to love the truth of salvation, of nature and grace, of good and evil, brings with it a temptation to hubris and arrogance. To argue that Winthrop and the Puritans were guilty of such arrogance cannot but be true. These were real men and they would undoubtedly admit to their own partiality, vice, and sin—perhaps even with a dour enthusiasm. Yet to argue that their conception of society is at bottom hubristic and arrogant and proud is to make a subtle mistake. To argue thus would mean first conflating all claims to universality and subsequently rejecting them all based on the account of the Puritans. To argue that the Puritans were imperialistic confuses the universality in their political and historical thought—which is present in various forms in all Christian thought—with the universality present in imperialism, which is of a different character. This confusion is a failure to distinguish between the relevance of universality to cognition or belief, on the one hand, and to action, on the other. Winthrop's conviction that the universal mind of God is discoverable by the particular mind of man in the particular events of history may be false. But arguing for the falsehood of Winthrop's view need not relegate all views containing an element of universality to the same category of falsehood.

John Winthrop and the colonists were not making claims to American exceptionalism in founding their colony. Neither were they making claims excepting their colony from some set of rules governing history. The rules of history, in their mind, were written by the ruler of history, and though its course might perhaps be discerned partially, the purposes behind it were surely not knowable with any sort of finality.[84] But their faith and their knowledge of history led them to believe that the setting up of the colony was a project willed by God. They were to be an example to behold, an example to be imitated—an exemplar to history and to the world. But being hailed as an exemplar is fundamentally different from conquering and ruling an empire.[85] The difference is as wide as the character of submission that attends each: submission in one is voluntary, and in the other it is not. The Puritans were exemplary, not imperial exceptionalists. Under one, similarity is achieved through obedience or inspiration. Under the other, it is achieved through coercion.

Perry Miller notes that though Puritan theology is often thought of as deterministic, "we are always in danger of forgetting that the life of the Puritan was completely voluntaristic. . . . The man into whose soul grace had been infused was liberated from that bondage and made free to undertake the responsibilities and obligations of virtue and decency," which is not possible under determinism. This was, in part, a practical and theoretical rebellion against the absolutism of the Stuart monarchs, Miller thinks, which further buttresses the argument that the Puritans were not about to begin forcing involuntary compliance with their rule. The Puritans wished to inspire obedience, not coerce it.[86] Ignorance of the line that divides exemplary and imperial exceptionalism makes more plausible the bristling stand often taken against Winthrop's universalistic words. Yet Winthrop's universalism is of a wholly different kind from the universalism of empire.

We have seen the role God was thought to play in Puritan society and the implicit views on history that that entails. We have seen the deep correspondence of the Puritan synthesis of theology and history to views of American exceptionalism. We can now begin to see that the contemporary idea of American exceptionalism would not have been possible except for its germination from the seed of the early Puritan synthesis. But it has also been made clear that contemporary imperialistic conceptions of American exceptionalism have not come directly from Winthrop and the Puritans. The idea has undergone major alterations and we are now prepared, after understanding this initial account, to understand the nature of those changes over the course of American history.

3

THE FOUNDERS

A Providentially Guided, Temporally Bound Country

Some of the most prominent commentators on the question of American exceptionalism have argued that the principal figures of America's founding generation were ardent imperialists in word and deed.[1] The claim is well established, it is supposed, by the vocabulary of key figures of that period in American politics. The use of the word *empire* to describe the new country from the Philadelphia convention onward is said to prove the founders' expansionist ambitions.[2] This, they say, belies claims to the limitedness of America's polity, along with the country's expansion across the face of the continent (a policy that was hotly contested at the time).

Historical scholarship is often tricky, not least because of the ambiguity and fluidity of language. The relationship between words and actions is even trickier. If some modesty and moderation are introduced into the case, it becomes obvious that what has occurred from the time of the American founding to today is not a constant line of imperialistic tendencies and actions but a change in the meaning of the word *empire*.[3] What is truly needed, rather than a simplistic argument based on vocabulary, is a thorough examination of the deep meaning of the most important documents of the period. Only then will the question of the founders' imperialism be answerable.

In the previous chapter the Massachusetts Puritans' understanding of God's role in their political order was outlined and shown to be an element of future conceptions of American exceptionalism. John Winthrop's "exemplary exceptionalism" was shown to have paved the way for imperial exceptionalism because of the elements of universality contained within it. Confusion about the role of universality in politics made possible the use of Winthrop's "exemplary" rhetoric for imperial purposes. From today's vantage point in history, we hear the imperial ring of Winthrop's words. But this imperial ring was superadded to Winthrop; his meaning was not originally imperial but came later to be taken as such. If anachronism can be avoided, then we see that those Puritans were not, in their time, imperialists at all. The same will be seen in the crucial documents of the American founding period.

The imperial exceptionalism seen later in American history had not yet developed in the minds of the constitutional generation. Far from imperialistic, the framers' conception of American order was continuous with the Puritans' in many ways. One can see, however, some differentiation of the Puritan symbols: biblical symbols, for example, though scarcely less powerful and prevalent in late eighteenth-century America, played a different role in discussions of political order.[4] Rather than serving as a strict blueprint for the manner in which society would run, these symbols provided inspiration and rhetorical flourish to the founders' words (which were rooted in the extant political tradition and in practical experience). The place of God in politics, it will be seen, had changed, and this affects the framers' conception of history. The simple manner in which government and God were related for the Massachusetts Bay colonists is no longer the case for the Americans of the constitutional generation. A "differentiation" has occurred, and exploring the nature of this differentiation is a new but necessary task in this chapter.

The pivotal years of the 1770s and 1780s see the composition and adoption of America's most cherished documents, and it ought to be explored whether these contain the kind of imperialistic exceptionalism so evident in later American history. In the course of examining the basic symbols of the American political tradition, I will argue that the evidence cannot support what some have supposed—that the founders aspired to be, or hoped their country would later be, an imperial power on the world stage.[5]

One of the most prominent features of the Massachusetts Bay Colony's conception of government—the explicit conception of their political community as a literal covenant with God—disappears from the political order of the American founding generation. The Puritan view faded relatively quickly: the 1639 Fundamental Orders of Connecticut have already abandoned the language of "covenant."[6] Yet it is not the fraying of the previous order that leads to the disappearance of this language. Rather, it is the increasing strength and embeddedness of that order that lead to the absence of the language of "covenant" from the Fundamental Orders. The political order has not been reconceived as something other than a covenant; its covenantal character is now so integral a part of the political order of the colonies that it may be taken for granted. It is not absent, but implicit.

The implicitness of the idea of a covenantal political order is said to be due to the fact that "the Mayflower Compact has become a symbol so familiar and meaningful that it is capable of merely tacit evocation."[7] The Fundamental Orders introduce two new symbols into the American political tradition, namely, "to maintain the peace" and "union." The symbols from Winthrop's "Model" discourse persist in the Fundamental Orders' new way to "assimilate the political and religious order."[8] "Chosenness" and the ambiguity attendant to it had already become a key part of the Massachusetts tradition by the time of the Fundamental Orders, and it is this very notion that lies at the heart of Connecticut's "new way." The necessity of maintaining unity is tied to this. Unity is the dominant symbol and thrust of Winthrop's discourse. The Puritan community was based on being radically "one," and the maintenance of unity was the means to this peace.[9]

The introduction of the Winthrop symbols into the main vein of the American political tradition poses a problem for the interpretation of that tradition. Namely, the degree to which the Fundamental Orders differs from the other documents—arising out of the Winthrop deposit—raises the question of whether a derailment has occurred in the tradition, rather than merely a differentiation. Kendall and Carey argue emphatically that the Fundamental Orders are a derailment: "[F]rom the standpoint of the later development, Connecticut here offers us an example of what Voegelin would call a 'derailment' of the original symbolization, and, at the same time, let us note, a move away from the language and spirit of moderation."[10] A few things should be said here before laying aside these points for the time being.

First, arguing that the Winthrop tradition is a derailment would mean arguing that the other line of the development—from the Mayflower Compact through the Massachusetts Body of Liberties and to the Constitution—constitutes a path of unproblematic sequential differentiation. Such an understanding lacks qualification and nuance. Whole documents, it should be said explicitly, need not belong wholly to the categories of derailment or differentiation. Any single document may contain elements of each. This is largely due to the second main point: these documents are not themselves symbols but *contain* symbols. Symbols—for example, unity—are the main unit of analysis in this inquiry. Once the relevant symbols are gleaned from the founding period, a determination of derailment or differentiation is possible; the discussion must be put off until then. Third, this discussion of derailment and differentiation lies at the heart of an adequate account of the

American political tradition, because it is a key part of tracing the origins, nature, and development of the self-conception of the American people.

Already with the Fundamental Orders of Connecticut and the Massachusetts Body of Liberties, religion's relation to the political realm begins to become distinct. Though the Fundamental Orders possess characteristics that are not part of the rest of the tradition according to Kendall and Carey, the document nonetheless articulates a somewhat ambiguous new relationship between God and the colony. Recall again the difference between the Pilgrims and the Puritans in regard to religion and politics. The political community, it seems, has been singled out by God for *some* reason.[11] It is possible that many peoples—or all—are called to service and a mission not dissimilar to the one pointed out in the Fundamental Orders. But this sense of uniqueness is not the main aspect of this articulation of religion and politics relevant here; rather, politics is in some sense the servant of religion. Put another way, the political community governed by the Fundamental Orders still understands politics as an instrument of God's plan in history, not unlike Winthrop nine years before. Yet there are palpable changes already in the 1639 document.

The peculiarly American symbols are, with the Fundamental Orders, becoming more defined. The "better ordering" of the Mayflower Compact has become the "orderly and decent government" of the Fundamental Orders. With this comes the innovation of a written constitution, not present previously as a single document. It is with the Fundamental Orders of Connecticut that the representative assembly is first symbolized in the American political tradition, and from here onward the legislative body is considered supreme.[12] An emphasis on legislative supremacy is all the more evident in Kendall and Carey's treatment of the Massachusetts Body of Liberties, in which "[o]ne might well say that the 'better ordering' and the 'thought-to-be-meet-and-convenient-for-the-general-Good' symbols of the Mayflower Compact have differentiated out into the symbols of an omnicompetent and legally omnipotent deliberative assembly."[13] This does not mean that the Massachusetts Body of Liberties is a move toward positivism; government is not held to be the sole measure of "justice" and the "general good." Rather, the Massachusetts Body of Liberties is an enactment and self-articulation of the supremacy of consent for politics.[14] Seen in this light, the continuity with the Mayflower Compact is obvious. This point is all the more persuasive when the circumstances surrounding its adoption are recalled.

The colonial period in New England was characterized more and more by a tendency toward self-government. From the early move toward white male suffrage in 1633 to the move for codification of the rules of government almost a decade later, even the Massachusetts Bay Colony—striving so much to remain radically one—no longer found the path to unity exclusively through representation in a single figure like John Winthrop. Unity is now achieved through documented mutual subordination not to a single man's wisdom and guidance but "to the transcendent truth of the soul and of society, and because it has demanded of the persons who are individual components that by 'signing' they signify their subordination, as persons, to that truth."[15] Representation itself is reconceived in this period, so that government itself undergoes changes accordingly. If we no longer consider a single man as sufficient to "represent" us as a community, the institutional change is evidence of the change in self-conception. Understood in this way, the change was effected by the Fundamental Orders of Connecticut and the Massachusetts Body of Liberties.

In these colonial documents, then, the people begin to understand an assembly as their "representative." The unity that has ever been the goal of all the political orders considered so far is now considered most appropriately achieved by the election of a supreme representative assembly. This new understanding of "representation" in particular is also a new understanding of politics in general, since politics is, under these documents, not considered a grant of the king but an activity of the people themselves for the people's own benefit.[16] Here it is not the end that is unique or new—it had been the consensus of most Western political thought for centuries that the end of good government was the good of the people—but the means: the representative assembly.[17] This is a symbol that, though modified in the Constitution to come, will not disappear from the American political tradition.

Kendall and Carey rightly believe the Massachusetts Body of Liberties to be continuous with the Constitution on the question of religion and politics. The Virginia Declaration of Rights similarly separates the two realms; it "drives a *wedge* between philosophy, which is the symbol to which it appeals when it speaks of justice, moderation, etc., and religion; and, with recognizably symbolic intent, drains the latter, religion, off for separate treatment."[18] The distinction between questions of "philosophy" and "religion," or between the "sphere of government" and the "sphere of society," is the "definitive American differentiation" and is already evident in the Virginia Declaration of Rights. "In the sphere of government, in short," Kendall and

Carey write, "religion is to be given the status it enjoys in the Constitution, which is to say *no* status at all."[19]

This Virginian understanding is not competing with the Massachusetts Body of Liberties, even though the latter contains much religious language that the former lacks; but they do "understand a Christian commonwealth to be a different sort of thing from what it was in Massachusetts; in the very act of symbolically disestablishing the Christian religion, by separating it from government, they establish it as the religion, the public truth, of American society, a status which (we believe) it continues to enjoy."[20] While perhaps the ubiquity of Christianity as the "public truth" of American society could be questioned today, Kendall and Carey's basic point about the understanding contributed by the colonial Virginians need not be. Kendall and Carey are arguing that the Virginians, rightly or wrongly, believed themselves to be establishing a Christian political order, even as they established one that claimed no competence on matters of religion.[21] This point invites reflection on the founding generation's conceptions of the relation of God and government. On this point, James Hutson is particularly instructive.

In an article aimed at making sense of the founders' beliefs about religion and society, Hutson finds remarkable unanimity on what might be called the sociological view of religion and politics. Such radically different figures as Thomas Paine and Theophilus Parsons believed the *effect* of religion on society and government to be salutary. This was due chiefly, Hutson shows, to the effect of the belief in a "future state of rewards and punishments," which was thought a vital component of the rule of law.[22] The base of the unanimity detailed by Hutson is, however, telling; it is founded on an *indirect* relationship of religion and politics in which the two are integrally connected, but only through the medium of society. A distinction in the spheres of religion and politics has been made since the time of the Puritans; whether the people act in their political or social capacity, these capacities are no longer one and the same.[23]

The Declaration of Independence

The first major document of American self-understanding from the founding period is one that has long been cherished as central to the American political tradition. The Declaration of Independence has admitted a very wide range of interpretations. Some consider it a charter of the elementary freedoms and rights of all mankind, while others see it as a simple indictment of a wayward ruler by a people steeped in the procedures, traditions, law, and experience of self-government.[24] For many, the Declaration has coequal status with the U.S. Constitution as America's two principal founding documents. These and many other interesting points about the Declaration—especially questions about the importance of equality and the existence of fundamental rights—have long been discussed in both peer-reviewed journals and more popular fora. But the old words must be read with new eyes.

Most Americans, scholars or not, would take it for granted that the beginning of the Declaration of Independence makes strikingly universal claims about the nature of government and human existence. Yet some words of context and qualification may cast doubt on these impressions.

The Second Continental Congress adopted the Declaration of Independence on July 4, 1776, in response to increasing acts of aggression by the British Crown. First penned by Thomas Jefferson and then amended in committee with John Adams and Benjamin Franklin, the Declaration was further amended in Congress before the final vote. Thus the Declaration was a decidedly corporate document, not the work only of Jefferson's admittedly able hand. "The more alterations Congress made on his draft," Pauline Maier notes," the more miserable Jefferson became." More important for our purposes is Maier's point, following Jefferson, that "[a]s a statement of political philosophy, the Declaration was therefore purposefully unexceptional in 1776."[25] The Declaration was intended by Jefferson and Congress to be a *summation* of widely held American views and beliefs, not a document meant to foment a revolution that would not have otherwise occurred. Thus the Declaration is intended as a representative document, though I will argue that the representation is one of circumscribed purpose.[26] This point is significant because it makes even more plausible the idea that the Declaration is representative of the whole people; rather than one man's political thought, it is the political act of a corporate body. The body of Congress was its author in a very real sense because only in its adoption, amendment, and promulgation were the words fully operative, fully what they were—a declaration of the several states' independence. As words, they were little more than ink on paper. But these words were also, taken together and pronounced by the people in Congress, an act. In adopting the Declaration, the American people were declaring themselves united for "action in history." Theirs was a coming together for one purpose, the purpose detailed in the Declaration: formal separation from the king and people of Great Britain.

Rather than its universality, the most striking feature of the Declaration is its fundamental particularity. After the introduction and preamble, there are no less than twenty-nine separate charges of wrongdoing brought against the king. Each is concrete and definite: his failure to rule his subjects by law; his encouragement of "domestic insurrections" in the colonies; his answering the colonists' repeated petitions for redress of grievances only with "repeated injury."[27] Many of the charges point to the main symbol of the whole American political tradition: these crimes constitute contraventions of the colonists' ability for deliberate self-rule by a representative assembly.[28]

A reading of the Declaration in its context answers, chiefly, two questions: who are the people speaking, and what are they doing? Immediately, we see that this document is "[t]he unanimous Declaration of the thirteen united States of America."[29] The document in hand is a joint statement of thirteen distinct entities. These entities, the states, are, however, unanimous in regard to the statements in the body of the document. No matter the manner in which the Declaration is taken afterward—whatever purposes it might later serve—the evidence from the text shows that it is a uniting document not unlike the Mayflower Compact and Winthrop's "Model" discourse. Though it will not set up a new structure of government, the document *is* the common action of these thirteen states. The speaker-actors have identified themselves. What are their purposes? If they are not undertaking to found a new political order, why have they come together? In short, the thirteen colonies come together to "declare the causes which impel them to separation" from the English, a people to which these states have formerly been tied with "political bands."

The announced purpose of the document, then, is to both enact and explain the states' separation from England. What follows next is the explanation, which is, first, an accounting of certain political principles upon which the founders base their action and, second, a list of the "long train of abuses and usurpations" that demonstrate the concrete historical circumstances that lead them to the practical conclusion of political separation. This third part of the Declaration constitutes what was traditionally the fourth and last part of such documents in the American political tradition up to this point.[30] The reason for this can be detected in the difference between this portion of the Declaration and other, similar documents. This portion of the Declaration takes the form and tone of an indictment. Rather than a positive statement of the principles of American government, we actually have a negative statement of the myriad ways that the colonies have been tyrannized. Rather than a treatise on good government, we have an indictment of bad government, which, though it is not the same thing, serves the same purpose in this case.

Implicit in the indictment, of course, is a vague picture of good government—a picture we might have already been able to paint, even without reference to the Declaration of Independence, because of the presence of such an account in the colonial tradition well before 1776. But there are good reasons for leaving the principles of good government implicit. First—and perhaps this is surprising given the most common interpretations of the document—the Declaration of Independence is just what it says it is: a declaration that enacts and explains the independence of the several American states. As such, the members of the Second Continental Congress, on behalf of the people of the thirteen colonies, tread no farther than is necessary to accomplish their stated task. The document's efficiency in regard to its task is patent. There are moments of waxing eloquence, but every last word is aimed at the double goal of enacting and explaining American independence from Great Britain. Everything present there serves this end.

Though later years of scholarship have accreted layers of meaning to its various clauses and vocabulary, the plain sense of the document cries out for a straightforward interpretation. Such an interpretation is further buttressed by the Declaration's ultimate and culminating paragraph that includes "the oath creating the body politic." Here we must exercise the same caution as in the middle part of the document: the Declaration does not so much create a "new body politic" as unchain one from the other, or, more precisely, one England from thirteen colonies. The only explicit relation between the colonies themselves is the unanimity in this one particular act. No further provision for political order *among* them is provided. Yet this smaller act is no less political for not being constructive. Indeed, the absence of constructive clauses, it would seem, suggests the lack of necessity for such construction in a document otherwise very focused on what is absolutely necessary and politically expedient. The last part, the "oath," is clear and simple and resembles closely a resolution offered days earlier by the Virginia delegation: "[T]hat these United Colonies are, and of Right ought to be Free and Independent States; that they are Absolved from all Allegiance to the British Crown, and that all political connection between them and the State of Great Britain, is and ought to be totally dissolved." Though the largely negative character of this oath is rightfully noticed and maintained, Congress does take a few words to explain, in a tone less than negative, what they mean by the colonies' new rights as "Free and Independent States": they "have the full Power to levy War, conclude Peace, contract Alliances, [and] establish Commerce." Note that this is not a list of ends to be accomplished by some newly formed government institution or body. It is a clarification of what was meant by the phrase "Free and Independent." Though the imperialists around the turn of the twentieth century hearken back to the Declaration for justification of their imperial project, they do not dream of allowing their annexed territory in the Philippines the power, itself, to "levy War, conclude Peace, contract Alliances, [and] establish Commerce." This will be done *for* them. This double standard in regard to the interpretation of the Declaration can be taken as a sign of these imperialists' stance outside the mainstream of the American political tradition.

Though the Declaration does not establish or found a new political entity, it does establish a new political order. Rather than create new government structures, it relies on the thirteen such structures already in place, recognizing that each of them holds the "separate and equal station" of a "Free and Independent" state. When the Fundamental Orders of Connecticut, the Massachusetts Body of Liberties, the Virginia Declaration of Rights, or even the Mayflower Compact were articulated, none of them presumed to begin ex nihilo. Each was an alteration of existing structures, effected by parties responsible for their upkeep. Just so with Winthrop's discourse: his blueprint for unity and order might have been taken as mere oratory had he not already been invested with the authority to guide the community and set the people on the path he announced. Each time the change was not from nothing to something but from one set of arrangements to another similar one. This is part of what is comprehended under the term *differentiation*, though that discussion should again be postponed until all the documents are examined. Suffice it to say that the Declaration alters but does not entirely create or destroy an order by itself.

The questions of universality or theories of history may be dealt with quickly and side by side. The second paragraph of the Declaration seems to make numerous universalistic claims, claims that have been interpreted as a kind of charter of human rights. While the literature on the question is vast, the text itself cannot bear this more expansive interpretation. Despite the apparent use of blanket statements in the Declaration's second paragraph, each is modified by that paragraph's very beginning. No matter what influences the founders countenanced in setting down the words as they are, all of them are chastened and subordinated to the concrete aim of the document by the words "[w]e hold." Though what is held are "truths" and though these truths are held as "self-evident," it cannot be said that the claims of the second paragraph serve any purpose but to legitimate the thirteen former colonies' separation from Great Britain and to recognize their dignity as sovereign states. The Declaration is a concrete document of political action, and the universalistic tone is subordinated to particular aims. Thus, interpretations of the Declaration of Independence as a charter of rights for all nations are not in keeping with the understanding of the founders. Long cited as one of the grandest and most universalistic documents of the American political tradition, the Declaration is, to the contrary, one of the most limited and concrete, even in its most rhetorically memorable passages.

We know what the aim of the Declaration is because it is stated explicitly: separation. We learn in the first paragraph that we are dealing with a people that is not English. The second paragraph is a recitation of the main outlines of then-common social contract theory. The debates surrounding the Declaration's composition and revision show how much care was put into each syllable, and so we can say with confidence that the claims of the second paragraph are included *in light of* the first, not in spite of it. In other words, these rights asserted—so often controversial and so often nowadays said to be individual rights that are ever expanding—are in this document referring to the people of the United States as a whole, as a unit. This "unanimous declaration" is, again, not a treatise of political philosophy, not a statement of the universalistic principles of good government for all times and places, but the justification for the United States to be independent of and separate from Great Britain.

These considerations about the universalism present in the document have, in turn, a profound effect on the document's implicit theory of history. In short, there is none. The extent of the document's historical consciousness is nearly exhausted by its opening words: "When, in the course of human events, it becomes necessary . . ." The phrase implies that it is not *always* necessary to undertake the kind of action about to be undertaken; it is *sometimes* necessary. The concrete charges that follow indicate that late eighteenth-century America was one of those times and places. There is no air of inevitability or notion that this move is the last, first, or middle term in any inexorable historical syllogism. What happens in the thirteen states, it seems, stays in the thirteen states. And the message is reinforced by the only use to which the Declaration puts history: as a repository of various political happenings on this side of the Atlantic. There is no grand force of history here, and the document does not situate itself in any kind of line with a future destiny or mission. It should not be said, however, that the document is wholly without reference to things transcendent.

There are two places in the Declaration that speak of God. One is the particularly famous "Laws of Nature and Nature's God." The other is near the end, when the people appeals to the "Supreme Judge of the world for the rectitude of our intentions." God, in this latest act of the drama of the American political tradition, has been passed over for the lead, relegated to a merely supporting role. The first invocation refers to God's role in creation. It is a nod, perhaps, to the numerous debates on politics and the state of nature, on the one hand, and to the belief of many Christians that God ordained the necessity of government from the beginning of time, on the other. For all the connotations, however, the plain sense of the text must again be recalled. The first appeal to God in this document is a baseline statement of what allows the thirteen new states to become "Free and Independent." God, in other words, makes possible their action. He even makes it appropriate. But he is not a direct, acting partner with them. He is passive rather than active, his role modal rather than causal. The later mention of God in the Declaration is not dissimilar to the first. God is being called upon as a witness to the otherwise secular act being undertaken in the Declaration. Here we see in sharp relief the distinction between the political and religious spheres, which I will discuss later. The Second Continental Congress adopts the Declaration "in the Name, and by the Authority of the good People of these colonies." Authority to separate from England and act as one is not a supernatural ability (except in the scanty sense of the Declaration's first line). Congress acts on the authority of the people it represents. This authority is given to all distinct peoples corporately and is exercised in America in Congress, that is, by the states' convening. But the representatives recognize that their intentions could be impugned. The later appeal to God is a testimony to the people's upright intentions. He serves as proof against detractors, a character witness in the court convened by the just-issued Declaration-indictment of the British Crown. These features, and their difference with the old Puritan symbols, will be discussed. But first, the other major political documents of the founding generation must be taken up.

The Articles of Confederation

In seeking the chief symbols of the American political tradition, one would be remiss in not pointing up the advent of the first government of the United

States as a single political entity.[31] Though the Declaration was certainly an act of the states together, it should be said that in 1776 the states spoke the same words in unison rather than with a single voice. The same can be said of the new document the Continental Congress passed the year after the Declaration, when the same body adopted the "Articles of Confederation and Perpetual Union" and sent those Articles to the states for approval. For various reasons—not the least of which were border disputes among the states—the Articles did not become operative for four years. Until 1781, then, the thirteen former colonies acted in the manner each one saw fit. Problems with commerce and foreign relations led the colonies to eventually concede the necessity of a common government.

As for symbols contained in the Articles, the document is nearly all bones and no meat. Very few points of interest are present. Its main purpose for us is found in deepening our understanding of the nature of the political order as it existed just before and just after the Articles' adoption. In this capacity, the Articles serve to confirm the picture given by a plain reading of the Declaration. Article II makes abundantly clear that "[e]ach state retains its sovereignty, freedom and independence." We remember the "Free and Independent" formulation from the Declaration; it is now officially and operatively recognized and preserved in the erection of the new common government.

The states enter into a "firm league of friendship with each other, for their common defense, the security of their Liberties, and their mutual and general welfare, binding themselves to assist each other, against all force offered to, or attack made upon them, or any of them, on account of religion, sovereignty, trade, or any other pretence whatever." Here we see the states' purpose in coming together and, as might be expected in the midst of a war, the chief concern is the "common defense" and binding each to the other so that none will lack the assistance they may, and will, come to need. None of this sounds very different from the Declaration's formulations; it even sounds much like the Constitution's. But the chief difference concerns the *manner* in which the states come together, which, as Article III plainly indicates, is "severally." This is reinforced by the identification of the speaker-actors at the head of the document; we are dealing with the "Articles of Confederation and perpetual Union *between the states* of New Hampshire, Massachusetts-bay Rhode Island and Providence Plantations, Connecticut, New York, New Jersey, Pennsylvania, Delaware, Maryland, Virginia, North Carolina, South Carolina and Georgia" (emphasis added). The document that follows is an action undertaken *by the states*, not the people. It is a "confederacy," not a single country. It is a conglomeration rather than an integrated whole.

The states come together in Congress in the same manner they had in the summer of 1776—as sovereign and independent states—but with a slightly different goal. They come together, once again, for a qualified and limited purpose. In 1776 this purpose was independence. In the midst of fighting for that independence, they have come together to better equip themselves to resist their common aggressors. Though the Articles contain provisions prohibiting independent commerce and foreign policy, these provisions are routinely flouted in the coming years, paving the way for further calls to union and, eventually, the U.S. Constitution.

The U.S. Constitution

We come now to the document that undisputedly lies at the heart of the American political tradition. Though, like the Declaration, much ink has been spilled in the Constitution's interpretation, there are immediately recognizable lines of continuity and divergence from the tradition that leads up to it, lines that we have already begun to see emerge. Those lines are the chief concern here. Just as at the head of the Declaration of Independence and the Articles of Confederation, we have, first and foremost in this document, the identification of those speaking and acting: "We the People of the United States." Here already is one of the most pertinent differences between the Constitution and the other documents of the tradition. Though the Declaration and the Articles were documents spoken and enacted by the states "severally," the Constitution is for the first time an act undertaken by the American people as a whole.[32] Here the states speak not in unison—as with the Declaration of Independence and the Articles of Confederation—but with a single voice (or, rather, the people of the several states speak with a single voice). Here the old political problem of reconciling the "many" into a "one" comes to a new resolution. Here the "many" are not "one" only in action but in a more fundamental way. This new government rests, finally, on what the Declaration took as its justification: acting "in the Name, and by the Authority of the good people of these Colonies." The people have come finally to represent themselves in the creation of this document, of this new political order.[33] Indeed, this seems to be first among the reasons that "the people" now undertake the adoption of the new order.[34]

We know who has come together in the U.S. Constitution; now we must

ask: to what end? Whereas with the Articles of Confederation the first reason for coming together was for their "common defense," the Constitution
is "ordain[ed] and establish[ed]" in order to "form a more perfect Union."
Some have seen in these words an attempt by the American people to form
a best-possible government; the "more" perfect union of which they speak
is, however, only ultimately conceived in grammatically comparative, not
superlative, terms. The union they are forming with the adoption of the
Constitution is comparatively more perfect than the union that obtained
heretofore—the Articles of Confederation—especially in terms of unity.
With even a cursory awareness of the history of interstate relations from
1776 to 1787, one can hear the exasperation conveyed in the phrase. Wars
among the states arising from tariff and border disputes, the lack of a single
currency or foreign policy, and the inability for the national government to
enforce its own decisions were serious obstacles to political cohesion under
the Articles.[35] The Constitution was aimed at solving these problems, in
part by addressing the most basic of political questions: how are we to live
together? The answer given to that question is somewhat new.

The American people will no longer be unified, be one, only in *acting*
together. They will no longer merely *act* as one, as with the Declaration of
Independence and the Articles of Confederation, but, with the adoption of
the Constitution, will *be* one. They will be one people and govern themselves
as such. The whole people of the thirteen states will, by this act, be a politically relevant body. With the Declaration and Articles the states remained
the units of political action; with the Constitution the people, taken as one,
as a whole, will act together whenever political action is needed (and as
circumscribed, of course, by the complicated new state and federal jurisdic-
tions in the body of the Constitution).

The Constitution contains symbols because it is the means by which the
American people come together for action in history. This coming together
is different in character from that of the Puritans, but it is not radically so.
On the question of history as such, however, the Constitution seems to be
silent. Much as was implied in the long title of the Articles of Confederation—that the union would be "perpetual" and hence its existence in history
is ambivalent—there is little in the Constitution that suggests the role of the
new body politic in history. The Constitution, like the Articles before it, has
nothing to say about the country's role in any history but its own.

A few words about the rest of the Constitution's preamble will shed light
on the document's scope and whether its provisions are applicable more

particularly or more universally. After noting the purpose of the present document to "form a more perfect Union," several additional purposes are added, though none will come as a surprise to the reader here. The new Constitution will help "establish Justice, ensure domestic Tranquility, provide for the common defence, promote the general Welfare, and secure the blessings of Liberty to ourselves and our Posterity." The symbol of justice has been constitutive of the American political order from the Mayflower Compact onward and little more needs be said here than has been observed by Kendall and Carey. Though under the Articles of Confederation the administration of justice seems to have been implicitly the province of the states, the symbol is now adopted by the American people as a whole. "Domestic Tranquility" has long been an aim in the American political tradition, though it has gone by the name of "maintain the peace" in other documents. This symbol shows just how circumscribed the new government was to be; not international or universal peace but domestic tranquility is the goal. After this, the "common defence," "general Welfare," and securing of "Liberty" are mentioned, in direct echoes of the Articles. Here again it is instructive to notice that these three goals are each explicitly aimed inward, much as one would expect from a document focused exclusively on political union. The "common defence" is to be provided for, not the protection of all or the salvation of the world.[36] The "general Welfare" of the union is another purpose of the new government, but the generality of this clause could scarcely be said to extend beyond the borders of the already established states; there is simply no reason to conclude otherwise from the text. The "blessings of Liberty" are explicitly to be secured for "ourselves and our Posterity." More than with the other clauses, the scope of the Constitution's action is here clearer than ever. The new government structures are aimed at the unity of the people creating them. This is no wide-ranging project in human liberation. The "people" here seek only to provide a just and lasting government for themselves and their descendants. The "people" who undertakes to do this simply does not comprehend other peoples under these provisions. Surely, the particular rules and provisions of the Declaration, the Articles, and the Constitution serve to circumscribe the institutions they affect and create. They cannot apply to Japan or Brazil, for example. But even the purposes of the union in the preamble cannot be accurately construed as betraying an impulse for empire. One might also remark that the organs of government are arrayed decidedly against the centralization and concentration of power that would be necessary for the success of imperial policies. Hamilton notwithstanding, the presidency is no imperial office in the Constitution.

The mention of "Posterity" reintroduces briefly the question of history, but we find immediately it is in a sense equivocal to that found in the Puritans. While Winthrop indicated the place of the Massachusetts Bay Colony in the wide sweep of history, the "people of the United States" only presumes to provide for "ourselves and our posterity." With this new government—though this is not unambitious—this aim ultimately amounts to a hope that the government will be "decent and orderly" and that it will persist as such into and beyond the next generation.

The Constitution thus is not particularly universal in scope and has little to say on the question of its own place in history. Likewise, the Constitution is nearly mute on the role God might play in the new order. Much as was implied by the Declaration and the Articles, the real authority for undertaking political action here is the people. When present in this period, God has so far served as a witness to the rectitude of the people's intentions or the guarantor—from the far-off moment of creation—of the legitimacy of self-government in general. Some of this silence on the place of God is broken in the indispensable supplement to the Constitution, the *Federalist*, to which we now briefly turn.

The *Federalist*

The outlook of the *Federalist* is very similar to that of the Constitution. Noting Carey's point that the *Federalist* does not tell us the *meaning* of the Constitution but only how and on what basis the government is supposed to work, many of the *Federalist*'s numbers are not directly relevant to the evaluation of the Constitution's universal scope or its place in history or the role of God in the new political order.[37] A few passages will suffice to shed further light on the aims of the people in the Constitution's adoption, and it is these that are, above all, relevant to the present discussion. In the first comments of *Federalist* No. 1 we see already an awareness by Publius of the real consequence of the new Constitution's ratification. The opening passage demands scrutiny from anyone examining the founding generation's thought on American exceptionalism. Two elements of the first sentence should be pointed up.

First, the "insufficiency of the existing federal government" is recalled, perhaps to reinforce what will be (as has already been seen) first among the reasons for the adoption of the new Constitution. A new one is needed because the old one—the Articles—is insufficient. Second, Publius calls his reader to "deliberate" upon the new Constitution. As far as Publius is concerned, his writing is intended to draw all his fellows into this moment of reflection and choice. And this, perhaps, is the point at which Publius could be said to support or articulate an idea of American exceptionalism. He posits it passively:

> It has been frequently remarked, that it seems to have been reserved to the people of this country to decide, by their conduct and example, the important question, whether societies of men are really capable or not, of establishing good government from reflection and choice, or whether they are forever destined to depend, for their political constitutions, on accident and force. If there be any truth in the remark, the crisis at which we are arrived may, with propriety, be regarded as the period when that decision is to be made; and a wrong election of the part we shall act, may, in this view, deserve to be considered as the general misfortune of mankind.[38]

Here we hear Publius putting the moment of the Constitution into historical context. More than in the Declaration or the Articles or the Constitution itself, we seem to see an awareness of the grand importance of the task they confront. In an apparently unconscious allusion to this passage, Godfrey Hodgson argues that "the Constitution was exceptional not only in its intrinsic skill and wisdom but also because it was almost unique in its historical contingency. Rarely, if ever, had men been able to sit down and devise de novo, on a clean sheet, a new political system for a territory as extensive and as rich in resources as the new United States."[39] Of course, the colonies' 150-year political history was anything but a "clean sheet." Their experience in self-government was immensely important for the order instituted by the Constitution, to say nothing of the British and Western influences. The somewhat common view that the Constitution came out of nowhere, "de novo," is belied even by Hodgson's own words in a different passage: "[T]he United States did not emerge like Athena from the brow of Zeus, or by a kind of geopolitical virgin birth."[40]

Analysis of the *Federalist*'s contribution to the understanding of the idea of American exceptionalism cannot proceed before its representativeness is established. Unlike the Declaration, Articles, or Constitution, the

Federalist is not the product of a representative assembly (or, in the case of the latter two, several assemblies). While the first three documents may qualify fairly clearly as the source of the American tradition's symbols in a relatively straightforward manner, holding up the *Federalist* similarly requires argument.

The *Federalist* is designed to persuade. In reading and understanding its arguments, this point should be taken to heart; it is easily illustrated in examining the passage already quoted. We know that Publius's aim is persuasion: he says so explicitly at the end of the first number, and this may leaven the analysis already begun.[41] If Publius is primarily focused on persuasion of his readers that the new Constitution should be adopted, an emphasis on the importance of the present moment would help Publius's case by helping dissuade the reader of the idea that the status quo is acceptable or preferable to change. Thus he attacks those two points in the opening lines.

It could be argued, then, that Publius's words just *cannot* be representative of the people—and thus cannot be mined for symbols—because Publius presumes in his very posture his own words' lack of support and representativeness. The point is difficult but not impossible to counter. Understanding why this argument does not preclude us from holding the *Federalist* side by side with the other documents requires a deeper understanding, once again, of the nature of symbols. Kendall and Carey treated symbols that were, admittedly, easy targets. Such was the nature of their effort. It is easy to determine whether some phrase or idea or document was a means to the "coming together" of a people if, in the text of the document itself, such was the explicit claim. All the documents they examine fall into this category—all except the *Federalist*. What reason do they give for its inclusion? The *Federalist* supplies the answers to some of the puzzles presented in the Constitution. The quick adoption of the Constitution suggests these puzzles little troubled the founding generation. And so the *Federalist*, as a written repository of the tradition that the founding generation carried in their hearts, can help us to see the Constitution with the founders' eyes. The *Federalist*, then, is a part of the Constitution in a sense—the part that was assumed in its drafting and adoption but not written into it.[42] And if that was not enough, the *Federalist* has itself taken a high place in our pantheon of venerated national documents. It is a reminder of how Americans wish to govern themselves, and the relationship is similar to the relation of law and morality.[43] Though it does not have the operative force that accompanies passage out of a representative assembly, the *Federalist* operates in a fashion very similar to this, having attained a sort of adoption by acclamation over time. This suggests something important about the nature of symbols.

Symbols, it seems, need not be only rigorously approved, official, and explicit as such. If the *Federalist* can in some sense be incorporated into the text of the Constitution, then the way is paved for nearly any document, idea, or feature of the political system to become a symbol in the tradition, so long as it can pass the muster of that most democratic of political tools, acclamation. This point will be readdressed in the next chapter when considering the most famous speech in American history, Lincoln's Gettysburg Address. The sense in which that speech may represent the American people—note, not an official declaration of the people through a legislative assembly—*seems* to drain Kendall and Carey's method of some of its potency. If, in other words, the *Federalist* can become an operative political symbol without first being adopted by the people in a manner similar to the Declaration of Independence, the Articles of Confederation, or the U.S. Constitution, what is to stop the addition of other potential symbols into that canonical group? Kendall and Carey allude to this point as a possible wrinkle in their account when they write, "And while there are many ways of looking at the Constitution, each with an accompanying morality, Publius' 'reading' of the Constitution has gained such wide acceptance over the years that most individuals find it difficult to read the Constitution with an 'innocent eye.'"[44] But they do not sufficiently explain why under this rule the *Federalist* is acceptable—that is, is a mere differentiation—and other documents like the Gettysburg Address are not acceptable (and must, therefore, be considered derailments). One sees again the importance of the distinction between differentiation and derailment in the frequency with which it breaks through the argument. It must again, however, be laid aside temporarily.

Only a few passages from the *Federalist* are relevant to the development of the idea of American exceptionalism. Its opening passage, quoted above, was seen to be somewhat ambiguous, even as it does suggest a place for the American people in the grand sweep of history. A more rigorous look at Publius's words, however, draws this into further question. The passive construction already distances the author from the claim being made: "It has been frequently remarked . . ." and "in this view . . ." More pivotal than this, however, is Publius's own choice of words, which places the claim not into the category of theories of history but as a statement of political *modality*. Publius notes the "important question" of "*whether* societies of men are really *capable* or *not*, of establishing good government from reflection and choice."[45] The passively recalled remark is not about the historical significance of the American situation but more generally about the *human* capacity for good government. Implied, perhaps, is the idea that America is giving this modality its best chance to date. But, read closely, we see Publius is not at all speaking historically. This is further reinforced later in the same passage where Publius urges even "wise men" who are "well persuaded of being in the right" to the prudence of proceeding cautiously and moderately. This is a far cry from the typological view of history taken by Winthrop and the Puritans, whose certainty in the will of God and its evidence in everyday events caused them to undertake the peril of settling and taming an unknown wilderness. Yet the hand of God is not wholly absent from Publius's thoughts about his country.

In *Federalist* No. 2 Publius notes the degree to which "Providence" has blessed America. After first speaking only to the good fortune of America's various soils and streams and the abundance and opportunity they afford, he goes on to write of America's people. "With equal pleasure I have often taken notice," Publius writes, "that Providence has been pleased to give this one connected country, to one united people; a people descended from the same ancestors, speaking the same language, professing the same religion, attached to the same principles of government, very similar in their manners and customs, and who, by their joint counsels, arms and efforts, fighting side by side throughout a long and bloody war, have nobly established their general liberty and independence."[46] Here Publius seems to see something very similar to what Winthrop saw before him: the hand of God in the concrete events of history. Publius goes on:

> This country and this people seem to have been made for each other, and it appears as if it was the design of Providence, that an inheritance so proper and convenient for a band of brethren, united to each other by the strongest ties, should never be split into a number of unsocial, jealous and alien sovereignties.
>
> Similar sentiments have hitherto prevailed among all orders and denominations of men among us. To all general purposes we have uniformly been one people . . . each individual citizen every where enjoying the same national rights, privileges, and protection.[47]

The United States, Publius argues, has long been "one" because of the actions and activities it has undertaken even before the Articles of Confederation: "As a nation we have made peace and war, as a nation we have vanquished our common enemies: as a nation we have formed alliances and made treaties, and entered into various compacts and conventions with foreign states."[48] This much was true, Publius argues, *before* the Articles. Then came that important document: "A strong sense of the value and blessings of Union induced the people, at a very early period, to institute a federal government to preserve and perpetuate it. They formed it almost as soon as they had a political existence; nay, at a time, when their habitations were in flames, when many of them were bleeding in the field, and when the progress of hostility and desolation left little room for those calm and mature inquiries and reflections, which must ever precede the formation of a wise and well balanced government for a free people."[49] Publius seems to speak here as if the American people came to be, as such, with the Declaration of Independence. This would seem to be the moment he has in mind in saying that the Articles came to be "almost as soon" as the people gained "political existence," which would contradict was has been said before about the founders' view of that document. There is a good reason for this. Keeping in mind Publius's aim in writing the *Federalist,* it makes sense to downplay the sense in which the Constitution is an innovation on the extant order. If Publius argues that the Articles themselves were a union of all the American people as a whole and that the Declaration of Independence was the American people's moment of new political existence, the Constitution appears as a mere modification of an existing relation rather than a new relation altogether. This would be easier to stomach for any of his readers who sought to avoid any radical changes to the political system. Yet the Declaration and Articles are clear in their preservation of the several states' sovereignty. It is clear, then, that Publius is here either speaking imprecisely or stretching the truth in order to make his case more persuasive. The Constitution, it must be reiterated, even thinking with the mind of Publius, is the chief and foundational moment for Americans.

The Articles, "instituted in times so inauspicious," stand in need of the remedy supplied by the Constitution. Here we have in *Federalist* No. 2 something old and something new. Again Publius appeals to the tradition and the importance of deliberation for good government. This is Publius the salesman, once again. So, too, with his points about Providence. But successful salesmen must necessarily operate within the bounds of basic truths. Pitches do not work unless the buyer already believes the premises on which they are based. Thus we can glean at least two things from Publius's arguments here: one, readers probably already believed in the role Providence played in the American founding and, two, they certainly believed in the vital importance of deliberation in politics (as has already been seen in their longstanding emphasis, through years of history and many documents, on the representative assembly). The particular details of these beliefs are, however, paramount for their relevance to the idea of American exceptionalism; it is the details that will link together or separate apart the founding fathers from their Puritan forebears.

From Puritan Society to American Society

Understanding the nature of the founders' belief in Providence—especially its degree of intelligibility—is crucial for understanding the development of the idea of American exceptionalism and its relation to the self-conception of the American people. In the *Federalist*, just as with the other documents considered from this period, there is little evidence that the old Puritan worldview persists. Their notions of universality, history, and the relation of God to politics are altered chiefly by a revolution in thinking on politics that separated the single Puritan religio-political realm into the two spheres more familiar to us today.

Recall briefly the three characteristics found at the heart of the Puritan political order. First, the Puritans conceived of the universality of the truth operative in their lives in the same way this relationship was conceived for much of human history. A given society could not survive, it was often thought, without affirming some particular account of the truth, and so governments had a vested interest in church doctrine, orthodoxy, and the silence of heretics. Puritan society dealt with these problems in the same manner in which they had long been dealt: orthodoxy was enforced with the coercive force of the state. If persuasion or threats did not work, then exile was a viable option, as with Roger Williams.

Second, the Puritans were particularly suited for such thoughts and actions because of their unique conception of history—specifically their conviction about its clear intelligibility. History's meaning and course were evident with a proper reading of scripture, they thought, and this certainty meant for them a politics unburdened by the processes of wide deliberation and consensus. The consensus on which the Massachusetts Bay Puritans based their community had to do with its covenantal foundation and a strong belief in its inwardly focused mission. All else, it seems, was mainly a matter of execution, which was delegated to a small group of prominent citizens.

Third, the Puritans' views on history and universality were tied intimately to their views on the role of God in their politics. For them, God was intimately involved in the genesis and maintenance of their political order. His divine sanction was detectible in numerous ways, they thought, beginning with their safe arrival on American shores. He was not merely a beneficent preparer-of-the-way but an intimate partner in the world-changing work they undertook. Much of this, we see, has changed by the time of the constitutional generation.

The most important documents of the American founding have little to say about the place of the American people in history, the universality of their task or aspiration, or the role that God is to play in their polity.[50] This much has been seen in the course of these documents' brief examination. The stark contrast between the Puritan and founding periods suggests a deep and significant change has taken place. Though the character of the change will be easier to see in subsequent chapters because of the increase in points of comparison, a few points are clear already.

Unity in Massachusetts, Unity for the United States

The relative absence of religious symbols in the major documents of the founding generation suggests that the people who now unite for action in history is a different one from before or at least that something is different about it. The paramount good of the Massachusetts Bay Colony's political order was the radical unity for which Winthrop argued. It was requisite for the colony's success. The small, homogenous group of settlers could brook no dissent, because their small number and the hard conditions of their life meant any disharmony was a threat to the perpetuation of the community and a threat to their own lives. Unity was the only safeguard for them against the chaos of Indian wars, brutal winter, disease, and an unfamiliar countryside; the contributions of all colonists were vital to the community. For the Puritans, dissension or jealousy were always possible straws on the camel's back of the community's existence; this made the choice between orthodoxy and heterodoxy in effect a choice between earthly life and death.[51]

The American founding generation confronted a much different problem; threats from without were its main worry. The thirteen colonies faced a choice between a life of submission to an increasingly tyrannical king, on the one hand, and open war against his military, one of the most formidable in the world, on the other hand. Their customary life was threatened and interrupted. Their ability to have a say in their own political affairs was under siege. But they had available to them a development in the tradition that was not present in the early Puritans. A distinction in the spheres of politics and religion allowed a different, wider, and more effective union. A series of small, cohesive communities, no matter how unified, would be no match for the British army and navy. All the individual states would need to unite in order adequately to face their common enemy on the battlefield. But union of such a diverse set of people required much more latitude in their unity than was seen with the Puritans. Thus the federal Constitution was both innovative and traditional. It fell in line with the lived tradition of self-government and the widely held American belief in the natural ability of free and virtuous peoples to submit to the rule of a deliberate assembly under God. But it did so while bracketing off portions of political life that up to then had not been separated. The separation would not be effected at all levels of government for some time, but I am not arguing for a pattern of secularization here. The point here is the separability of spheres, a step that is taken in this period and one that is one step in the thinkability of American imperialism.

Though Publius extolled the degree to which the thirteen states were already one, a distinction is necessary to contextualize his statement. These states that he speaks of as so unified are the same ones that, though they had a common Congress, persisted in wars, border disputes, and commercial conflict. Though the population was Christian and English on the whole, there were already pockets of foreigners and several states had different established Christian religions. The several states' inhabitants were certainly not "one" in the manner Winthrop thought necessary for good government. Yet Publius points up their unity in ancestors, language, religion, political principles, and customs.[52] It would be unfair to charge Publius with ignorance of the variation and diversity of the American people on these counts. The reason for his observation is readily found: unity is affirmed because they are as "one" as is necessary for political action. It could perhaps be said that, for the Puritans, the only sphere relevant to politics or religion was the same one, that is, the sphere of truth. By the time of the American founding this one sphere had been distinguished along religious and political lines, at least at the national level, the level of the oneness in question.[53] Even pious religious observers could be in union with the impious in the

American order, provided certain baseline political agreements were made. The constitutional regime is the product of a bifurcation: what is right or expedient or true in one sphere need not create interpersonal conflict in the other. The ravings of a heretic may indeed be harmful to the cohesion of a community, but for the purposes of political union this need not concern the community created by the Constitution. Whether the several states may hold themselves to a more Winthrop-esque standard of close cohesion is irrelevant, since it is clear that this question is left out of the picture for the new federal government.[54]

The Founders on Universality, History, and God

The view of the American founding generation on the question of universality in politics should now be somewhat clear. The political sphere operates according to a standard different from the religious sphere. While not irrelevant to politics, the religious sphere need not be consulted on the best way to "establish Justice" at the federal level. Put so plainly in the Constitution's preamble, the people is saying, in effect, that justice would be fairly well in hand once the body of the Constitution is enacted and followed. Ensuring "domestic Tranquility," too, along with providing for the common defense, promoting the general welfare, and securing the blessings of liberty, seem to be considered principally political tasks—both by their presence at the head of a solely political document and in their straightforward articulation without significant qualification. None of these tasks comprehends a people or project greater than basic good order, according to the understanding that had been constant in the colonies for more than a century. Their time as coequal, sovereign states and colonies had led to disputes and conflicts among themselves, and their security against an external threat required a change in the order at home. The conflicts that might have prevented their unity were dissolved once the spheres of politics and religion were distinguished. Religious questions could be handled by religious leaders according to the rules and beliefs of the various denominations, but political questions could be handled together, as one. On political questions, consensus—ever the goal—was now easier to achieve because its scope had been narrowed. Agreement on political questions had become easier because political questions had become more circumscribed. Rather than a perfect Christian community designed to usher in the millennium, the goal was now a political order decent enough to allow each to pursue his own goals. The Declaration, the Articles, and the Constitution are not documents authored by a people on a mission. They are the articulations of a way to achieve political order and stability that, in turn, allows for a variety of good ways to live.[55] These documents show a distinction that divides human life according to its more transcendent and immanent ends, religion pertaining to the former and politics to the latter.

Misconceptions are possible in light of this distinction. It should not be thought that the founding generation is arguing, as a people, for the irrelevance of religion to political life. There are numerous easy proofs against this view. As was seen above, many of the most prominent citizens of the period argued that religion must be robust in their country in order for the new government to be successful. No less an authority than George Washington is famous for asserting the vital importance of religion to good government:

> Of all the dispositions and habits which lead to political prosperity, Religion and morality are indispensable supports. In vain would that man claim the tribute of Patriotism, who should labor to subvert these great Pillars of human happiness, these firmest props of the duties of men and citizens. The mere Politician, equally with the pious man, ought to respect and to cherish them. A volume could not trace all their connections with private and public felicity. Let it simply be asked: Where is the security for property, for reputation, for life, if the sense of religious obligation *desert* the oaths which are the instruments of investigation in Courts of Justice? And let us with caution indulge the supposition that morality can be maintained without religion. Whatever may be conceded to the influence of refined education on minds of peculiar structure, reason and experience both forbid us to expect that National morality can prevail in exclusion of religious principle.
>
> 'Tis substantially true that virtue or morality is a necessary spring of popular government. The rule, indeed, extends with more or less force to every species of free Government. Who that is a sincere friend to it can look with indifference upon attempts to shake the foundation of the fabric?[56]

In this passage from Washington's Farewell Address, one can see the distinction of the two spheres. "The mere Politician" and the "pious man" seem to be, if not different people altogether, at least logically distinct.[57] It is just this distinction that lets George Washington and his peers erect a government that stands in line with the tradition preceding it but innovates within its bounds to create a government and social order robust enough to stand up to serious challenges for more than two hundred years.

Neither should it be thought that this separation necessarily portends secularization. As the term is usually used today, secularization entails chiefly a decline in religious practice and belief. In this, America was anything but secular or secularizing on the eve of the Revolution. "Indeed," writes historian Jon Butler, "one of the great transformations of the eighteenth century centered on the renewal, not the decline, of the state church tradition in colonial America. . . . [T]he state church apparatus found itself strengthened, not weakened [in the founding period]."[58]

The separation does not mean that the founding generation's religious background did not influence its political thought and practice. As Barry Shain has pointed out, it is perhaps the founders' Christianity and Protestantism that made bicameralism palatable (unicameralism was thought more proper to an Enlightened society). Further, Shain argues, Americans did not view Christianity as an impediment to good government and society but rather a boon: "In short, Enlightened authors had embraced an anthropocentrism and anticlericalism in opposition to America's continuing theocentrism and broad public respect for pious religiosity."[59] The very structure of American institutions, then, displays the vitality of Christianity on political questions at the time of the founding.

Finally, it should not be thought that the distinction was wholly new. After all, John Winthrop was his colony's governor, not a religio-political priest-king. Ministers were hired by political bodies in colonial Massachusetts; they were not one and the same. Yet their work was viewed as one. And though the founding generation's views—like the Puritans'—cannot be said to be monolithic, they were at least unified enough for us to see a distinction between their way of life and the Puritans'.[60] The distinction has been much discussed throughout the chapter, especially in terms of differentiation and derailment. A direct discussion has long been in order and is finally possible.

Derailment or Differentiation?

The shift in understanding so evident between the Puritan and founding periods is not a total shift in direction or meaning. There are points both of continuity and distinction, and distinguishing the change as a derailment or differentiation is no simple task. If a continuity in the principal symbols of the tradition could be found, this would serve as an easy answer to the question of differentiation or derailment. The observed difference would be a change more in appearance than substance, and we would see that no derailment had occurred. Yet might not the radical distinction of the relevant spheres of politics and religion lend credibility to an argument in favor of derailment?

The principal symbols of the tradition, even in regard to the question of American exceptionalism, have not changed from the Puritan period to the period of the founding. Transcendence and universality have not been abandoned, but they have been separated out of the political sphere, except at its periphery. A typological theory of the intelligibility of history has changed to the view that "Providence" has—note the passivity, new in this period—arranged the current circumstances for a certain purpose, which may or may not be entirely known. This more moderate stance is nonetheless continuous with what came before, being a difference in the degree of certainty and intelligibility rather than a difference in kind from certainty to uncertainty.[61] Accordingly, the role of God has changed—he is more passive than active in politics and history—but he is not absent from society and life.[62] George Washington's thought on religion and politics was, we know, largely typical of even otherwise very divergent figures like Theophilus Parsons and Thomas Paine.

The distinction of the spheres presents a profound change from the Puritan to the founding generation. But it is a change that does not alter the general course of the American political tradition. No longer is politics the vehicle for man's transcendent purposes, but it can facilitate those purposes by refraining from meddling in them.[63] The spheres of politics and religion are no longer considered identical, but neither are they independent. A differentiation has occurred, but its product is not yet different enough for the change to be considered a derailment. The distinction between derailment and differentiation is made based on the degree of consistency from one period to the next. The continuity here is too great to see in it a derailment, but this judgment will be rendered more plausible in comparison with subsequent periods. This makes even more obvious the status of differentiation and derailment as judgments of historical phenomena. Judgment as to one or the other may be made only from a distance in history. The flow of events, influences, and lines of development must be traced over more than a few points of data in order truly to see the trends for what they are.

All four periods examined here are required to present a full picture of the development of the idea of American exceptionalism. At this early stage, however, a relatively limited judgment about the continuity so far may already be made, even if it will be rendered more plausible with more time.

The Founders: Imperial Exceptionalists?

Now that the changes between the two periods taken up so far have briefly been analyzed, an early judgment may be made on the central question of the present project. Is there anything in these changes that paves the way for later generations' claims to American exceptionalism, particularly the more aggressive, imperial variety? The answer is yes, though the reason why will fully be seen only in subsequent chapters.

In chapter 2 I argued that characterizations of the Puritans as closet (or, for some commentators, quite open) imperialists were due to confusion about the nature of the universality present in the written accounts of their political life. In this chapter I have shown that the founders, too, were anything but imperialistic, and this is for two main reasons. The Puritans were certainly unable *practically* to found an empire; no one believes or argues otherwise. The claims about their imperialism usually imply they justified empire theoretically or philosophically. This, with close reference to the inward focus of their project, was seen also to be false. It is just the same with the founders.

Though emerging as a distinct sovereign power with the ability to resist one of the world's great empires by force, the United States was set up not to expand but to last. Its principles of self-government and local control were aimed at circumscribed goals that involved only the order of their own lives and societies and the preservation of that order. Such is on display from the people's very mouth. Their only "mission"—as articulated in their most important documents—is order, which is necessary for securing the blessings of liberty, along with their other circumscribed aims. But if the founders were not explicitly imperialist, might they have been so in secret, building into their government the future possibility of a great empire? This, too, can be rejected, for if the people were truly to set themselves on the road to expansion, particularly of a more virulent kind, the institutions they created do not lend themselves to it. The best possible facilitator among U.S. institutions is the office of the president, about which little is said in the Constitution save his role in executing the will of the people as pronounced in the laws of Congress. Any evidence for the founders' imperialism is necessarily found, then, outside the most important documents of the period.

Thus, neither the Puritans nor the founders were philosophically or practically equipped for the kind of imperial exceptionalism that develops later in American history. But key developments in this period will, in time, be seen as ingredients for the imperial exceptionalism that emerges around the turn of the twentieth century in America. The thoughts, changes, and actions of the American founding generation do not constitute and did not cause the later development of American exceptionalism. But the latter could not have happened without the former. Yet to understand this fully, we must move to the next relevant period in American history, the time leading up to and including the Civil War.

4

ABRAHAM LINCOLN

An Ideally United, Potentially Unbound Union

Up to this point we have moved from the western shores of England to the eastern shores of New England and farther south to Philadelphia. The movement has run from the early seventeenth-century American wilderness to a thriving city in the late eighteenth century. The next jump requires yet another plunge into a new century and milieu, into a time and situation of great consequence for the country: the Civil War.

What changes, if any, have occurred from the founding period to the Civil War period in regard to the self-conception of the American people? To determine this, we will examine the articulations of the latter period's most prominent spokesman: Abraham Lincoln. Now that the project has gained some trajectory from the materials already examined, the way forward is fairly clear. After a consideration of Lincoln's representativeness, three major speeches of Lincoln's presidency will be taken up and examined according to the criteria already established.

Sources of the Idea of American Exceptionalism

An analysis of the writings of John Winthrop yielded three main elements by which he could be called the father of American exceptionalism. The Puritans' particular conceptions of the role played by universality, history, and God in their politics seemed to foster a worldview that is one of the sources of the idea. The unity of the new colony was the main concern, for it was the only way to achieve their end, the founding of a new kind of community and politics that would be an example to the world. The sense in which unity was to be maintained was in their common work and belief. All were to work for the same religio-political end via the same particular means: submission to the covenant laid before them in the early days of the colony. The tremendous cohesiveness required by the covenant represented, perhaps, a fatal flaw in the system; the initial unity did not long persist.[1]

By the late eighteenth century a broader unity of a different sort was thought necessary for the preservation of the extant order. Though the preservation of the colonial order by means of apparently fundamental changes seems counterproductive, the colonists saw the acts and emerging patterns of imperial Britain as radically and unacceptably innovative. Guarding against pernicious innovation required casting off British rule altogether and setting up a new kind of government. The American federal structure of government was neither wholly old nor wholly new. It was an attempt to balance the efficacy necessary to a nation that was seeking to establish its rightful place among the nations of the world—particularly in matters of commerce and war—while maintaining deference to local control and existing structures that had already been governing the former colonies. This new, limited unity was a political aim very different from the radically cohesive oneness of the Massachusetts Bay Colony, but it achieved some of the same basic purposes. Even in its youth as a country, the United States became increasingly secure economically and militarily and was able to meet the challenge of an admittedly distracted and weakened England. Even this limited oneness was not uncontroversial, but it was made possible through particular compromises that circumscribed it within definite boundaries, as shown in the new union's Constitution. Yet the nature and conditions of the bond enacted in that document were, by the mid-1800s, under serious dispute.

At the center of the debate, then and now, stands Abraham Lincoln. His words and actions determined both the course of the conflict at the time and how that conflict has been viewed ever since. The latter is particularly of interest. For, though the symbols we are able to discover in the most consequential speeches of his presidency are corroborated by the various actions undertaken by the government while he was in that office, the depth of our understanding regarding Lincoln's place in American history and the history of the idea of American exceptionalism remains the primary concern. We are here not concerned, then, with the constitutionality or morality of Lincoln's actions.

Neither is the present chapter an evaluation of Lincoln's greatness or efficacy as a chief executive or commander in chief—such books have been written and rewritten. Furthermore, I am not concerned with treating whether Lincoln himself was an exceptionalist—just as in the previous chapter I did not conclude one way or another whether the American founders were believers in American exceptionalism as we know it today.[2]

The concern throughout has been to uncover the ground on which the late claims to American exceptionalism might be founded, especially in terms of the symbols of the American political tradition. Lincoln plays a role in making such claims possible, though it is not a direct and deliberate role. The kind of American exceptionalism we will see most clearly in the Progressive period is still not present in Lincoln's own thought or time. Yet it is telling that some of the most prominent figures of the Progressive period were infatuated with all things Lincoln. Tracing a direct link, however, is not my concern.[3] Of considerably more interest is the degree to which Lincoln represents a new moment in the coming together of the American people— a second founding or refounding, a fixing of the mistakes of the founders eight decades before.[4] Most important in this respect is the reordering and reinterpretation of America's founding documents and the consequent new view of the manner in which political unity was achieved in America and is to be maintained. George D. Fletcher has argued in *Our Secret Constitution* that the country's central constitutional event, the event from which it has received its present meaning, is not the original founding but the Civil War. In the opening passage of this interesting book, Fletcher writes that the Civil War "began with one set of purposes and ended with another. The original motive for resisting Southern secession was preserving the Union. The resulting and final idea was to abolish slavery and reinvent the United States on the basis of a new set of principles." The change is evident in and effected by Lincoln's main presidential speeches.[5]

Lincoln's speeches may be evaluated in two ways. We will first seek to understand whether any changes have occurred in the basic symbols of the tradition. Upon examination, it will be clear that Lincoln's use and interpretation of the Declaration of Independence is very different from those that came out of the Continental Congress. The change amounts to a derailment of the tradition, as the previously basic symbols are displaced by new ones.[6] This is the first main view we will take of Lincoln's contribution. But this view raises serious questions and leads to another.

Looking ahead in American history shows just how much more prevalent Lincoln's understanding of the Declaration is over its original composers' intent. The now-joined "Lincoln-Declaration"—which, since it widens the scope of the task of government, amounts to a new operative reading of the Constitution—displaces previous accounts of what America is. Thus, from a point of view after Lincoln, he seems to be wholly in line with the "American political tradition"; the changes he effected have helped to bring about that tradition as it is known today. In other words, Lincoln is viewed as *central to* the tradition because he has become the main authoritative interpreter *of* the tradition. But here arises a problem. Different judgments of the phenomena are made depending on which perspective is taken. If we view the tradition from the perspective of the founders, Lincoln appears as a divergence from the principal symbols of the tradition; if we view the founders from the perspective of Lincoln, then Lincoln seems to be in perfect harmony with the tradition, which makes it appear as if no derailment has taken place at all. Our point of evaluation in history, coming after the derailment, views the derailed "tradition" as the tradition; the previous line to us appears somewhat foreign. The advantage of the current project's approach, however, is that this distinction between the main line of the tradition and its derailment can be seen more clearly, showing each stage in American history for what it is.

Understanding whether Lincoln represents a differentiation or a derailment of the original tradition presupposes both a thorough understanding of the original tradition, already undertaken in chapter 3, and a thorough understanding of the nature of Lincoln's representativeness, which is now in order.

In previous chapters I discussed the varying criteria used to find and evaluate symbols and their representation. Some documents examined previously have been obvious representatives of the oneness of the American people—none more so than the U.S. Constitution. The Constitution has been in continual force for more than two hundred years, and the official changes it has undergone do not amount to any great change in the identity of the people who acts as its author. While Kendall and Carey seem satisfied on these grounds that the question of the American political tradition is consequently a settled one, a serious challenge is posed to this view if only the scope of representation in the American political tradition is widened slightly.

The founders made the amendment process difficult by design in order to avoid the kind of quick, sweeping changes that might easily imperil a popular form of government. Yet changes in the letter of the document are not the only factor affecting the way the document is received or operated. Attitudes toward a law, if changed, may change the way it is interpreted and enforced. Such changes need not pass muster in front of a legislative assembly but need only be so widespread that the new view becomes authoritative and operative. This is precisely what happens with Lincoln.

It should be said that though the U.S. president serves in a primarily executive position in the order of the Constitution, he also stands in nowadays as representative for the country as a whole. His speeches may give a contemporary sense of the meaning and nature of the Constitution, then, in a way that approximates the process of making symbols. If widespread attitudes toward and interpretations of the country's founding documents and symbols affect the meaning and operation of those symbols, then the very influential words of a president should be examined to see whether a shift in the country's unity and identity has taken place. I wish to argue that this is just what happens with Lincoln.[7]

To avoid mistakes in interpretation, a president's own concrete political aims ought to be pointed up so that there is no confusion between the aims of one man and the intentions of the whole people. Reinhold Niebuhr notes the interplay between personal conviction and public purpose:

> Lincoln's passion for saving the union was viewed by some critics as a personal concept of the irrevocable character of the covenant of the Constitution. A very high-minded leader of the secessionist states, Robert E. Lee, had a different conception: though he detested slavery, he felt himself bound in loyalty to his state of Virginia rather than to the nation. Since the Civil War itself, not to speak of the many unifying forces which made the nation one, subsequently altered the loyalties of our citizens, making state loyalty subordinate to national loyalty, it is safe to say that if Lincoln's conception of the irrevocable character of the national covenant was a personal conviction, it was eventually transmuted into a national one. In his first inaugural address Lincoln argued in favor of the irrevocability of the covenant in words which many of his contemporaries did not accept but which we take for granted.[8]

Though Niebuhr is correct about both what Lincoln means and the change that occurred in the wake of the Civil War, Lincoln's interpretation is inaccurate, making the change not necessarily an ambivalent one. Nonetheless, I provide this passage to show the relation of Lincoln's personal influence on the nation's course and shape, even long after his death.

If Lincoln's speeches are to be taken up, however, then just which ones?

A president's inaugural addresses and annual messages to Congress would seem a natural fit, as these are the occasions upon which, more than any other time, he would make statements in his official representative capacity. An examination of his annual messages to Congress, however, yields few relevant passages.[9] Though they contain some memorable phrases, Lincoln's annual messages do not have the force of the speeches examined in this chapter. A case in point is helpful for understanding. The famous phrase in which Lincoln seems to call America the "last best hope of earth" occurs in one of these annual messages. Yet context makes it unclear whether this is a statement generally about liberal democracy or, even more generally, about liberty in the abstract. Such considerations prevent scrutiny of these speeches from being fruitful. Nevertheless, as William Lee Miller observes, speeches are potent tools of political action, and Lincoln was known to be keen to use them as such. His inaugural addresses and his Gettysburg Address have an altogether different character and much more easily bear the weight of representation, particularly after their delivery and subsequent absorption into the American political tradition. Of his inaugural addresses, the second is better known than the first. Yet the first inaugural is important for the understanding it gives of the nature of the American union. The Gettysburg Address, the most famous speech in U.S. history, cannot fail to make the list of relevant speeches. It rings still in American hearts and minds, painting a specific picture of who we are as a people, our role in history, and our place under God. The second inaugural is said by some to be an emendation of the Gettysburg Address; it will be treated primarily in this capacity.

Lincoln's words are neither few in number nor narrow in scope, nor generally lacking in usefulness, erudition, insight, or interest. I am tempted, as are all who take up Lincoln, to draw upon all his speeches, letters, addresses, and proclamations in order to sketch a picture of the man often regarded as America's finest statesman. I hope, however, that it is obvious already that such a course would take me far afield from my main purpose; in taking into view only those most prominent and influential pieces, the Lincoln who is representative for us today is made so manifest as to justify the truncation of the full Lincoln of the historical record.

The First Inaugural

Upon reading Lincoln's first inaugural address we are struck, first, that there is much of profit to be found. As Lincoln indicates early in the speech, his

chief concern is to soothe the anxieties of those who had worked strenu-
ously against his election because of their fear of losing their property or
way of life. After assuring his hearers that he was elected by law and intends
to execute the law as it stands—referring to the fugitive slave clause of the
Constitution, and so on—he moves on to the imminent "solution" already
undertaken by several states before he took office: secession. He rejects secession as a "legal impossibility." Lincoln then gives a thorough account of
the nature of the American political order in light of these considerations.

Basing his argument on a consideration of the nature of all governments,
Lincoln concludes that it could not be lawful for any one member state of
the United States to disconnect itself from the others. Such a disconnection
would amount to a toppling of the American political order, and it would
be achieved by a vast minority power. This scenario is especially disturb-
ing, Lincoln argues, in light of the importance that the American order
accords to the rule of the majority. Therefore, secession is impossible and
"the Union of these states is perpetual."[10] Thus far Lincoln's considerations
are more general than particular.

Seemingly anticipating his de-emphasis of the U.S. Constitution in the
Gettysburg Address and echoing the many previous speeches in which he
emphasized the constitutional role he saw for the Declaration of Independence, Lincoln speaks of the manner in which the American people brought
forth their government. "The Union is much older than the Constitution,"
Lincoln says. "It was formed in fact, by the Articles of Association in 1774.
It was matured and continued by the Declaration of Independence in 1776.
It was further matured and the faith of all the then thirteen States expressly
plighted and engaged that it should be perpetual, by the Articles of Confederation in 1778. And finally, in 1787, one of the declared objects for ordain-
ing and establishing the Constitution, was 'to form a more perfect Union.'"[11]
Lincoln goes on to argue that if the union could indeed be unmade "by one,
or by a part only, of the States," it would be "less perfect than before the
Constitution, having lost the vital element of perpetuity." If the perpetuity
of the union was actually truncated or eliminated with the adoption of the
Constitution, Lincoln argues, then one of the Constitution's aims is subverted
in its very adoption, which is absurd. Those who argue for the legality and
propriety of secession, then, are inconsistent because they accept this inconsistent conception of the union. But this raises the question of whether
Lincoln's own corresponding view—that the union can be properly said to
begin in 1774—is sound. Many have remarked on the somewhat "mystical"

quality Lincoln attaches to the union.[12] Yet in taking Lincoln at his word we see what he considers the nature of the union in "legal contemplation," that is, by law. He seeks to uncover the juridical origins of the country in history and pinpoints the Articles of Association of 1774—one of the early acts of the First Continental Congress—as the moment of origin.

Pointing to this moment is, however, somewhat disingenuous. A lawyerly tone draws the attention of Lincoln's hearers away from his actual argument; his story of the gradual development of "the Union" is consequently emphasized. The dates and the documents are familiar to nearly all—all except the relatively obscure moment that Lincoln argues is the true point of origin for the country. The manner in which he lists the various events and dates draws attention away from the fact that Lincoln uses the term *union* in several equivocal senses in the succeeding sentences. But to understand this, we must understand the sense in which each was meant to bring about a political "one," which varies with each of the moments Lincoln lists. The "union" of the U.S. Constitution was certainly preceded in time by the Articles of Confederation, the Declaration of Independence, and even the Articles of Association, but these documents do not enact, reenact, or institute the same political order at their respective moments. The progression Lincoln gives, rather than a continuity, is one of change. Admitting such a change would, however, undermine Lincoln's point.

The union he now headed as president was, compared to the Articles of Confederation, distinctly different and new. The Articles marked the first moment on Lincoln's timeline that there would be a government with a truly national identity. Yet these Articles were not in effect until their late ratification by Maryland in 1781. Lincoln's date, 1778, was the year that the Continental Congress passed the Articles of Confederation for consideration by the several state legislatures. The Articles preserved the prior sovereignty of each member state, unlike the 1789 U.S. Constitution, which established a truly national sovereignty for the first time. And if the Articles of Confederation did not speak of the same particular political order as the Constitution, neither did the Declaration of Independence nor the earlier Articles of Association. These two moments were particular political acts—done in concert, assuredly, but each for limited, particular purposes. Neither the Articles of Association nor the Declaration of Independence presumes to set forth a new political order, which is easy to see upon reading them, though both seek the cessation of a certain political order. Thus Lincoln supposes the various "unions" he lists to be merely stages in the same union; this is, however, an equivocation because of the very different character of the unions indicated.

If the union of which Lincoln speaks is equivocal, even in "legal contemplation," then why pursue this line of reasoning? His purpose is made clear at the end of the paragraph. The object of the U.S. Constitution was, among other things, to "form a more perfect Union." Rather than acknowledging that the union had heretofore been imperfect—the clear implication of the preamble's words in the context of the Articles' operation—Lincoln seizes upon the apparently necessarily perpetual quality of governments in some general philosophical remarks. The particular case he wishes to make cannot be supported by the political tradition, so he moves to generalities. Lincoln points to the use of the word *perpetual* in the long title of the "Articles of Confederation and Perpetual Union between the states of. . . ." Finally, Lincoln emphasizes the superlative quality of the word *perfect* in the Constitution's preamble. Now, anyone wishing to emphasize the perpetuity of the Articles of Confederation has to reckon with the fact that only six years elapsed before there was a successful attempt to begin scrapping them. Lincoln does not do this. Neither does he explain what the possible difference in meaning might be between *more perfect* and *perfect* in the context of the preamble. It had been conventionally understood that the union among the states was not previously robust enough to achieve the true purposes of such a union; the last phrase of the preamble implies this and suggests that the new document it heads, the Constitution, is a fitting remedy.

Note also that Lincoln cites 1787 instead of the Constitution's ratification date of 1788—again giving the date of the document's passage rather than its date of operation; it is, again, easy to see why. Any concession by Lincoln that the states are the primary agents in the creation of the union would make him more vulnerable to the arguments of the secessionists. Since the first inaugural is, in the main, an argument against secession, Lincoln's choice of dates is anything but arbitrary or merely inaccurate. In trying to make his point, he alters the relevant dates in his timeline. Thus the purpose that Lincoln has in mind, the establishment of the legal impossibility of secession, colors his argument. "The Union is unbroken," Lincoln says on his own narrow technical grounds, despite the fact that six states had already declared their own independence from the union.

Lincoln's supposedly "mystical" belief in the American union has, at least here, given ground to the perpetration of a legal fiction. He wants to persuade his hearers that the states had little role per se in the creation of the union and that they cannot, therefore, achieve its undoing. It is difficult to establish this with reference to the relevant documents. With a new interpretation of the same old documents, however, Lincoln's favored conclusion is more easily drawn.

The existence of "the Union" before the Constitution is an interesting political problem. Lincoln gives a view contrary to the founders', who, before the adoption of the Constitution, saw the states as "one" only for a few specific tasks—first independence and military resistance, then coordination of foreign policy, a uniform currency, and so on. Lincoln does not wish to leave open the possibility that the union was the creation of the preexisting colony-states. This would mean that the states, at least arguably, could in some way "alter or abolish" the union they created (in the words of the Declaration). But, Lincoln wishes to argue, if "the Union" is itself the creator of the political order, not only of the U.S. Constitution but also of its precursors, then there could not possibly be a constitutional means for destroying the order created in the Constitution, except as provided by the amendment process. Granting this, Lincoln seems to implicitly argue, abolishing the Constitution would only revert the states to the previous order under the Articles of Confederation, which was the order of "the Union" before the Constitution. But here Lincoln's logic encounters a problem: if "the Union" came before the Constitution, where did the union come from? Recall that Lincoln answers clearly, if implausibly: the Articles of Association of 1774.[13]

For the Lincoln of the first inaugural, it was from 1774 forward that the states were in some sense "one" and "the Union" was born. This line of reasoning gets Lincoln where he needs to go constitutionally, but the "in some sense" is all-important. The qualification of the colony-states' "oneness" varies from moment to moment in the 1770s and 1780s. It moves on a sliding scale in documents Lincoln mentions here.

The Articles of Association of 1774 were drafted, passed, and signed by the Continental Congress in order to persuade the king of Great Britain to repeal the Intolerable Acts. They were aimed at "redress[ing] the grievances" of the colonies; more specifically, the articles aimed to stop those acts "which threaten destruction to the lives, liberty and property" of the colonists.[14] One hears already the formulation famously modified by Jefferson. But, very different from the situation with the Declaration of Independence, these representatives in Congress address their grievances to the king and in the same breath profess continuing allegiance to him. They convene "a continental congress." Their purpose is circumscribed and limited. They want to vindicate and regain their traditional rights as Englishmen—trial by jury and so on—and they say so. All of this is done in the same way they will later declare their independence—in Congress, in writing, above the signatures of those present—reenacting what is by the time of the Constitution the particularly American way of conducting joint action. The important difference between the Articles of Association and the rest of the documents is that in 1774 the Congress has still not asserted independence. They still claim to be "*his majesty's subjects* in North-America."[15] Far from constituting themselves as a people distinct from the English, this body is in this act seeking resolution and reconciliation with Britain after being wronged by it. This is not the act of a distinct people or a people wishing to become distinct from their fellow subjects in England. They want continued union with the Crown.

Though Lincoln asserts that "the Union" is born with the adoption of this document by the Continental Congress, all that really results from these articles is a politico-economic act in concert, differing little from the Declaration of Independence in form, though it is different in content. Just as with the Declaration, no new order or government is set up. Even where the Articles of Association instruct representatives to be elected, it is explicitly for the purpose of enforcing the "non-importation, non-consumption, and non-exportation agreement" set forth here. Further establishing the character of this union is one of the last few clauses, which encourages the various colonial legislatures to pass any measures that are further required to enforce the present agreement, which would be unnecessary if this body were now in the position of speaking for, coordinating, and ruling the union as a whole.[16]

I will only briefly recall here that the Declaration of Independence is a similarly definite, rather than indefinite and "perpetual," political act. Rather than an act of founding and origination of a political order, it is the opposite: the cessation of a present or previous political order. To be sure, any act declaring a certain order over and done with implies by negation the rising of a new one. Yet as was seen before, the new order of the Declaration is one in which the several states are now "free and independent." And far from becoming one—except in the particular act then being undertaken—the sovereignty of the several states is asserted and affirmed. In geometrical terms, the Declaration of Independence is the endpoint of a line segment along a continuum of time rather than the beginning of a ray.

The Articles of Confederation and Perpetual Union much more resembles a geometric ray, to further pursue the analogy, but itself quickly becomes a line segment. The order of the Articles of Confederation, argue the framers of the Constitution, was plagued by the problems arising from their preservation of local sovereignties. The 1787 convention in Philadelphia started somewhat anew. Thus, though Lincoln asserts the long perpetuity of "the Union," the truth of his statement requires a repeated equivocation of the central term. Such an equivocation drains Lincoln's argument about secession of its persuasive character.

Lincoln's argument, though it is built on some unsteady ground, is not wholly wrong. Secession may in fact be legally impossible, but the union need not have preexisted the Constitution in order to establish this. The Constitution is not properly undone by any one state or any group of states, just as Lincoln says, because it contains within it the means for altering or abolishing it, by which none of the secessionists wished to abide. This means that the lawful way of altering the extant political order was avoided altogether, weakening the hand of the secessionists. These considerations will be more important when I discuss the Gettysburg Address. Before this may be done, however, there is more to say of the first inaugural.

Lincoln's next argument in the first inaugural concerns the nature of the principles of the Declaration—which he clearly has in mind but does not cite by name—and their relation to the Constitution and the then-present political order. "All profess to be content in the Union," says Lincoln,

> if all constitutional rights can be maintained. Is it true, then, that any right, plainly written in the Constitution, has been denied? I think not. Happily the human mind is so constituted, that no party can reach to the audacity of doing this. Think, if you can, of a single instance in which a plainly written provision of the Constitution has ever been denied. If, by the mere force of numbers, a majority should deprive a minority of any clearly written constitutional right, it might, in a moral point of view, justify revolution—certainly would, if such a right were a vital one. But such is not our case.[17]

Here Lincoln discusses the claims and arguments of the Declaration of Independence on the right to revolution. He says that if some "clearly written constitutional right" is denied, then revolution is justified "in a moral point of view." Lincoln's modification of the terms is interesting. Though the Declaration speaks of a government becoming "destructive" of the Creator-bestowed and "unalienable" rights of "Life, Liberty and the Pursuit of Happiness," Lincoln speaks of a "clearly written constitutional right." These are not identical. The Declaration's rights seem to be natural rights, rights that are certainly political in that they form the bedrock foundation of politics but are not necessarily written out explicitly and officially. But if this is so, then what the Declaration holds to justify revolution would not in fact do so on Lincoln's terms. Lincoln—often seen as the champion of the Declaration—seems to foreclose the possibility of extraconstitutional revolution.

If Lincoln is here arguing that the principles of the Declaration point to the irrevocability of the constitutional order (except by constitutional means), then he would seem to be of one mind with the founding generation—though with an important caveat. The distinction between what seems like a "natural law" justification of revolution contained in the Declaration and the constitutional justification mentioned by Lincoln is eliminated when the founders' full understanding of law and constitutions is made explicit. As Philip Hamburger has written forcefully in another connection, the general principles of the natural law were not thought to be extraconstitutional by the founders. Far from it. The amorphous nature of the British constitution had taught our founders that not all laws necessary to the good of the people could be provided for ahead of time. The law carried with it an understanding of the natural law as a necessary part of the very constitution they wrote out and ratified. Just so, when Lincoln argues that only the violation of a "plainly written provision of the Constitution" might justify revolution, he argues for a fairly positivistic understanding of the U.S. Constitution, which the founders would have rejected.[18] Such an understanding allows Lincoln to conclude that secession is not constitutionally possible. And if a positivistic understanding of the Constitution is the right one, then he is right. But if the founders' understanding of the Constitution is not so positivistic, then here lies a point of divergence between them and Lincoln. And since in this address and in all public statements Lincoln was always careful to convey his precise meaning, it can only be concluded that he is here rejecting the founders' broader constitutionalism. We must take Lincoln at his word and conclude that the more positivistic interpretation of Lincoln's words is the right one.

Returning to the general nature of the union and its relation to government, Lincoln says that "unanimity is impossible." The only real choices are (1) majority rule, (2) despotism, and (3) anarchy. No one would willingly choose despotism, it seems, and Lincoln sees the secessionists as choosing anarchy—an intransigent minority's only live option. The only constitutional option for the majority in this situation is for the union to "constitutionally defend and maintain itself," which, being spoken by Lincoln here, suggests the possibility of action by the president.[19] Lincoln says that he will not antagonize the intransigents unnecessarily and that, among other things, the mail service will continue even in those states that have voted for secession. But with knowledge of subsequent events today's reader is perhaps not mistaken in hearing Lincoln's words as a threat—or at least a promise that secession is not to be the final word on the nature and requirements of the Constitution.

Union will be maintained on Lincoln's watch, then, either by acquiescence of the minority to the majority or through some other means available to him as president. The nature of these other means is not specified but can be imagined. Further clarifying and reiterating his meaning throughout the address, Lincoln says that "whenever they [the American people] shall grow weary of the existing government, they can exercise their *constitutional* right of amending it, or their *revolutionary* right to dismember or overthrow it." He welcomes amendments because that means the perpetuation of the union, even if its operations change. This is to the advantage of those involved, he says, considering the very sure disadvantages of disunion.[20] He does not favor revolution and speaks of it in drastic terms.

Beginning his conclusion, Lincoln reiterates that he is not seeking to resolve entirely the disagreements now flaring up because of his rise to the presidency: "The Chief Magistrate derives all his authority from the people, and they have conferred none upon him to fix terms for the separation of the States. The people themselves can do this also if they choose; but the executive, as such, has nothing to do with it. His duty is to administer the present government, as it came to his hands, and to transmit it, unimpaired by him, to his successor."[21]

Thus leaving the fate of the union ultimately in the hands of the people, he also alludes to the people's "ultimate justice," which will bring about a peaceful outcome. Lincoln raises the possibility that only one or the other of the North or South can have God on its side; in either event, he says, "that truth, and that justice, will surely prevail." Lincoln lays the challenge before his "dissatisfied fellow countrymen" to avoid civil war. Gazing ahead beyond the present conflict, Lincoln is confident that the union will persist once all have been touched by the "better angels of our nature."[22]

The main change from the Puritan to the constitutional period was a differentiation of the spheres of religion and politics from one another; in Lincoln's first inaugural we have no reason to believe this separation has changed. (The same cannot be said of the Gettysburg Address.) If Lincoln can be supposed to offer a definition of who we are as a people in this address, it is not yet clear that the definition differs significantly from the founders' in terms of universality. It might perhaps be said that the universality to which he appeals here is a general or more philosophic kind of universality, as opposed to a Christian or theological kind. Though differentiated into political and religious spheres, the universality of the founding period seemed everywhere still to be the universality of Christianity. Here Lincoln seems to try to speak from a more generic point of view, attempting drastically to widen the scope of American politics. Although Lincoln calls on "Christianity" (by which he seems to mean the moral codes it inculcates) and "a firm reliance on Him, who has never yet forsaken this favored land" to temper the hurry that might lead to bad decisions by some, the main thrust of his words indicates a broader, more philosophical basis. The scant evidence so far weakens such a conclusion. More definitive evidence will be found below. Thus the picture from this first speech is muddled. For God's role in the polity, Lincoln has something in mind similar to the founders; God will be active only insofar as he influences the citizens privately—but this activity is vital for the public good.[23] The gesture towards angels in the last line is not narrowly Christian; it connotes as much a humanistic as a Christian point of view. Little here seems to be said of America's role in history, though this and the other two themes will figure largely in the second and third speeches considered in this chapter.

The Gettysburg Address

In the best-known piece in all of American oratory Lincoln captures a particular vision of America's origin and future and how these two were linked in the war he was then prosecuting. In considering what has been called "the American manifesto," we see that Lincoln speaks at once to who we are as a people and who we ought to be.[24] While volumes have been written on the Gettysburg Address, I confine myself to the role played by this speech in the development of a new American self-conception and the derailment of what went before.

The opening lines of the Gettysburg Address serve not only to situate the speech in American history but also to frame and interpret American history as a whole. In saying that "[f]our score and seven years ago our fathers brought forth on this continent, a new nation," Lincoln points to the adoption of the Declaration of Independence as the moment of birth, the moment of union for "the Union." While this very claim has already been problematized, there can be little doubt that Lincoln means to argue just this: the Declaration of Independence was the defining point of origin for the United States, and that moment gives the union its course in subsequent history.[25]

In the first inaugural Lincoln argued in contrast that 1774 marked the advent of the union. His purposes there were clear: he wanted to establish the constitutional impossibility of secession. Here, too, Lincoln's aim is clear, though different. In framing the Declaration as the founding moment in American history, America can be given an original and abiding mission that culminates in the war he was currently waging. In saying that the nation was begun with the Declaration, Lincoln can also say that the nation has been and ever shall be "dedicated to the proposition that all men are created equal."

Now, many critics have seized on the ambiguity of this formulation.[26] These critics react largely against the notion that America was ever supposed to seek, as a country, to ensure economic, racial, or any other sort of equality as a lived condition of every individual citizen. While it cannot be said that any aspect of the Gettysburg Address has gone unnoticed or underanalyzed, I want to make a different point and call attention to the most important feature of this first sentence for my purposes.

Lincoln claims that the country was, from its beginning, a nation "dedicated" to a "proposition." The particular content of that proposition is not my main concern; more important is the very notion that a nation could be dedicated to a proposition at all. It could be argued that Lincoln did not come up with this particular interpretation of the Declaration of Independence himself but that he merely popularized it. Because it was both in the air in the Republican circles he ran in politically and in the Republican Party platform even before his time as its head, Lincoln's role in this very substantial change could be minimized.[27] Yet for my purposes, what matters is precisely that Lincoln *popularized* this view—not that he thought of it first. My purpose is not mere intellectual history but a study of the real changes wrought in American history and American political thinking by a powerful idea. Whether or not it was original to him would not change the fact that the argument has found its locus classicus in his line from the Gettysburg Address. I do not wish to argue that no one admires or agrees with Lincoln when he says this. Today, most do. Based on what we have seen with the previous analysis of the Declaration and the other central documents of the American tradition, however, I wish to argue that, in saying this, Lincoln is wrong about the United States. The aim of the United States was not at all operatively formulated as a reified proposition until Lincoln did it here.

Students of the Declaration, as I have argued, need not and indeed should not follow Lincoln's interpretation, despite the ubiquity of this interpretation in the scholarly literature and popular imagination.[28] It can be seen with a careful reading of the Declaration that such an interpretation relies on either a partial reading or a deliberate misreading of the documentary tradition.[29] Rather than seeing the Declaration in terms of its own sources, Lincoln exhorts us to consider it as a gift "brought forth on this continent." From where? This detail is left ambiguous. The first inaugural's emphasis on generality, however, leads the hearer to conclude that the ambiguity is perhaps a device intended to suggest, unargued, an abstract philosophical origin for the Declaration. "Brought forth" from where? Usually, it is supposed, from Thomas Jefferson's reading of John Locke's political philosophy.[30]

With these words Lincoln has achieved single-handedly what in his first inaugural he encourages the Southerners to work for legislatively: a recasting of the political order of the United States. But he has achieved it not by law but by altering the meaning of the law and Constitution in the opinions of the citizenry. Lincoln gives the United States a new origin in 1776—rather than in the gradual development from a centuries-long tradition of self-government and self-understanding—and with this comes a mission. The country, previously dedicated only to its own perpetuity, is now set on a course for the realization of a state of universal equality. And you need only recall Lincoln's testimony as evidence: perpetuity is the aim of all governments. Where before the union was concerned only with its own order, it is now concerned with the concrete realization of an abstract idea. Now, in other words, the union may in principle become preoccupied with the order of the entire world.

With this claim, Lincoln epitomizes a point made by Voegelin and echoed by Kendall and Carey with special reference to the American tradition: "[P]olitical philosophy, as most political scientists understand the term, is a tardy development in the history of a people, and, moreover, a development precisely out of the stuff of symbols and myths." The authors continue,

We must not, when we stand in the presence of an original compact set of symbols, look for what we fashionably call political principles; the principles come only later, as a result of what Voegelin calls critical clarification of the symbols—or, if you like, as a result of what happens to the symbols when political philosophers and pundits go to work on them, and spell out their content in what we may call propositional form. The critical clarification, which may be skillful or unskillful, faithful to the original symbols or unfaithful to them, etc., comes later, after the symbols, but always proceeds with the symbols as its raw material.[31]

Lincoln seems to be not interpreting the symbols but reifying them in a way that changes their operative meaning. Thus in one stroke Lincoln achieves a refounding of the country in a manner contrary to his own preferred means of avoiding the Civil War. Rather than deciding together, constitutionally, how the American people is to be "one," Lincoln has revised the Constitution himself with this recasting of the Declaration.

Now to be sure, Lincoln has not done this without the consent of the American people—he persuades them to adopt his view. Though persuaded and not coerced, a change is wrought nonetheless. Union is now thought to be achieved not through juridical means of representation and consent but in common dedication to a common idea. Whether a recent emigrant or the scion of one of the country's oldest first families, all citizens are now "one" only in this belief in the idea of America. Rather than through common deliberation, Lincoln's radical unity is attained by reducing all parties to a predetermined uniformity that stifles the possibility of deliberation. This is the nature of propositions. Where the previous symbol was deliberation, which presupposes an open-ended outcome, the new symbol is radical, complete, abstract uniformity in both principle and action. Where the tradition previously held up a process of common decision making as its central symbol, now a universal end takes that spot. America is now not a people, as the Constitution had it, but an idea.[32]

While for my purposes the conception of America as an idea is by far the most important aspect of the Gettysburg Address's influence, several other clauses and ideas in it are relevant, too. The second paragraph begins with the framing of the entire Civil War as a world-historic test of the possible success of the kind of venture Lincoln just described. While this point seems to echo the passage from *Federalist* No. 1 discussed above, Lincoln's phrase has a more ultimate meaning. While Publius, too, seems to believe that America's success is an important test case for the possibility of freely chosen government ("conceived in liberty," in Lincoln's words), Lincoln attaches to that same notion the possibility of any government being dedicated to a *proposition*—but these are two distinct ideas. Lincoln places America at the pivot point of world history in regard to the success of this kind of political-propositional venture. Lincoln and Publius differ in regard to what they consider the venture to be. Publius speaks of whether a government may be based on "reflection and choice"; the success of the Constitution will show whether man is capable of self-government through deliberation. Lincoln, on the other hand, frames the Civil War as a test of whether a free country that is dedicated to a proposition "can long endure." It might be said that Lincoln's "conceived in liberty" carries the same meaning as Publius's emphasis on "reflection and choice." That may be so, but it does not change the fact that Lincoln has appended to his "conceived in liberty" the additional qualifier "dedicated to the proposition that all men are created equal." His meaning at best includes Publius's and goes beyond it, which means that they do not at all have the same meaning.

Lincoln's test is different from Publius's because Lincoln's conception of America is different. Lincoln believes that America is primarily an idea and that the present conflict is a test of whether this unique human venture can succeed. Publius sees America as a concrete political union, arising from and based on a particular instance of "reflection and choice." Publius believes not that America stands at the fulcrum of world history but that it occupies a uniquely advantageous position for the possibility of the establishment of government by deliberation, in contrast to the usual route of "accident and force."

Likewise, Lincoln draws the fallen soldiers of Gettysburg into his new idea of America. In doing so, Lincoln succeeds in adding considerable persuasive force to the account. Not all who heard Lincoln's words, however, were persuaded. Contemporary accounts show that some were aware of what Garry Wills has called Lincoln's "open-air sleight of hand." Rather than dying to "uphold the Constitution, and the Union created by it," wrote one newspaperman in the wake of Lincoln's address, the president supposed that the soldiers died "to dedicate the nation to 'the proposition that all men are created equal,'" which the writer considered offensive, innovative, and absurd.[33]

Some have noted the absence of the words *under God* from Lincoln's prepared text alongside their widely remembered presence in his delivered remarks. This is seen as a sign that this addition was an afterthought, vindicating the postmortem accusations of Lincoln's profound, lifelong skepticism. Though I do not wish to insert myself into the controversy over either these words or the even-larger debate about Lincoln's personal religious belief, I can say that their presence here reflects well, at least, on Lincoln's grasp of and representation of the American people.[34] Americans, before him and still today, seem to wish to hear that God has a role to play in our history—whatever it is.[35]

Lincoln famously closes the Gettysburg Address by saying that those who would give witness and honor to the war dead ought to take on the dead's supposed mission in life: ensuring the perpetuity of a nation dedicated to the proposition of equality. Though he does not use the same words, a similar meaning rings through the Gettysburg Address and the first inaugural. "Shall not perish from the earth" and "perpetuity" both have the quality of a geometric ray, to recall the earlier analogy. Yet here in the Gettysburg Address the image is not so dry and mathematical. Standing up to dedicate a cemetery on the very ground where so many died, Lincoln seeks to honor the dead by persuading his hearers that the dream of those fallen soldiers might yet be realized—and that if it is not realized there would be drastic and dire consequences for all governments, both now and in the future, for all mankind. Rather than a detached consideration of the nature of governments in general, as with the first inaugural, in the Gettysburg Address Lincoln seeks colorfully and forcefully to persuade his audience of his particular interpretation of the United States' history and future. As has been noted by Garry Wills and others, Lincoln seems to try and effect a total revaluation of the entire American political order—past, present, and future. As has also been observed, English usage is enough to confirm Lincoln's lasting influence. While in its youth as a republic, the United States was referred to in the plural, which is today considered awkward and incorrect. The United States changed to a singular noun in the wake of this president and this speech.

It is clearer with the Gettysburg Address than with the first inaugural that Lincoln's conception of universality is not merely a Christian universality differentiated into religious and political spheres as the founders' was.[36] Here Lincoln sees the United States in ultimate terms: it is to play a role in world history, that is, both within the concrete events of the political world and in history itself. Its success is the first link in the chain of the world's future political possibilities. America, in Lincoln's contemplation, stands at the center of history, at least in respect to the question of liberal democracy. As William Lee Miller has noted, "Lincoln was himself not only a thoroughgoing believer in the founding's universal moral truths, but [also] their most eloquent spokesman." This is reflected, Miller notes, in the universal significance Lincoln gives to American success at the end of the Gettysburg Address. But this is not without its problems:

> But there certainly is the danger of pretension in all that. An Englishman, for example, might have objected to the idea that the continuation of the United States was the sole test for the whole history of liberty, not for this nation or this continent but for the entire earth and for any nation "so conceived." Citizens of many other countries might find it overreaching for an American to claim that his country is the last best hope of earth. The proud claim that we are the bearers of a universally valid form of government, and even that we are the sole bearers, has had its unfortunate effects upon this country's behavior before and after Lincoln.[37]

This is a position that will ultimately determine the fate of many around the world, and though it has become ubiquitous and orthodox as the interpretation of the Declaration and the American founding, all ought to question whether this was the intention of the founders or was rather an innovation upon their words.[38] Universal significance is given to the particular moment in world history. This moment and the actions taken at that moment are thought to affect all subsequent history. As Glen Thurow has argued, Lincoln's words are aimed at giving politics in America a new and much more expansive meaning: "The viewpoint of the [Gettysburg] Address, which takes its bearings by the nation founded 'four score and seven years ago,' expands politics until it absorbs even the meaning of life and death."[39]

Lincoln's Second Inaugural

Thirty months of war and controversy separate Lincoln's first inaugural address from the Gettysburg Address. Eighteen more months elapse before the delivery of his last major speech. Lincoln's second inaugural address is the only speech ever to challenge the Gettysburg Address for the top spot in the American imagination, though the former cannot be said to have overtaken the latter in influence. With a bloody victory all but assured, Lincoln speaks mostly of the future reconciliation of the two warring sides.

Insofar as the second inaugural represents a departure from or a contradiction to the Gettysburg Address, it may provide symbols that advance the present inquiry.[40] If the symbol presented by the Gettysburg Address is that of a country dedicated to an abstract proposition rather than one ruled by the deliberation of a virtuous people under God, then in some sense the second inaugural paints a still-different picture.

One of the chief themes of the second inaugural is the reconciliation of North and South, though even in his consideration of this theme a more fundamental theme lies in the background: "The Almighty has his own purposes." Up to the point in the speech when he utters that sentence, Lincoln has concentrated on treating the South with forbearance and a degree of generosity; the rest of the speech after that sentence indicates that a particular view of history, specifically God's role in history, is the principle that allows for this generous treatment. God, Lincoln affirms, is in charge of even terrible events like the war that North and South are passing through. This fact makes the war no less terrible, but it does render the two sides more equal in the wake of the war than a victor would typically concede or allow. Though Lincoln himself says early in the speech that one side "would make war rather than let the nation survive; and the other would accept war rather than let it perish," he immediately follows this juxtaposition with a passive formulation: "And the war came."[41] The war, terrible as it is and had been, was more an act of God than an event in purely human history. The terribleness of the war, even the occurrence of the war itself, falls equally on the shoulders of both sides because it is, simultaneously, equally the fault of both sides and neither side.

I do not need to dwell on the theological soundness or implications of Lincoln's argument here. For my purposes, it is enough to understand his meaning. The whole second inaugural is an antidote for the poisonous aspect of victory, that tendency to absolve oneself of any wrongdoing when a terrible contest has been won. Part of that is accomplished by explaining how, because God is in control of these events, the guilt of the participants is reduced. Lincoln need not have been so generous toward the South in this speech. He was, in fact, vilified for it in his time. Lincoln is humble in regard to the North's actions and motivations in the war. He is humble in the face of the South's positions and institutions: "[L]et us judge not . . ." And he is humble in regard to whether man can ever know God's purposes in this life: "If we shall suppose . . ."[42] Lincoln is again humble in not claiming for his side the righteousness and vindication that a victor might be tempted to claim: "Both [North and South] read the same Bible, and pray to the same God; and each invokes His aid against the other. . . . [T]he prayers of both could not be answered; that of neither has been answered fully. The Almighty has his own purposes." Far from claiming God's favor for either North or South, Lincoln calls attention to the hubris involved in any belief in one's own chosenness.[43] God's will in history is, for Lincoln, a fairly inscrutable thing. We may speculate on it, but certain knowledge is not for us to have.[44] This does not mean, however, that we are left without direction.

In Lincoln's chastened or qualified view of what God allows us to see, there seems to be a glimmer of light: "with firmness in the right, as God gives us to see the right." We should have "malice toward none" and "charity for all" because God does, in perhaps limited and indefinite ways, give us some knowledge of what is right. This is the ground on which Lincoln can show the way forward out of the human-created terribleness that was the Civil War. We must "bind up the nation's wounds," "care for him who shall have born the battle, and for his widow, and his orphan." God gives us our direction here: charity and reconciliation.[45]

It has been supposed that the somber, backward-looking second inaugural in some sense contradicts the Gettysburg Address's forward-looking focus on the mission of the country. Yet the core meaning of each—at least insofar as each tells us who we are as a people, insofar as each contains symbols—need not be inconsistent. The circumstances of the two speeches are very different and this gives to each a very different aim. In the midst of war a commander in chief gives ultimate meaning to the sacrifices just made and the others that are sure to follow. Though at his second inauguration Lincoln had not seen the last deaths of the war, he could see they were on the horizon. This was no longer the time to rally the troops. Now was the time to "bind up the nation's wounds," which could only be done as one. The oneness of the two sides had been torn, and healing this rift was possible only with a superabundance of the qualities and virtues Lincoln extols. It is vital that this happen, even on the standard and with the concerns of his earlier speeches. The separateness that was the conviction and aim of the secessionists, Lincoln seems to say, should not be allowed finally to triumph because the partisans of "union" refused to humble themselves back into unity with their former enemies. And so we see in the three major speeches of Lincoln's presidency an enduring theme: the union is paramount and should be preserved at even a very dear price—in blood and in the humility of the victor.

What, then, does the second inaugural add to our understanding of the American people's new understanding of themselves? How does it affect their conception of the role of universality or God in government? Where does it place them in history? We have to say that, as a historical judgment, the second inaugural does not add much to our account.

If, as Thurow has argued, the second inaugural was in some sense intended as a rejoinder to or contradiction of the Gettysburg Address, then the address was not completely successful. Lincoln's uncommon generosity toward the South would not be matched by his successor or the decades of decisions after him. This lack of correspondence between the verbal symbol—that is, charity, generosity, and forbearance for one's enemy—and the policies that came after it disqualifies the second inaugural from full force as an operative symbol in the tradition. The Gettysburg Address, on the other hand, has been enormously influential in the ways that the government acts. The increased and ever-increasing centralization of power, the alteration in how the federal structure of government has been viewed and treated, even our patterns of speech have been affected by the Gettysburg Address. Everywhere America became more an idea than a people.

Lincoln's Conception of America as Derailment

Because the Gettysburg Address has won out in terms of symbolic power and influence, a definite change has occurred in the conception of universality from the founders' period to Lincoln's. In the Puritan period all in society aimed at the same transhistorical religio-political goal: the Massachusetts Bay Colony would be a new way of life for all Christians. The new balance and structure of government would please God and bring many blessings on the venture. By the time of the founding generation these views had changed. It was not so much that questions of government and religion had come to be answered differently, however; it was more that they had come to be seen as different and separate questions. Political and religious questions were separated, which, while leaving intact a similar, chastened view of the possibilities for government, changed the way government was thought of. With Lincoln we have another change.

The spheres of religion and politics were, for the founders and for many over the course of politics in the West, divided along transcendent and immanent, spiritual and temporal lines. In Lincoln's time this distinction, having already been made, made possible a new confusion. In a moment when the events of a temporal or political sphere seemed to *need* to acquire universal or transcendent significance, Lincoln made it so in the Gettysburg Address. A quality previously reserved to the religious sphere in America, human achievements with universal significance, was infused into the political sphere. In an instant Lincoln achieved a relation of these spheres that, because of the shape of their Christian worldview, the founders would not have tolerated. Their Christianity led them to keep the political sphere from encroaching on the religious sphere, protecting the latter. Purposefully or not, then, Lincoln effects a move away from a more Christian conception of universality in government to one that is less so.

If the political and religious spheres are in some sense fused back together, it might seem that the conception of universality in the Gettysburg Address is a hearkening back to the old Puritan tradition of holding the spheres undifferentiated, holding them as one. Just as John Winthrop and the Massachusetts Bay colonists saw themselves as enacting an aspect of salvation—that is, universal history—so also it appears that Lincoln places America as a nation at the center of this kind of timeline. Once the change from the Puritans to the founders had occurred, however, the primitive order could not be returned to in precisely the same manner. The undifferentiation of the spheres would require more than infusing politics with a transcendent mission.

In fact, Lincoln's move is possible only after such a differentiation because the Christian worldview that informed the original differentiation would not have allowed this kind of pseudoreligious mission to be given to government. The Lincolnian move requires a misunderstanding of the distinction of the spheres and their relation, which requires the distinction's prior occurrence. This misunderstanding is achieved both in the moment of and in the wake of the Gettysburg Address.

It should be noted that the second inaugural does not place America at the center of universal history; its logic rejects all thinking along these lines as hubris. Far from placing America at the fulcrum of history, the second inaugural places America on a vast sea, listless and under the near-total control of whatever storms God wishes to send. Water may surely be treaded in such circumstances, but there is no illusion that this affects the course of the water or the size or direction of the waves.

Even treading water has limited influence on one's position and cannot be kept up indefinitely.

It seems that Thurow's judgment of the contradiction of the two speeches is somewhat accurate. But, recalling what Voegelin said of political philosophy, it ought to be asked whether, in regard to America's self-conception, such a contradiction matters. Political theorists often seek a systematic quality in their subjects and theories. Contradictions are sometimes considered weaknesses and sometimes considered necessary. But for politics, are they problematic? In this case, the answer is no. The American people developed a handy way of admiring both the Gettysburg Address and the second inaugural: they simply adopted one as politically operative, as a new symbol in the American tradition (though no one now sees it in its newness) and forgot about the other. This is not to say that the second inaugural has been forgotten in the canon of great American oratory. But it has not given direction to American politics as the Gettysburg Address has.

A few more words might be said of Lincoln, the founders, and the Puritans. If the Puritan covenant contained both blessings and curses and if the founding generation was supposed to have dropped God's curses out from the political realm, it might be supposed that Lincoln takes a combination of these approaches. It would be easy to mistake the mission of the Gettysburg Address or the woe of the second inaugural as similar to the Puritans' covenantal blessings and curses, respectively, but each lacks a necessary quality for the comparison. In the Gettysburg Address Lincoln seems to have given America a transcendent mission, though without either being charged with its execution by God or becoming beholden to God for any failure in it. In the second inaugural Lincoln speaks of curses, of punishment, of woe; but none of these are delivered intelligibly by a personal God, as they were for the Puritans, according to the terms of any covenant or any conceivable reason. Far from a previously agreed-on consequence of the covenant's breach, the woe of the second inaugural comes from beyond the veil of human ignorance. "The Almighty has his own purposes," and these are inscrutable to man. Thus, while some elements of Lincoln's speeches might roughly appear to correspond to the old Puritan framework, they are very different in character, and this affects what they say about mid-nineteenth-century America's sense of the role of universality, history, and God in the life of their country.

It remains now only to reiterate why, by and large, the "Lincolnian" contribution to the American tradition is a derailment of that tradition.[46]

The differentiation of the spheres of politics and religion is more complete and more total with this new way of conceiving who Americans are as a people. No longer is America only a people seeking a political order that would make possible lives of Christian and traditional living, as it was for the founders. Neither does the worldview Lincoln articulates go back entirely to the undifferentiated union of the two spheres. Now each sphere seems to be put in the service of a single, abstract, transcendent mission. Thus there is a confusion of the spheres.

A further question about the nature of the distinction between derailment and differentiation is brought to mind in a passage from Lincoln's own first inaugural. Lincoln reflects on the relationship between the force of law and the consent of the people: "[T]he fugitive slave clause of the Constitution, and the law for the suppression of the foreign slave trade, are each as well enforced, perhaps, as any law can ever be in a community where the moral sense of the people imperfectly supports the law itself. The great body of the people abide by the dry legal obligation in both cases, and a few break over in each. This, I think, cannot be perfectly cured."[47] Because the basic symbols of the tradition are such by virtue of the consent and practice of the people—indeed, by their declaration in word and deed that such and such is a law unto themselves—then such symbols seem open to new interpretation and even revision as the result of a change in the temperament or opinion on the part of the people. If all cease to believe in and obey the law, it could become a dead letter. It may cease to be politically operative and effective. It perhaps ceases to be a symbol. If, as has been pointed up, the Gettysburg Address's interpretation of the Declaration of Independence and the American founding is now the orthodox opinion, how is it that they do not now represent only a differentiation of the tradition, a new iteration of the American people's self-understanding? The answer, interestingly, lies elsewhere in Lincoln's first inaugural and depends on the nature of the union as a concrete political act and entity.

Early in the speech, speaking of the various silences or ambiguities in the Constitution, Lincoln says, "If the minority will not acquiesce, the majority must, or the government must cease. There is no alternative; for continuing the government, is acquiescence on one side or on the other."[48] We must decide in common, as one, the fundamental questions of our common life. As Lincoln rightly says, unless we do this, we do not answer the challenge of the present moment but avoid it—and are left only with the choice of despotism or anarchy. This must be viewed from another perspective. The secessionists have, in refusing to acquiesce at all, precluded the possibility of their own self-government.

When some disagree with the general or specific direction that our common government takes, the minority has already agreed, at the people's primordial point of union and origin, that their disagreement would not be grounds for separation. This is the very essence of a symbol: it is a coming together for action in history. It is an outward statement of who a people is, and when some seek later to renege on their ancient agreement, the others must call them to account. Just as Kendall and Carey wrote of the signers of the Mayflower Compact, so also Lincoln asserts the following of any who are party to an act of political union:

> We the signers will, we are saying, keep on deliberating about what is for the general good; we the signers accept that—it is as old as Aristotle—as the standard to which we must subordinate our deliberations; but decisions do have to be made about the matter from time to time, and the best we can hope for at any moment is not laws that are meet and convenient to the purpose named but laws thought to be that. What we promise to obey, then, off in the future, is the results, fallible and subject to revision as a matter of course, of future deliberations of a certain kind—so that, if, off in the future, one of us the signers is to take exception to a law on the grounds that it is not for the general good, not meet and convenient, he will be told: We did not promise laws that are meet and convenient, but only such laws as are thought to be; it is enough if a given law reflects the general thinking amongst us as to what is meet and convenient; it is that which you have promised to obey.[49]

The ancient consent that still binds the government together in Lincoln's time and ours is not revocable on the grounds that it is not the best possible government. One must accept the bad with the good. Lincoln understands this. He must abide by it. We must hold him and his followers to account by arguing that his speeches truly do represent a derailment of the American political tradition. For all the continuity of the first inaugural with the previous tradition, the Gettysburg Address is a fundamental break with the previous tradition. The latter represents, among other things, a foreclosure of the deliberation that is the tradition's central symbol. Lincoln's images and words and interpretations do amount to a derailment, and if this is still seen as problematic, a further reason illustrates why it is not.

It might be supposed that Lincoln's contribution cannot properly be called a derailment because it does not fit the bill of a true symbol. It is not representative of the people in the same way as the Declaration of Independence, the Constitution, or any of the obvious choices. Yet Kendall and Carey, and I following them, include the *Federalist* as a symbol in the tradition. Or, to be clearer, the *Federalist* is a symbol in the American political tradition insofar as it modifies the way the Constitution is seen, which it surely does. We do not see the Constitution alone when we look at its articles and clauses. We see the *Federalist*-Constitution. We live under the *Federalist*-Constitution because it is not the Constitution, simply, that determines how we act in concert; it is the Constitution as modified by the *Federalist*.[50] Now, in just this way, Lincoln's contribution modifies the central symbols and documents of the American political tradition. Just as "we cannot look at the Constitution with innocent eyes" because we have read the *Federalist*, neither can we look at the Declaration of Independence without hearing Lincoln's interpretation of it.[51] The charging of those words with a universalistic mission is superadded, but we do not any longer see it as superadded, and we certainly do not act like it. We act as if what Lincoln says of the American political tradition just is the American political tradition. And this is so even though, as we have seen in this and previous chapters, there are serious discrepancies between the two.

We have here a new account of America as primarily an idea. And this means that the country has a new potential to expand the scope of its government at home and abroad. When America is an idea rather than a people, the previous criteria for what it means to be an American—territory, community, partnership, tradition—have been removed. This amounts to a redefinition of America, a new account of who each of us is as an American.[52] The union is now thought of as "brought forth" abstractly and philosophically. It is "dedicated" to a proposition. This is what, to most, it now means to be an American. And it is in this, as we will soon see, that Lincoln is one of the chief sources of what will become the idea of imperial American exceptionalism.

5

ALBERT BEVERIDGE

A Racially Defined, Imperially Aimed Nation

From the beginning of this book, the argument has been building toward a contemporary conception of American exceptionalism. The objective has been constant: to identify the various elements that seem to make up the idea and then to trace their evolution through the course of American history. Though the ideas do not cease to change after the turn of the twentieth century, the particular combination seen at that time is recognizably similar to today's imperial conception of American exceptionalism.

A floor speech by Senator Albert J. Beveridge of Indiana has come to be regarded as the locus classicus of the period's justification for American imperialism. It was delivered in support of a resolution he introduced, which called for the annexation of the Philippine Islands as American territory. After examining that speech, a brief treatment of some official statements by Presidents Theodore Roosevelt and Woodrow Wilson are sufficient to show that Beveridge was by no means alone in the period or in government. Political decisions were based on this account of Americans' self-conception, and understanding this self-conception will help us to understand where the ideas and policies came from, what they entail, and where American political thought might go from here.

The Theoretical Problem of a Derailed Tradition

Continuing with the line of analysis that has so far been pursued presents a challenge, though not an insurmountable one. In looking at a period of American history *after* its political tradition's derailment, how is it that anything substantive remains to be said of that tradition? A derailed tradition is something different from what it was before. Pointing up the derailment seems to be among the last possible things that could be said, based on this pattern of thought. Indeed, something like this point seems to have stood behind Kendall and Carey's apparent satisfaction with treating only the "basic symbols" of the tradition and not moving beyond the effects of the derailment in the wake of Lincoln's presidency. An analogy helps further to illustrate the methodological problem at hand.

If a tightly spun thread begins to unravel, it often happens that the unraveling thread has no clear core. The thread is not what it previously was; its unity has turned into a plurality, and though it is still loosely connected, the loosened strands can no longer perform the function they previously did as a unit. If the American political tradition were a thread traveling along an axis of time, the unified strands would represent a certain settled account of the way politics was conceived in the tradition. It need not have become what it was all at once—such a simultaneous birth and maturity is decidedly *not* what happened in America. The strands cohered over time. That maturity and unity, especially when put into political action, could be called "the tradition" and could represent a way to sort out what is truly traditional from what is not. But as I have argued, there was a time when the tradition unraveled, or became derailed. And this presents a problem for treating "the tradition" at any point after its unraveling. The difficulty is especially apparent if you see that it is problematic even to speak of the tradition being derailed, since even this seems to indicate that some things change and some do not, without indicating the nature of the change.

Derailment seems to indicate that the vehicle of tradition keeps moving, but in a new direction. It seems that, in this analogy, what changes is the vehicle's direction rather than the vehicle itself. Yet the tradition just *is* a vehicle. A lived political tradition is constituted by a set of symbols that help explain how, why, and to what extent a people is politically one. It is a means by which history, and a particular people's role in it, is rendered intelligible. Now, derailment also connotes the cessation of motion or, more specifically, a crash. The vehicle of the tradition, not being designed to go in this new direction, or "off the rails," has run aground and cannot continue. To move forward requires rebuilding the vehicle so it can function in a new way. To push the implied metaphor to its limits, this would mean building a car from the parts of the now-useless, derailed train. We see, then, that this analogy is becoming inadequate.

The image of an unraveling thread seems much suited to the phenomenon. Wholeness is lost, but the elements are not wholly discarded. They are still present, though now coherent with each other to varying degrees;

they are certainly no longer a unit. Broad agreement on the symbols that make up the tradition is gone, not to mention a consensus *interpretation* of those symbols. And so the various elements of the old, unraveled tradition can be clung to with varying degrees of coherence. The original unity may be achievable in principle, even if it is difficult to achieve in practice. But more likely is a diversity that seems, to each particular group, a matter of one orthodox position against a number of heterodoxies. To speak more plainly, the unraveling of a tradition presents an opportunity not only for a new consensus but also for the advent of multiple new, separate consensuses. Where once there was unity, there is now plurality. This seems to be what happened in the wake of the American tradition's derailment. Widely divergent accounts of who Americans are as a people are now possible, each with some real grounding in the people's imagination.

Now, the derailment or unraveling of a tradition is the cessation of its being, if not the cessation of the being of the elements that make it up. The strands may still intersect and, in some ways, reinforce each other in a now less coherent set of separate unities. But they cannot serve as a robust source of guidance for the political life of the community as a whole. That is the real consequence of a derailment or unraveling of a tradition. The tradition ceases to be viable as a vehicle that can move a distinct people through history. Each competing account of the tradition will increasingly seem to rest on solid ground (to mix metaphors) rather than to form a single account possessing exclusive foundational status. To speak once again of the American tradition, we are left with multiple constitutional moralities, each entrenched and assured that it has a monopoly on the truth.

Any analysis of the frayed thread, that is, the American political tradition after Lincoln, must be conducted without the illusion, then, that it represents a compelling, coherent, consensus unity itself. The symbols reused in constituting a new unity are not necessarily coherent in the same way as before, or even coherent at all. It may be, to return to a much earlier analogy, as new wine in old wineskins; the old skins may burst from the character of their new contents. The new purposes for which the old symbols are now deployed—the Declaration of Independence as a document justifying the liberation of the world by the U.S. military, for example—may so stretch those traditional elements as to make them less coherent, less compelling, less attractive as the representative, consensus account of the American political tradition. In a word, such developments make the tradition less livable and so contribute to the destruction of the tradition itself. The result of this destruction is a move toward something completely and purposefully new, à la the new articulations of many prominent Progressives or a move toward Realpolitik or some other architectonic and simplistic theory of politics. Thus, in the wake of such an unraveling the task of understanding takes a slightly different tack: we are left to examine the now-plural unities, or self-conceptions, that are the result of a tradition's unraveling. Imperial American exceptionalism is just one of those self-conceptions and stands now alongside the others—particularly "exemplary American exceptionalism"—as ideas in search of adherents. Each corresponds, if imperfectly, to particular actions taken by the community and can, therefore, be treated as a symbol for this reason. The difference is that these new symbols are symbols, comings-together, only for a part of the people. There is no single people any longer. But there is still a logic and a perceptible self-conception that can be gleaned from major political actions and actors of the day. They are new and form another possible source of operative self-conception today.

The myriad strands making up the thread of the American political tradition in this period will not be unfamiliar; some of the old threads persist into the new unity. The Declaration of Independence, the Constitution, and the notion of America as a chosen nation are present here. But there are new elements as well, and even these old ones are infused with new and different meaning. Though we are no longer, in other words, dealing with the "American political tradition" properly speaking, since we took that term to refer to the coincidence of action and articulation before the derailment in Lincoln's presidency, we are nevertheless dealing with some of the same old elements of that tradition, elements the reader will find familiar, even if they are combined in ways that fall outside the tradition. Ultimately these new combinations are necessarily outside the tradition because the line of continuity and understanding has been broken. This calls into question, of course, the privileging of any particular settled order *as* a tradition. If there seems to be a settled order, and if that settled order cannot be called something *other* than American, then how could the order of the founders be *more* American or *more* traditional than the order of the Progressive Era? The answer is necessarily found in the analysis, with recurrence to the principle of continuity over time.

We finally come to a moment in American political life when the idea of imperial American exceptionalism is recognizable. Or, to take into account what has just been said about the delicacy of discussing unraveled traditions, we will see in this period around the turn of the twentieth century an array of ideas we mostly recognize as the contemporary conception of imperial American exceptionalism. It should be clear that, though in this period the American political "tradition" is a derailed tradition, the tradition as it was still constitutes a rich store of symbols and understandings of life, politics, God, history, universality, and other concepts that can be recombined in more or less traditional ways.

In the previous chapter we saw that the period of Lincoln's presidency presented an apparent problem: it was difficult to know which documents to include and exclude. But in Lincoln's presidency there was no new American political order put in place in an official document. Rather, Lincoln's recasting of the existing documentary heritage effected a revision—that is, a derailment—of the tradition as it was. His words have achieved, especially since his time, a status similar to the *Federalist* in coloring our view of the Constitution and Declaration of Independence, though, unlike the *Federalist*, Lincoln's coloring seems to change rather than merely qualify the original symbols. The problem of choosing which documents to examine persists in the period now under consideration, since there is again no explicit re-founding document in the Progressive Era. But the solution, too, is similar to that in the previous chapter.

Symbols correspond to and articulate political action. Whether the action is a relatively easy case, as with the "coming together" of the U.S. Constitution, or a harder case, as with the several wars and actions undertaken around the turn of the twentieth century, the actions are accompanied by articulations of their meaning. These articulations, first, detail what is being done and, second, evoke the nature of the people doing it and the nature of their political union. Beginning with the outbreak of the Spanish-American War and continuing through the entrance of the United States into World War I, the American people see themselves very differently than they had in the previous periods examined. The different self-conception is evident in their actions.

The Spanish-American War

On April 19, 1898, the U.S. Congress passed a resolution declaring war on Spain.[1] It was the culmination of some months of agitation for intervention in Cuba, famously stirred up by the interception of unflattering Spanish diplomatic documents, the sinking of the USS *Maine* in Havana's harbor, and the exaggeration of Spanish atrocities in the "yellow journalism" of William

Randolph Hearst and Joseph Pulitzer II, which popularized the call for war.[2] President William McKinley signed the declaration of war the next day, and the Spaniards declared war on the United States within one week's time. But just what did Congress seek to achieve in war?

Congress summarily declared Cuba an independent political entity, demanded Spain leave the island, and authorized the use of force by the president to enforce this resolution:

> A joint resolution for the recognition of the Independence of the people of Cuba, demanding that the Government of Spain relinquish its authority and government in the Island of Cuba and to withdraw its land and naval forces from Cuba and Cuban waters, and directing the President of the United States to use the land and naval forces of the United States to carry these resolutions into effect.
>
> Resolved, etc., First. That the people of the Island of Cuba are, and of right ought to be, free and independent.
>
> Second. That it is the duty of the United States to demand and the Government of the United States does hereby demand, that the Government of Spain at once relinquish its authority and government in the Island of Cuba and withdraw its land and naval forces from Cuba and Cuban waters.
>
> Third. That the President of the United States be and he hereby is directed and empowered to use the entire land and naval forces of the United States, and to call into the actual service of the United States the militia of the several States, to such extent as may be necessary to carry these resolutions into effect.
>
> Fourth. That the United States hereby disclaims any disposition or intention to exercise sovereignty, jurisdiction, or control over said island except for the pacification thereof, and asserts its determination when that is accomplished to leave the government and control of the island to its people.[3]

In doing this, Congress considered more than two dozen bills and resolutions, all eventually referred to a single House committee. Though the various debates were not unreflective about the gravity of such an international political undertaking, the resolution itself makes no mention of the authority by which Congress acts. Indeed, though some found in the country's foundational documents an abstract justification for a right to revolution—and this is implied when the resolution mimics the Declaration of Independence in saying Cuba is "and of right ought to be, free and independent"—it must be admitted that the "liberation" of another state from colonial rule is fundamentally different from America declaring *itself* to be free and independent.[4] We see already part of the major change in American self-conception evident in this period: the final paragraph of the Declaration has been radically universalized. Rather than the stirring conclusion of a compelling indictment-act, Congress now implicitly affirms that the Declaration is a charter of independence for all peoples and that the United States is willing to put its diplomatic and military power to this task. Note that, though the universalization of the Declaration was begun by Lincoln, it could scarcely be said that he intended the interpretation that is operative in these international interventions. Nonetheless, the relationship between his interpretation of the Declaration and the American founding does seem to pave the way for just this sort of action because of the great expansion in scope it gives to our government and the universal and historical significance of America that then becomes his legacy.

After naval routs in Cuba and the Philippines—the latter was also caught up in the conflict with Spain—Spain accepted provisional terms for a truce on August 2, paving the way for an "independent" Cuba and a subjugated Philippines.

Though all did not go well in Cuba, the case of the Philippines was both more problematic and more telling in regard to the change in America's self-conception. The country was divided against itself on the question of empire. But "the public was, by and large, faced with a *fait accompli* that, although theoretically reversible, had the initial impetus of its very existence to carry it along."[5] In the peace treaty Spain had "ceded" the Philippine Islands to the United States.[6] What was to be done, then?

> There seemed to be four possible ways of disposing of the Philippine problem. The first, returning the islands to Spain, found favor nowhere. The second, selling or otherwise alienating the Philippines to some other power, seemed to invite a general European war; and it would hardly be more justified than remaining in possession ourselves. . . . The third possibility, leaving the Philippines to themselves and giving them the independence [that formerly exiled leader and now prospective native governor] Aguinaldo's men had been fighting for, was equivalent in the minds of most Americans to

leaving them to anarchy or to conquest. . . . The final possibility was American possession, in the form of a protectorate or otherwise.[7]

The last option was ultimately pursued, but only after vigorous and fruitless debate in Congress. In a speech on the floor of the Senate, Albert J. Beveridge of Indiana delivered what has come to be viewed as a crystallization of the new imperial self-conception of the American people, justifying the annexation of the Philippine Islands as U.S. territory. Beveridge is perhaps the clearest articulator of the actions undertaken, and for this reason it is all the more appropriate to take up his articulations as the proximate source of new symbols for imperial American exceptionalism.

Beveridge's Imperialism and the Philippines

Senator Beveridge took to the Senate floor on January 9, 1900, to speak on behalf of a joint resolution he had introduced only a week before. Relatively simple in expression, the resolution reads, "Be it resolved by the Senate and House of Representatives of the United States in Congress Assembled, That the Philippine Islands are territory belonging to the United States; that it is the intention of the United States to retain them as such and to establish and maintain such governmental control throughout the archipelago as the situation may demand."[8]

Beveridge begins his address by noting that certain "hurtful resolutions" had been introduced in the Senate and that "every word" of these debates "will cost and is costing the lives of American soldiers."[9] Beveridge then moves on to found his argument on the Constitution, which he says calls the Philippines "territory belonging to the United States." Now, the Constitution does not single out the Philippines particularly, as Beveridge suggests; his hearers would know this, which means simply that Beveridge is hereby referring to the part of Article IV, Section 3, that gives Congress the authority to legislate in regard to territories, as opposed to states, which have their own legislatures and are guaranteed a "republican form of government." Beveridge is beginning, then, with the premise that Congress has the power to regulate the Philippines. But this is problematic.

If, as he asserts, Congress already has the power to rule over the Philippine Islands, then presumably Beveridge's resolution is moot. If the Philippines are already U.S. territory, then the Constitution does clearly allow Congress to regulate them. But, as is obvious from the very fact of his introduction of the resolution, the Philippines are not being treated as territory of the United States. He takes for granted the very action that he hopes to effect. If his argument were correct, the action he urges would be unnecessary. If his argument were wrong, then the action he urges would be inadequate. Beveridge is being somewhat disingenuous. Now, it is true that the peace treaty with Spain that ended the Spanish-American War "ceded" the Philippine Islands to the United States. But a treaty does not have the same legitimacy as a law duly passed by Congress. Beveridge knew this and was trying to remedy the problem with this joint resolution.

The speciousness of his constitutional argument quickly gives way to one of two main arguments in favor of annexation. I will discuss the relation of Beveridge's racial theories to his imperialism momentarily; while those points are woven throughout the speech, Beveridge dwells on the economic impact of annexing the Philippines in a more concentrated passage near the beginning.

Beveridge's main economic argument is found early in the speech and is a kind of précis of what he will elaborate on in the body. "Our increasing trade henceforth must be with Asia," he says. "More and more Europe will manufacture what it needs, secure from its colonies what it consumes. Where shall we turn for consumers of our surplus? Geography answers the question. China is our natural customer. She is nearer to us than England, Germany, or Russia, the commercial powers of the present and future. They have moved nearer to China by securing permanent bases on her borders. The Philippines give us a base at the door of all the East." Beveridge continues, "These islands are a self-supporting, dividend-paying fleet, permanently anchored at a spot selected by the strategy of Providence, commanding the Pacific. And the Pacific is the ocean of the commerce of the future. Most future wars will be conflicts for commerce. The power that rules the Pacific, therefore, is the power that rules the world. And, with the Philippines, that power will be the American Republic." One can see already that Beveridge has notably departed from the American political tradition in several ways. Basing his argument on the expansion and aggrandizement of American political power is very different from the American political tradition evident in previous periods of American history. Yet there are elements that are similar, even if, as a whole, his view is very different. Weaving together the themes we have already seen in the other texts pertaining to the idea of American exceptionalism, Beveridge sees the movement of history, guided by God, as giving to America, first, a mission and, second, the ability to accomplish it. "We shall not dispute the divine meaning of the fable of the talents," Beveridge says later on, arguing in effect that *because* we have "been given the Philippines by God," we should use them to increase either our material wealth, or our power on the world stage, or our territory, or all of these.[10] Beveridge proceeds to make a long list of the natural resources and material advantages that would accrue to the United States if it annexed the Philippines. Good farming, abundant coal seams, copper, gold, lumber, fibers, a vast expansion of the customer base for U.S. manufacturers into Asia: all these could be gained with the passage of this resolution, he argues.[11] Empires, it has long been noted, have as one of their chief features the kind of economic colonialism here on display.[12] A concentration of power over vast tracts of land means that the riches of any one area come to be employed for the sole good of the imperial center. Resources from the provinces are appropriated to enrich the center; excess goods are sold back to the provinces whence their raw materials came, adding another mechanism for the centralization of wealth. Such is often the reality of imperial operation, if not always one of the main justifications or features of its self-conception. Yet here Beveridge is unabashedly imperial. These are not, however, the only arguments he gives in favor of annexation; there are numerous noneconomic arguments as well.

The congressional debates over Beveridge's and similar resolutions invariably include recourse to the supposedly intrinsic superiority of the "Teutonic" or "Anglo-Saxon" race over others. It is a key feature of Beveridge's speech, echoing a prominent line of thinking around the turn of the twentieth century. After briefly giving the economic argument above, Beveridge looks to the case of Hong Kong, where, he says, "our constructing race has builded [*sic*] one of the noblest cities of all the world," despite the extreme tropical conditions.[13] Since Hong Kong was a British colony, it is clear that Beveridge's racial thought is by no means confined to Americans only; it is race, which is held in common with the British, that is the important factor for understanding his arguments.

It should be noted that many racial theories at the time were tinged with a strong sense of geographic determinism. The climate, it was thought, produced the character of the people and their ways. Beveridge is seeking to make his racial argument over and against these deterministic arguments, saying that it takes only the right race to civilize areas previously thought incapable of it. Thus climate should in no way give Americans pause in taking possession of the Philippines. Dorothy Ross puts it succinctly:

American writers often linked their national history to the account of Anglo-Saxon liberty developed in England. American self-government was attached to a continuous inheritance that went back to the Teutonic tribes that vanquished Rome. Its institutions were carried by the Saxons to England, preserved in the Magna Carta and the Glorious Revolution, and planted in the colonies, where it reached its most perfect form in the American Revolution and Constitution. The American Republic was the latest link in the chain of Teutonic liberty, and the exemplar of liberty to the world. Originally this view of liberty was understood as a chain of immemorial custom, and it still encouraged a flattened conception of historical change by reading current institutional forms back into earlier periods. The millennial destiny required the same static logic and ancient lineage. The American Republic could hardly be understood as the product of merely local, temporary conditions, but had to be assimilated to a long-standing continuity of universal import.[14]

While Ross's account is not identical to Beveridge's, it hits some of the contours of his meaning while at the same time reinforcing one of the central claims here, namely, that over time the interpretation of these issues changed. Through anachronism and a sense of urgency not to fall into the European pitfalls, Americans like Beveridge molded the tradition away from its previous lines into a new way of thinking and formulation.

The Filipinos, Beveridge says, are a "barbarous race, modified by three centuries of contact with a decadent race," that is, the Spanish. A people barbarous by nature and influenced by decadence, he goes on to say, is totally incapable of self-government. Beveridge next suggests that "civilization" demands that the Filipino race "shall be improved."[15] Granting them self-government when they are ill-prepared for it "will drive us to our duty in the end," which is to rule over them until they are just as capable of self-government as the Anglo-Saxons, a feature that took "*us* a thousand years to reach."[16]

Beveridge continues his account: "Self-government is a method of liberty—the highest, simplest, best—and it is acquired only after centuries of study and struggle and experiment and instruction in all the elements of the progress of man. Self-government is no cheap boon, to be bestowed on the merely audacious." Interestingly, a similar argument to the *contrary* has come to be coupled with the idea of American exceptionalism in recent times, justifying the kind of imperialism of which Beveridge would approve but on grounds he would not. Beveridge argues that the Filipinos cannot simply be granted self-government; we must imbue them with it over a very long time. Repeating the same theme, Beveridge says that "in dealing with the Filipinos we deal with children," suggesting that an American takeover of the islands is salutary and necessary, though he gives no account of how the Anglo-Saxon race advanced without any similar tutelage.[17]

Now the believability of arguments like those of Niall Ferguson and others, who see America as imperial from the beginning, is easier to understand even in the face of the contrary facts presented above. The argument has been made for over a century. We encounter, then, something similar to what has happened in the wake of Lincoln. Just as Lincoln's revision and reinterpretation of the founding swept away the original views without calling attention to the changes, so also does Beveridge present his view—which we can see is new in important respects, having already thoroughly understood the main elements of the tradition in previous chapters—as the one true view of the American political tradition. I am trying to provide a more sophisticated view than one gets from uncritically taking the arguments of Lincoln, Beveridge, and others as true, since they are usually aimed at some concrete contemporaneous political end.

Nevertheless, Beveridge does perceive such an imperial obligation and wishes America to "do our part in the world-redeeming work of our imperial race."[18] It is the charge of "our governing race" to rule over peoples like the Filipinos just as America ruled the Indians and inhabitants of the Louisiana Purchase, in order to prepare them properly for the civilized enjoyment of American life. This is why interpretations of the Declaration of Independence that might forbid such imperialism are wrong, Beveridge says: they do not recognize that America has long held these racial views, which are implicit in the founding documents themselves.[19]

Not even the relatively dry proceduralism of the Constitution escapes the all-explaining principle of race: "You can not interpret a constitution without understanding the race that wrote it." Beveridge believes that the peculiar meaning of the Constitution is fully grasped only when it is recalled that "God has not been preparing the English-speaking and Teutonic peoples for a thousand years for nothing but vain and idle self-contemplation and self-admiration." He goes on:

> No! He has made us the master organizers of the world to establish system where chaos reigns. He has given us the spirit of progress to overwhelm the forces of reaction throughout the earth. He has

made us adepts in government that we may administer government among savage and senile peoples.

Were it not for such a force as this the world would relapse into barbarism and night. And of all our race He has marked the American people as His chosen Nation finally to lead in the regeneration of the world. This is the divine mission of America, and it holds for us all [the] profit glory, happiness possible to man. We are trustees of the world's progress, guardians of its righteous peace. The judgment of the Master is upon us: "Ye have been faithful over a few things; I will make you ruler over many things."[20]

The "senile peoples" to whom Beveridge refers could perhaps be the European mainlanders, for whom he hardly has any compliments, but could not plausibly be counted among the "savage" peoples. Thus all the main themes of Beveridge's speech—economics, geography, race—are interconnected, and it is not possible to speak of his views on race as entirely separate from his views on the nature of history or the place of God in the American political order. We turn now to those two elements, first examining them in Beveridge's own terms and returning later to note Beveridge's points of departure and continuity with previous American history.

Beveridge claims not only economic improvement and opportunity as a legitimation of the imperial act of annexation but also the sanction of God. God has, through the vicissitudes of political history, "been preparing the English-speaking and Teutonic peoples." And, further, he has not done so without a purpose in mind; he has given to them a mission to civilize the world, redeeming it. Thus we begin to see the role that the ideas of God and history may play in justifying imperialism.

Beveridge exhorts his countrymen to "gratitude for a task worthy of our strength" and urges "thanksgiving to Almighty God that He has deemed us worthy of his work." And it is clear to Beveridge, just as it was clear to the Puritans, that God spoke to America *through* the events and trends of history. "These islands," he says, "are a self-supporting, dividend-paying fleet, permanently anchored at a spot selected by the strategy of Providence."[21] God ordered the physical location and the character of both Americans and Filipinos, Beveridge avers, for the mutual benefit of each in a divinely inspired imperial relation. And the relation does not stop at material beneficence or political development.

In discussing the progress the British have made in Hong Kong, Beveridge challenges directly the charge of American imperialism: "If this be imperialism, its final end will be the empire of the Son of Man."[22] Whether Beveridge means that the Christianization of the Filipinos—many of whom were already practicing Catholics after centuries of Spanish rule—is the inevitable effect of America's economic and political largesse or whether he means that any unpleasantness associated with the means of Christianization is justified by that particular end, we see here that Beveridge claims for the imperial project the divine sanction of God. He takes the missionary component of the Christian faith to be identical or nearly identical to economic and political imperialism. Though the character of these views is very different, it is clear that there are points of correspondence with both the original and derailed American political tradition. Beveridge is taking threads from the now-unraveling tradition and seeking to braid a new cord.

Before discussing this further, however, it should be noted that it is Beveridge's conception of universality that makes the difference; it, too, is taken to justify imperialism. Evangelization was traditionally linked to conversion and, in turn, understood as primarily inwardly focused. Christian humility meant first seeking to remove the beam from one's own eye; now, to Beveridge, evangelization is taken to justify political imperialism. Whereas the universality of Christianity was, early on, an impediment to imperialism and expansionism in America, now Beveridge makes it the heart of imperialism's justification.[23]

Clearly showing his break with the specifically Christian character of the American colonial inheritance and political tradition, Beveridge argues, "It is not true that 'charity begins at home.' Selfishness begins there; but charity begins abroad and ends in its full glory in the home. It is not true that perfect government must be achieved at home before administering it abroad; its exercise abroad is a suggestion, an example and a stimulus for the best government at home. It is as if we projected ourselves upon a living screen and beheld ourselves at work." It will be instructive, in other words, and redound to the benefit of American self-government to try this experiment in the government of others. Interestingly, Beveridge acknowledges one of the central points of the present thesis: that America was not traditionally an expansionist political order. But he quickly brushes aside the point: "Self-government and internal development have been the dominant notes of our first century; administration and the development of other lands will be the dominant notes of our second century. And administration is as high and holy a function as self-government, just as the care of a trust estate is as sacred an obligation as the management of our own concerns."[24] Disregarding the American political tradition as it had been understood—and as he still understood it then—Beveridge openly and explicitly recognizes that the resolution he advocates lies outside of it. The old tradition may be used when it is convenient and should be discarded when it conflicts with the moment's (or the master race's) political will. This is precisely Beveridge's main point in discussing the Declaration of Independence and the Constitution.

Though the Declaration was a concrete political act of separation, this is not the usual view of that document today. Many, following the same lines of argument Beveridge traces, believe that that limited and particular document is, in fact, rather a charter of the political freedom of all peoples.[25] Thus it can be read to undermine Beveridge's point. For if all peoples are properly free and independent, then they should be able to frame a government for themselves, "laying its foundation on such principles and organizing its powers in such form, as to them shall seem most likely to effect their Safety and Happiness." We know already of Beveridge's estimation of the Filipinos' abilities in this area. He now speaks directly to such a point in regard to the Declaration of Independence: "The Declaration of Independence does not forbid us to do our part in the regeneration of the world. If it did, the Declaration would be wrong."[26] The Declaration of Independence may be discarded, he says, just as the Articles of Confederation were discarded. But in this Beveridge compares the supposed theoretical justification for the freedom of all peoples with a concrete political structure that hardly functioned and was replaced by the common consent of the bodies that controlled it, the state legislatures. To this Beveridge might respond only that his original point on self-government still stands: only those capable of self-government have a right to it, and the Filipinos are incapable of it.[27]

Beveridge has broken with one of the key features of the American political tradition, the hierarchy of the various forms of law. Written into the Constitution, and having been an operative tradition well before that, foundational documents and existing law were always treated with a modicum of humility and respect. Beveridge ignores this tradition and steps outside of it, and this is due to a familiar reason:

> And if the Constitution had not had the capacity for growth corresponding with the growth of the Nation, the Constitution would and should have been abandoned as the Articles of Confederation were abandoned.

For the Constitution is not immortal in itself, not useful, even, in itself. The Constitution is immortal and even useful, only as it serves the orderly development of the Nation. The Nation alone is immortal. The Nation alone is sacred. The army is its servant. The navy is its servant. The President is its servant. This Senate is its servant. Our laws are its methods. Our Constitution is its instrument.

This is the golden rule of constitutional interpretation: *The Constitution was made for the people, not the people for the Constitution.*[28]

Just as the Declaration should be abandoned if it gets in the way of performing "the regeneration of the world," so also should the Constitution be laid aside when it is counterproductive. Here we see stronger than ever the role race plays in Beveridge's thinking. Stronger than even the traditional role for the rule of law, considerations of race should govern how we act more than our previously given, covenantal word. The Constitution, in this view, is subject not mainly to revision according to its own provisions but according to the desires of the "Nation" that was its author, namely the Anglo-Saxon settlers of America. This rejection of history is, however, fairly selective.

There are times when Beveridge sees history as the unfolding of God's instructions for America. When he speaks of the "strategy of Providence" locating the relative proximity of America, the Philippines, and China, this is partly what he means: that God made it so with the purpose of guiding American actions. He also speaks of nature itself and the timely progress of technology, which now enables us to reach the Philippines relatively quickly through steam-powered ocean travel. The ease with which this can be done and the specific moment of this innovation strongly suggest to Beveridge that God has indicated *this* is the right course. Nature itself seems to demand it. And if this were not enough, near the end of the speech Beveridge lays bare one of the central assumptions of the whole set of arguments he is making:

Blind indeed is he who sees not the hand of God in events so vast, so harmonious, so benign. Dull indeed is the mind that perceives not that this vital people is the strongest of the saving forces of the world; that our place, therefore, is at the head of the constructing and redeeming nations of the earth; and that to stand aside while events march on is a surrender of our interests, a betrayal of our duty as blind as it is base. Craven indeed is the heart that fears to perform a work so golden and so noble; that dares not win a glory so immortal.[29]

The events of history manifest the "hand of God" and show us the way we ought to go. And make no mistake, Beveridge says, "Were it not for such a force as this the world would relapse into barbarism and night"; God has said to us, "I will make you ruler over many things."[30] Americans are the chosen people. They are the fulcrum of history, the right arm of God. They represent truth in its fullness. Disagreement must be pushed aside as the falsehood it is in order for their righteousness to triumph. That righteousness is the true and main concern, with all others taking a back seat. And lest it be thought that Beveridge is alone in these arguments, let it be noted that numerous other senators and congressmen join him in the debate.

Many disagree, and this shows that Beveridge does not express the unanimous declaration of America's self-conception in this period. Recalling, however, the analogy of the unraveled thread, we saw from the beginning that treating a now-derailed tradition was bound to reveal a lack of consensus. Those disagreeing with Beveridge and his views largely agree with the tradition, which shows that the American political tradition's derailment is not so much a transition from one consensus to another but the destruction of a consensus and the proliferation of numerous competing accounts, each with a number of adherents. What we have now is an unraveled tradition.

This means that part of the "symbol" framework is being modified. Unity or unanimity is no longer the case in American politics. One could also have said this in regard to Lincoln, but Lincoln's views became a near-consensus in the generations that followed. The same cannot be said of the imperialism of this period, which neither was at the time nor since has become a consensus view of who we are as a people. Thus there is no need to explore the degree to which Beveridge and his colleagues are representative, since no one view is any longer representative at all. But Beveridge's account has something that the competing accounts do not: execution and operation. Though the resolution he introduced never passed Congress, the plan proceeded largely as he wished. Congress's inaction allowed President McKinley to act according to his discretion, in which he yielded to Beveridge and figures in the administration like Theodore Roosevelt.[31] This set into motion a pattern notably followed by each of the presidents of the period, and a few illustrations are sufficient to show that the imperial mindset was not at all confined to Congress. It became the operative principle of American political action in this period, particularly in the presidency.

President McKinley and Theodore Roosevelt

In 1898 Col. Theodore Roosevelt was riding high. Having come home from the Battle of San Juan Hill as an American war hero, he set to parlaying his celebrity into the prize he wanted most of all: the governorship of the Philippine Islands, recently ceded to the United States by Spain in the war he just had helped to win.[32] Various intraparty political machinations led instead to the governorship of the State of New York and, in 1900, the vice presidency. Upon entering the country's highest office in September 1901 as a result of President McKinley's assassination, he inherited an administration that had already formed its habits of governance, including a set of policies on the Philippines.

The lack of a comprehensive policy toward the Philippines meant that there was, in fact, room for Roosevelt to blaze his own trail. As John M. Dobson has observed, "The possibility that American annexation [of the Philippines] might foment a long, costly, and bloody war with the Filipinos was not widely recognized at the time [i.e., the end of the Spanish-American War]. In the end, the decision was strictly an American one, arrived at on the basis of quite limited information. How and why the United States reached that decision are questions that have intrigued historians for ninety years, with no consensus in sight."[33] Never the theoretician, Roosevelt's words and acts in regard to America's imperial possessions largely maintained the status quo.[34] The main aim of a somewhat aimless policy was to acquire and maintain territory in the east that could facilitate trade and the increased exportation of American manufactured goods. Much like Beveridge, McKinley believed the United States was imperial only insofar as the Christian "missionary sentiment" could be called imperial. At the time many, including McKinley himself, believed that the United States would be welcomed as a liberator and savior after centuries of Spanish rule; the Americans would work "selflessly" to civilize the Filipinos, and these benefits would engender trust.[35] Any material gain, in this mindset, is considered either serendipitous windfall or just reward.

Teddy Roosevelt's presidential addresses are shot through with the same aims and expectations as Beveridge's speeches, beginning in his first major speech in office. In his 1901 "First Annual Message to Congress," Roosevelt says he wanted "to make them [i.e., the Filipinos] fit for self-government after the fashion of the really free nations." Just like Beveridge, Roosevelt believes that the question of others' self-government is tied to their race and their race's history: "[W]hat has taken us thirty generations to achieve, we cannot expect to see another race accomplish out of hand, especially when large portions of that race start very far behind the point which our ancestors had reached even thirty generations ago."[36]

Roosevelt says that the United States had been behaving and was continuing to behave with a "disinterested zeal," an example unparalleled in history. To leave abruptly, as some called for, would be to risk "murderous anarchy," he thinks, which would in turn be a "crime against humanity." This kind of undertaking, or any "wars with barbarous or semi-barbarous peoples," are a "most regrettable but necessary international police duty which must be performed for the sake of the welfare of mankind." In a policy formulation that would develop over time as one of the orthodox defenses of moves like the annexation of the Philippines, Roosevelt, already in 1901, says that he is merely applying the old Monroe Doctrine to a new situation: "In other words, the Monroe Doctrine is a declaration that there must be no territorial aggrandizement by any non-American power at the expense of any American power on American [i.e., North or South American] soil."[37] Though he applies this only to Cuba at first, by 1904 Roosevelt expands it to justify the "police power" of a reluctant United States against any "free nation" that does not, in the United States' estimation, use its freedom responsibly.[38]

Roosevelt is aware of the objection, mentioned above, that in adventuring abroad America is contravening Christ's admonition to first take care of ourselves before presuming to fix others:

> Ordinarily it is very much wiser and of more useful material betterment to concern ourselves here at home than with trying to better the conditions of things in other nations. . . . Nevertheless there are occasional crimes committed on so vast a scale and of such peculiar horror as to make us doubt whether it is not our manifest duty to endeavor at least to show our disapproval of the deed and our sympathy with those who have suffered by it. . . . There must be no effort made to remove the mote from our brother's eye if we refuse to remove the beam from our own. But in extreme cases action may be justifiable and proper.[39]

While recognizing with Beveridge that the traditional stance of America had been not to intervene in such situations, Roosevelt seems to make a different argument. The "crimes" committed are too great to ignore in this situation; the crimes of which he speaks are, however, not enumerated here and neither are the criminals. Though elsewhere Roosevelt acknowledges the material riches of the islands, like Beveridge, he does not use that as justification for taking or keeping the Philippines. Staying and continuing to hold the Filipinos in subjection is justified, he argues, because of the "good we are able to do in the islands," not least our effort "to develop the natives" so they can one day achieve self-government.[40] The mission, then, is civilizing them and cultivating them in America's own image—though without ever extending the possibility of statehood, a fact that Beveridge's opponents thought very telling.[41]

In Roosevelt's inaugural address he reflects on the special challenges and successes of the American political tradition. Though we inherited a tradition, we "have had to pay few of the penalties which in old countries are enacted by the dead hand of civilization."[42] The new century presents perils, "the very existence of which it as impossible that they [the founding fathers] should foresee." But these perils must be met with the same "spirit" as the previous ones, especially the maintenance of virtue, and with support for the order already regnant, which is good and should be maintained. We will achieve all this, Roosevelt concludes, by cultivating "the qualities of practical intelligence, of courage, of hardihood, and endurance, and above all *the power of devotion to a lofty ideal*, which made great the men who founded this Republic in the days of Washington, which made great the men who preserved this Republic in the days of Lincoln."[43] Roosevelt explicitly buys into and endorses, reflectively or not, the Lincolnian narrative that the most essential part of America is its ideality. He also lumps Lincoln together with Washington without considering that each operated according to a different interpretation of what America is. Furthermore, Roosevelt makes no distinction between the founding fathers' actions and the imperial actions he advocates.

Later in the same year Roosevelt delivered his "Fifth Annual Message to Congress" and sought to rebut the criticism that the Monroe Doctrine was expansionist. He was simply pushing the limit of the full flowering of the Golden Rule, which he says is the ideal standard in the international political order. Roosevelt denies outright that action in Cuba is imperial: "It must be understood that under no circumstances will the U.S. use the

Monroe Doctrine as a cloak for territorial aggression."[44] Yet he makes no parallel claim for policy toward the Philippines. Roosevelt, right through the end of his administration, denied self-government to the Philippines, which he thought remained incapable of it.[45] Roosevelt's words and actions, then, confirm each other and help to demonstrate a change in the operative American self-conception, away from the previous tradition. Though Roosevelt seems to have firmly set and expanded the policy of international policing in the presidency, he is not the last president to have acted similarly. Though Woodrow Wilson repudiates the racial aspects of Roosevelt's and Beveridge's thinking, this comes simultaneously with an even more grand and idealistic vision for the role of the United States in world affairs.

Woodrow Wilson and the Idea of American Exceptionalism

A relatively brief look at some of Woodrow Wilson's actions and words is sufficient to understand that he falls in a clear, if loose, association with Roosevelt and Beveridge on many of the ideas discussed above. His more ideal, more expansionist views are concentrated toward the very end of his political career. Even late in his career, on the occasion of his first inaugural address, Wilson sounds a decidedly conservative note. He advocates "restoration" over "revolution." "We shall restore, not destroy," he says. "We shall deal with our economic system as it is and as it may be modified, not as it might be if we had a clean sheet of paper to write upon, and step by step we shall make it what it should be, in the spirit of those who question their own wisdom and seek counsel and knowledge, not shallow self-satisfaction or the excitement of excursions whither they can not tell. Justice, and only justice, shall always be our motto."[46] This incremental approach and chastened worldview, however, have eroded by the beginning of his second term.

In his second inaugural address Wilson sounds much more like Roosevelt and McKinley in protesting any assertion that America works only for its own aggrandizement. It is not selfish motives but the tragic circumstances of the world that draw the United States to assert itself:

> We may even be drawn on, by circumstances, not by our own purpose or desire, to a more active assertion of our rights as we see them and a more immediate association with the great struggle itself. But nothing will alter our thought or our purpose. They are too clear to be obscured. They are too deeply rooted in the principles of our

national life to be altered. We desire neither conquest nor advantage. We wish nothing that can be had only at the cost of another people. We have always professed unselfish purpose and we covet the opportunity to prove that our professions are sincere.[47]

International problems may require U.S. engagement, since "[w]e are provincials no longer. . . . There can be no turning back. Our own fortunes as a nation are involved, whether we would have it so or not." And though the "principles" of nonconquest are "deeply rooted" in America, Wilson argues that, nonetheless, America can be absolutely sure of its righteousness: the "principles in which we have been bred" are "the principles of a liberated mankind."[48] We know better, perhaps, than other, nonliberated peoples what should be done. And if necessary, Wilson suggests, we will do it. The necessity came, at least in Wilson's mind, less than a month later, when he asked Congress to declare war on Germany.

In his request for the declaration of war, Wilson actually disclaims, unlike Beveridge and Roosevelt before him, American uniqueness in regard to righteousness. We are "only a single champion" of "right," not the only one.[49] Yet in stating the objectives and risks of the present situation, he suggests an ultimate goal as the guide: "We are glad, now that we see the facts with no veil of false pretense about them, to fight thus for the ultimate peace of the world and for the liberation of its peoples, the German peoples included; for the rights of nations great and small and the privilege of men everywhere to choose their way of life and of obedience. The world must be made safe for democracy. Its peace must be planted upon the tested foundations of political liberty. We have no selfish ends to serve. We desire no conquest, no dominion."[50] Wilson sets the country to war *not* against a particular enemy but *for* a universal and abstract goal. His own aim is not a particular cessation of certain unjust circumstances and actions—as we might expect would be his goal from his first inaugural address—but to "bring peace and safety to all nations and make the world itself at last free."[51] The finality of this goal approaches the same ambition that Beveridge had for a politically effected "regeneration of the world." The finality Wilson seeks is so fundamental and so ultimate that it could not be achieved except with the mobilization for total war, if even then.[52] Yet this result was not the sole product of Wilson's mind. It was the product of decades and centuries of change in the American political tradition.[53] He stands at the end of the process of the dissolution of the tradition, direct heir to Lincoln's conception of America as an idea: "Sometimes people call me an idealist," Wilson once said. "Well that's how I know I am an American. America, my fellow citizens, . . . is the only idealistic nation in the world."[54] He, along with Roosevelt, Beveridge, and their political allies during the period, takes the words of the founding and infuses them with new meaning: "The vision of America as the enforcer of justice and the scourge of tyrants is a noble one. It goes back, in rhetoric at least, to the early days of the republic and corresponds to the image of the United States as standard-bearer of freedom for peoples everywhere. It was not, however, until recently that this patriotic self-image was translated into a program of action and America was declared to have a responsibility to bring her concept of democratic self-government to peoples everywhere."[55] Recognizing that a change has occurred from America's earliest days to Wilson's idealist foreign policy, and having seen the key texts over the course of American history that epitomize this change, an analysis of these changes is now possible and proper.

Elements of the Puritans?

The imperial politics of the turn of the twentieth century seemed to possess an understanding of history not unlike that of the Puritans of Massachusetts Bay. Whereas the Puritans believed that events in history were telltale signs of the future—another book of God's revelation when coupled with the Bible—Beveridge and others in his period believed much the same, but without recourse to the Bible. When Beveridge speaks of the progress of the Anglo-Saxon race toward its present work of taking responsibility for the development of other races, he equates the particular circumstances and events of his time with the unerring plan of God.[56] Because it happened, Beveridge takes for granted that it was God's will.

The Puritans, however, did not take for granted that God's will would be achieved. They were highly aware that upon them much depended. They could fail, and if they did, the results would be calamitous. Nevertheless, God would assist them if they remained righteous. And though Roosevelt urges his fellow citizens to virtue in his inaugural address, this is as close as he comes to the Puritans' view of their own possible failure. The Puritans believed that God assigned to them a high mission to improve themselves and build a perfect community of Christian charity that would serve as an example to the world.

Beveridge and the others see their mission as directed outwardly rather than inwardly. It is evident that Roosevelt, perhaps the least ideologically pure of the three men examined in this chapter, perceives this distinction between an inward and outward focus when he refers to the biblical passage about the "mote" in another's eye.[57] But he allows that this admonition should not be so rigid as to prevent the United States from invading and governing other peoples as subjects or engaging in "international police action" when he saw fit. In other words, Roosevelt seems to stand for moderation in all things: even extreme acts of imperialism are sometimes permissible. Thus the least extreme of these three represents, still, an extreme departure from the main line of the American political tradition.

Though the political actors of this period are highly aware of and explicit about the role of God, that role is very different from the one conceived by the Puritans, and it leads to a very different practical outcome. One understanding of the "Christian sentiment" leads to the development and cultivation of a close-knit community focused on its own salvation; the other understanding leads to the takeover and subjugation of other peoples and the exploitation of their land and resources. It could be objected that the Puritans colonized New England and were imperial in regard to the "savages" there. This argument is taken up in the debate over Beveridge's resolution. Senator Richard F. Pettigrew of South Dakota makes a distinction between "expansionism," by which he means the westward movement of the United States across North America, and "imperialism," which pertains more to the Philippines and like situations:

> I might say here, Mr. President, that I allude to those who advocate the conquest of the Philippines as imperialists and not as expansionists, for the reason that expansion implies the enlargement of the same thing, the adding of more of that which you already have, the acquisition of countries holding a population capable of living and supporting our Constitution to be admitted as States into the Union; while the imperialist doctrine is the acquisition of tropical colonies where it is admitted that self-government can not exist, as we understand it under our Constitution; and therefore the people must be governed perpetually and forever as crown colonies of this Republic. The holding of such countries, the conquest of an unwilling people, their retention in subjugation by a standing army, means of necessity not a republic where all the people must be consulted, but a despotism where the will of one man can march armies, declare

war, and act with great rapidity. A republic is naturally slow in action, because the people must be considered and must be consulted.[58]

In one view of how Christianity affects political action, God plays a role that *limits* the actions of the people. In the other, God grants them full *license* to expand and rule over others. On the one hand, God serves as supreme judge and arbiter of all order, giving blessings and protection and expecting great strides toward community cohesion and holiness. On the other hand, the actions undertaken are said to have the full, unconditional endorsement and sanction of God's Providence, so that little could or should slow them. In one, the sense of universality serves as a check upon the scope of government and purpose of politics. In the other, the government is invested with much more than an exemplary significance; government is, in this period around the turn of the twentieth century, thought of as the embodiment of the transcendent will of God, and its triumph is his, swerving for no obstacles.

Abandoning the Founders

Just as key aspects of the Puritan worldview are taken up, in a modified way, by Beveridge and the others, so too are the founders both exalted and rejected in this period. Where the founders' words are thought to condone expansion, they are heralded. Where their words could be used to slow the imperial actions desired by Beveridge, he urges that they are merely "wrong."

The limitedness of the political sphere was a civilizational inheritance the founders both cherished and handed on. A Christian view of the world, though not enacted politically and formally, served as the governing principle on the relation of politics to life and the relation of America to the world. It was an operative principle of the Puritan regime that only an inward-focused excellence would have the proper outward effect. Such a reading of the Puritans requires an accompanying fresh reading of the founders. But there is evidence beyond the country's basic founding documents. This is exemplified in the famous Fourth of July oration by John Quincy Adams:

Wherever the standard of freedom and independence has been or shall be unfurled, there will be America's heart, her benedictions, and her prayers. But she goes not abroad in search of monsters to destroy. She is the well-wisher to the freedom and independence of all. She is the champion and vindicator only of her own. She will recommend the general cause by the countenance of her voice, and by the benignant sympathy of her example. She well knows that by once enlisting under other banners than her own, were they even the banners of foreign independence, she would involve herself beyond the power of extrication, in all the wars of interest and intrigue, of individual avarice, envy and ambition, which assume the colors and usurp the standards of freedom. The fundamental maxims of her policy would insensibly change from liberty to force. . . . She might become the dictatress of the world. She would no longer be the ruler of her own spirit.[59]

Abandoning this view required the theoretical moves that have already been discussed. But here we see an explicit articulation of the general character of America's self-conception in the founding era. For the founders, transcendent ends were not subsumed into the immanent, political realm. As I have shown, the separation of the spheres of politics and religion was put in place on Christian grounds and maintained by the conviction that this balance of transcendence and immanence was the best way to order politics. Such a view was rejected in the imperial actions of the turn of the twentieth century. The Constitution, Beveridge argued, should be wholly subject to whatever the people wished to accomplish. And in this it is clear that Beveridge rejected—or at least failed to recognize—that the separation and limitedness of government is precisely what the founders wished to accomplish. But such a recasting of the role of America in the world required first a recasting of the nature of America in general. Such was Lincoln's accomplishment.

The Embrace of Lincoln's Idea of America

When Lincoln spoke of America as "dedicated to a proposition," he set into motion a revolution in America's self-conception and its main symbols. He made it possible to think of America as "one" in a new way. Rather than because of the concrete political union that Americans had formed, Lincoln proposed that they were united by sharing the same ideas about America and being dedicated to them. This was seen as vital for a people whose previous concrete union had been rent asunder atop the altar of war. Lincoln held out the possibility for reunion if only all parties could change their minds and, as he had it, dedicate themselves in common to the idea of

America. But in making this move, Lincoln made it possible to conceive of America as something transcendent, as something detached from strictly historical events and circumstances. His recasting of America as an idea led to a consequence he may not have intended. In order to make the several states once more thinkable as a unit, Lincoln made it thinkable that anyone who adhered to an abstract belief could be politically "one" with the others. Lincoln changed America from a unique, concrete, particular country incapable of being copied into a creed that is by definition replicable and expandable. Lincoln made thinkable the idea that America was not at all "provincial," not at all subject to the "dead hand of civilization," as Wilson and Roosevelt, respectively, later put it, but an idea widely and easily held by any aspiring idealist.

The Elements in Place

After running through some of the most important moves in the history of the American political tradition, an answer begins to emerge to the question How did we get here from there? "Here" is the thinkability of imperial American exceptionalism. "There" is its initial unthinkability. We have seen that the difference between exemplary exceptionalism and imperial exceptionalism consists, in American history, in the difference between the respective conceptions of God, history, and universality that are operative in the political tradition.

What we mean by *American exceptionalism* today is often American imperial exceptionalism. That is the sense in which the term is most controverted and the sense with which it gains the most political traction. That sense of the term was distinguished from the other senses not treated here.

One arrives at the turn of the twentieth century and sees many of the same elements and developments observable at several stages of previous American history, but in new combinations and with new attendant interpretations. The now-disparate strands of the tradition do not seem to form a single coherent thread, though their loose association can be recognized as having come from a previous particular tradition. The strands are made more intelligible now that we have recognized their former coherence. The unraveling is clearer to us who have, in undertaking this inquiry, seen the thread of the tradition as it was before.

Before moving on to some concluding thoughts, the unraveling nature of the tradition at this point in history should be touched upon. My observation that the American political tradition seems to have collapsed in large part by the turn of the twentieth century is not unique. It is evident in the palpable sense of urgency in the debate over Beveridge's annexation resolution; it seemed as if the United States stood at a crossroads, or perhaps at a dangerous precipice. Walk one direction and the result is the dissolution of the republic. Walk the other way and hope may be preserved. On February 20, 1900, Senator Richard Kenney of Delaware delivered a rejoinder to Beveridge:

> Mr. President, does not this cry for conquest take us back through the centuries until we find ourselves in that time of the Roman Republic, when by the ambition and greed of some of her sons was begun her conquest of the world—the beginning of her end? In that history can we not see ourselves and read our future? New territories were conquered and their people enslaved. Military governors were sent to rule over them. Strange laws were enacted for their government and alien judges sent to administer them. The religion and manners of the conquerors were enforced; in a word, all the miseries which follow in the train of the conqueror and oppressor came to the peoples to whom Rome brought the blessings of her civilization. Rome then thought herself trusted of the gods for the civilizing of mankind throughout the world, but soon was taught her mistake. In her struggle to destroy the liberties of others she lost her own. Man's unalienable rights—life, liberty, and the pursuit of happiness—then, as many times since, asserted itself [sic] and the conquered became the conquerors, the slave the master. And Rome, the mistress of the world, repudiated and despised, passed—a page in history. In imperialism she found her end.[60]

The American political tradition was by this time no longer univocal. It had changed; it had unraveled; it now had no clear core.

When the ideality of Lincoln's account is combined with the now-limitless license of a Puritan worldview cut in two, and when the founders' government is no longer seen as wholly separate from more transcendent purposes and concerns, then the imperial politics of the turn of the twentieth century is possible. The evidence already shows that the humility of the Puritans is gone. The new ultimacy of the goals achievable by politics means the conception of what is possible for government has been drastically expanded from the time of the founders. And the Lincolnian view of the abstract foundation of the American political order made expansion even more thinkable on the grounds of realizing "lofty ideals." The argument here is not that the imperialism of this period *had* to happen but that the developments in American history traced in the previous periods were necessary to make this imperialism possible.

Conclusion

The Possibility of a New and Traditional American Political Order

The self-conception, worldview, and behavior of the American people underwent a great change by the turn of the twentieth century. The change, while radical, was piecemeal and sometimes slow; it proceeded nearly imperceptibly. The story is one of gradual differentiation from colonial times into the nineteenth century. But then, a crisis. The wounds of the Civil War required bandages not previously known because the war presented a problem—real disunion—that we had not encountered before. To solve this new problem, a new solution was ventured; we came to be bound up together in a radically new way. This new binding has had a lasting effect both on the way we think of ourselves and on the way we conduct ourselves at home and abroad. Who we are as a people, a question originally settled and unified in the central documents and symbols of the American political tradition, became an open question because the original symbols and documents were stretched beyond their limits.

In the Progressive Era there was no single consensus on Americans' self-conception. Great debates were waged on the floor of the Senate chamber between more imperial Republicans like Albert Beveridge and humbler-minded Democrats like Richard Kenney. Approaching midcentury, the arguments remained largely the same, though the parties switched sides; the Beveridge strand became more and more operative. This great change—from more humble, local, and inwardly focused to more brazenly imperial and centralized—saw manifestations throughout the twentieth century in the New Deal and Great Society. From midcentury and up until recent decades, the more centralizing and outwardly directed tendencies seemed to have been confined to the Democratic Party. As has now long been obvious, this more imperial cast of mind holds great sway on both sides of the political aisle and in virtually all corners of society.

Most now think about politics in terms of a highly centralized government, highly centralized solutions, and what America can do by itself and to its own advantage on the international stage. There is a large and increasingly settled consensus on a more imperial self-conception and operation in American politics—a consensus nearly opposite to our original and most basic symbols. Vast amounts of natural resources, capital, and human lives are allocated accordingly and put in service of an imperial worldview under which, despite ourselves, we still sometimes chafe. The day may come when Americans are completely at home in this imperial worldview, but even if we are not wholly so today, only a shrinking minority are willing or able to contradict the operative majority. Even then, the current minority, in tune with the traditional American position, are today completely out of tune with the principles of the tradition. Their nearly hollow accounts betray the great interruption of principle and symbol articulated in this book.

If there is any hope to be gleaned from this troubling state of affairs, it lies in the fact that a consensus may still be possible. The possibility of a new and more traditional American politics—which despite appearances is anything but a contradiction in terms, given the understanding of tradition advanced in these pages—may yet come to pass, because despite the fraying of the tradition there does seem to be a growing consensus of some kind, wrongheaded though it may be. If consensus is possible at all, then a change in its content is also possible. There is no impersonal and irresistible force behind this change. We citizens have done it together. We can undo it. But how did it come about?

Though I have so far mainly concentrated on what has happened—an imperial shift—a brief indication of how is also in order and will help answer the question, What now? The relatively new imperial American exceptionalism has gained ground due in large part to a particular group operating within the confines of party politics in the last decades, namely the group often called "neoconservatives." The group's particular ideology, its origin, or the causes of its ascendency are not my concern here. Books about this have been written; this is not one of them. Though the neoconservatives' influence on the trajectory of American politics has been considerable, some of their arguments have actually closely resembled those voiced by Beveridge a century ago.

Arguments by Beveridge and his allies in Congress and the administration that "self-government is no cheap boon, to be bestowed on the merely audacious" are bound to sound familiar to those who listened to the justifications of invasion and occupation in the wake of the Iraq War in 2003.¹ Beveridge's point then was that the government of the Filipinos could not responsibly be left to them; preparing them for self-government would of necessity require cultivation and development by an experienced ally, namely the United States. Just so with Iraq, we were told, because that political and social culture was not robust enough to stand upright against decades of political and social oppression.

The central question here is not whether self-government requires a sort of formation. Many agree that the difficult work of self-government requires habits and customs and reliable institutions in order to run smoothly. The central question is twofold: first, whether such habits, customs, and institutions may be imposed by a foreign power and, second, whether it is the particular responsibility of the United States to do so. The answer to these questions was formerly settled in an operative no. Later, in Beveridge's day, the country was fairly evenly divided between yes and no. Even if it might be said that a divide persists, it must also be said that an operative yes is nearly always present today.

Among others, one of the stated goals in the invasion of Iraq was to free it to govern itself, just as Beveridge, Roosevelt, and others argued in regard to the Philippines. But there was a big difference between the recent case and that of a century ago in the coherence and robustness of the opposition. Whereas Beveridge was eloquently and vociferously opposed in his day—such that no congressional action was ultimately possible, though the administration did end up carrying his plan through—in the twenty-first century opposition to a more imperial politics has had little sway or effect.

The similarity in the lines of debate is striking. If opposition was voiced, in Beveridge's day or in recent years, it was met with much the same response: rather than be bogged down in a drawn-out conflict, we would be welcomed as liberators in the sands of Iraq or on the shores of Luzon.² Thus, so went the argument, there would be little price to pay in American blood or resources. The Filipinos would accept us with open arms because of our "disinterested zeal," which was unparalleled in history, said President Theodore Roosevelt. Those advocating an exit were irresponsible, he said: immediate withdrawal would result in a surefire "crime against humanity."³ Belying the disinterestedness of the Americans was the frequent talk that the likely rewards—the goodwill of a well-placed new ally, safer trade routes, rich natural resources—were to far outweigh any actual losses. In both the Philippine and Iraqi cases, the calculus in lives and resources turned out wholly different.

Yet even if the risks and rewards had fit the proponents' accounts in the Philippines and in Iraq, questions should have remained. It might still have been asked whether this was the sort of thing that had characterized American leadership and behavior previously. If not, why was it right at *this* time? These arguments were raised by Beveridge's opponents in the Senate. But by the turn of the twenty-first century, the knowledge of the American political tradition that had fueled the opposition's arguments a century before had been lost. The elements that formed and evolved over centuries into the American political tradition as it existed from the colonial period onward had persisted in pockets within the citizenry and Congress up through the imperial invasions of the Progressive Era. A hundred years later, after still more decades of erosion, those elements had vanished. The old, traditional words could no longer bear the strain of being stretched over very different sorts of political action. The new wine of imperialism had finally burst the old wineskins of the American political tradition. No longer were defenses of foreign invasions primarily couched in terms of the Declaration—as Beveridge did, albeit inaccurately. The universalistic aspirations that could be misinterpreted from the Declaration have lain, to be sure, barely below the surface of some of the imperialistic claims and actions; but these are never faithful to the Declaration and the lived American political tradition. A new justification has come into use, which amounts to a new take on Beveridge.

A new theory of global politics and the new ideal of promoting democracy became the American symbols—the new basis on which we are to act as one and that partakes little of our rich political tradition. These new symbols—a world-historic triumph of democracy, for example—were advanced by elites like the neoconservatives; but such an untraditional account of the American political tradition can be so widely accepted only if there is a prior, great, and very wide impoverishment of the civic knowledge of the citizenry. Tocqueville observed, in remarking on the state of education in early nineteenth-century America, "If he pays attention only to the learned, he will be astonished by their small number; and if he counts the ignorant, the American people will seem to him the most enlightened on earth." The average American, being drawn into political conversation,

> will teach you what his rights are and what means he must use to exercise them; he will know by what practices the political world operates. You will notice that the rules of administration are known to him and that he has made himself familiar with the mechanism

of the laws. The inhabitant of the United States has not drawn this practical knowledge and these positive notions from books; his formal education may have prepared him to receive them, but has not provided him with them. It is by participating in legislation that the American learns to know the laws; it is by governing that he finds out about the forms of government. The great work of society is carried out each day before his eyes and, so to speak, by his hands. In the United States, the whole of the education of men is directed toward politics; in Europe, its principal goal is to prepare for private life.[4]

We do not learn and we do not know today the sorts of things observed here by Tocqueville. And though he could take for granted a great deal of familiarity with the political tradition because obtaining knowledge of it then had the urgency of current events, Americans today cannot. Our touch with the past, with our own tradition, with our own self-conception, is all but lost. But we need not leave the matter at that.

America stands at a fork in the road. We brought ourselves to our present state by discarding and disregarding the American political tradition as it was lived by our founders. We can move toward a new and traditional unity once again through a reacquaintance and reappropriation of those symbols that have ever defined us. We may eventually continue down the present path to centralization and an imperial posture. This is the more likely road because it is the easier one. But taking another path is possible. We can and should recognize the wisdom of those who went before us. We can and should pay heed to their reliance both on the lamp of experience and on their humility and virtue. We should take to heart that intuition put so well by Goethe when he said,

What you have as heritage,
Take now as task;
For thus you will make it your own!

We cannot make our heritage, our political tradition, truly our own without taking it upon ourselves as our own work and task.

This book is premised on a bit of violence, to use Allan Tate's memorable term.[5] In these pages I have sought to avoid anachronism and any privileging of a certain set of ideas over another. I wanted to chronicle, first, merely what happened in the course of American history in regard to the American political tradition, the American people's self-conception, its own account of American exceptionalism. But if a tradition is a dynamic thing, a thing that undergoes changes according to how its adherents act over time, then how could a given set of ideas be considered traditional at all? How could one set be called "the tradition" over and against later or earlier accounts of those or similar ideas?

Confirmation of the symbols I have pointed up has always been achieved by looking at the actual actions undertaken by the American people and listening to the articulations of the American people. This has allowed a clearer set of distinctions between derailments and differentiations, between "the tradition" and departures from it. My task, fully possible only at the end of the inquiry, has been to consider what use can be made of the American political tradition. This task is decidedly antitraditional, or at least not purely traditional, because it involves taking a stance on what is and is not traditional without advocating merely the status quo ante. In discussing our state of affairs, few would wish merely to turn back the clock. And even if that were possible somehow, we have seen too much today to become naïve once again, to keep from having an opinion on what is better or worse in regard to the possibilities opened up by the American political tradition. But enough of the nonsense about unthinking traditionalism. Just as an unproblematic Golden Age is the fictive fantasy of reactionaries, so also is the caricature of an ignorant past where uncurious men whiled away their days in unthinking repetition of whatever they received from their forebears. This is the portrait often painted of the medieval period in world history courses or of any aristocracy of any period. It is a poor likeness and so is the usual depiction of the American political tradition, what I will call the "usual account."

The usual account holds that the seed of the true American political tradition—equality, individual rights, progressivism, and so on—was planted in the inhospitable soil of British colonialism. This seed contained Jefferson's beautiful thoughts and turns of phrase (decoupled from their modification by his coworkers in the Continental Congress). The seed struggled to survive the long, cold American winter between roughly 1776 and (at least) 1861 but did last that long in germ form. By the time of Lincoln, or certainly by the dawn of the Progressive Era, the full American idea was allowed to germinate, grow, and bloom. Thereafter the seed could be reproduced and transplanted the world over in the soils of every land and the souls of every individual.

Contrary to this usual account, each age, each man, seeks to weigh the resources at his disposal against the problems laid before him. This is the same situation in which we find ourselves, although it must be granted that, to use Voegelin's vocabulary, the old "compact" solutions and understandings are no longer available to us at this later, differentiated stage. The alternatives we face and the balance we must effect have innumerable dimensions and each must be addressed if a new and plausible balance is to be found. You may ask, plausible to whom? The answer is: the American people. I have repeatedly zeroed in on three dimensions of this self-conception and so I wish to present each as a dichotomy. In this, it seems to me, part of the way forward may be glimpsed.

In the American tradition the role of God in the political order and the role of the political order in history go hand in hand. A certain position or commitment in one area requires a similar position in the other. Though ever at the heart of the tradition, when viewed as a whole the particular role God is to play in the American political order has varied. Is he the guarantor of the country's success? Is he America's unambiguous protector and bene-factor? Is America to be his special nation such that America's interests and God's will are, in any geopolitical or domestic situation, one and the same?

Or might it be, in a kind of updated or widened neo-Puritanism, that God could be said to treat the American political order not unlike he treats all of humanity in the Christian tradition, namely, that certain gifts are given, graces extended, and circumstances prepared with a view to special responsibilities undertaken by the possessors? If it is traditional or expected, as it seems to be, that God's role in American circumstances and advantages is to be acknowledged, might the acknowledgement take a form that recalls the Puritans' awareness that such blessings are also a burden? It is pos-sible. Lincoln speaks to this in his second inaugural. There are two ways to understand the role of God in American political thought and action, one more aggressive and unbounded, one more bounded and internally focused. Both are plausible given a certain reading of the tradition. But only one is well founded in the original tradition. Only the readoption of a humbler view of the role of God in American political life can return us to ourselves.

The part played by history in the American political tradition has also varied. A certain conception of history has the potential to inspire a hubris that tempts Americans to sweep aside those on the world stage who would contradict us. In a manner not dissimilar to the atrocities committed by Mao and Stalin, a confident subscriber to the idea that America is the apogee of world-historical development might be slow to rein in decisions and actions affecting the "backward" countries and peoples of the world. In this view of history, all American actions will ultimately be justified, even if they cannot quite be justified at present; thus all is permitted here and now.

Here again a slightly more sophisticated understanding of history could help to avoid this imperial frame of mind. If history is characterized by a progression from more compact to more differentiated forms rather than from less advanced to more advanced, then each change along the continuum of time can possibly be seen as improved and yet always incomplete, capable of further differentiation, further improvement. This, coupled with what Bellah called the "ambiguity of chosenness" in regard to God's role in the polity, is a decidedly traditional view of American politics that yet does not fall into the imperial American exceptionalism that today defines the usual account.

Americans' conceptions of how universality plays into their politics have also varied over the course of American history. If one's conception of universality is so clear and monolithic that a very low threshold permits the coercion of dissenters, then it might still be compatible with an imperial account of American exceptionalism or an imperial American self-conception. Yet even then, if human beings are held to possess a certain dignity to remain responsible for aligning themselves with the universal, then a brash imperialism might be forestalled. If, as an alternative to this reified conception of universality, it is held that the universal is intelligible and realizable only in the particular—with all the limitations that attend this—then such a sense of universality would be yet another bulwark against, rather than a pretext for, the imperial conception of America often heard today.

In our political acts we will commit to one or the other side of the variations of these three dimensions. But each is resolvable in favor of a decidedly nonimperial, completely traditional, renewed American self-conception. They are so resolvable if—and perhaps only if—a suppler, more sophisticated understanding of our political tradition is cultivated in the very wide body of the American citizenry. The problem is not in the neoconservatives alone, though I have singled them out. The problem lies primarily in the condition that made possible their rise to prominence: the loss of an adequate understanding of the American political tradition in the heads and hearts of the American people. This loss created a vacuum into which a new, imperial account was placed. And it happened without a debate or contest and so largely without deliberation or consciousness of the degree to which this new account differed from the way America conducted itself for generations. We forgot who we were, so that when we were told half truths, we could not recognize them as such.

Is this a call, then, only for more education or for an increase in its funding, and so on? No. Large-scale education initiatives are not the answer. The sort of education now widely available is not conducive to the more sophisticated understanding of history required for us truly to return to ourselves. Yet this understanding is necessary. The reinvigoration of the American political tradition can be made possible only, it seems to me, through a slow and concrete process characterized by deliberate encounters with both what is foreign and what is familiar, each in its own sphere and on its own terms. This is a job, in other words, not only for a more adequate civic education but also for a more liberal education. Today institutions of higher learning aim primarily to sell knowledge or skills that are useful for a career, or what Tocqueville called the "private life." But we need something more. A liberal education is the peculiar province of those who do not wish to and do not need to become bureaucrats or technocrats. It is a sort of education not widely available today but one that was widely available in our country's past. While it is not impossible to imagine a grassroots "Great (Books) Awakening" on a very wide scale, such an event does seem unlikely.

Even so, becoming a society of better, subtler, suppler thinkers does not *solve* the problem of the disintegration of the American political tradition; it only allows for the solution. It only provides for the solution's possibility. Education of the right sort opens up the modality of a nonimperial American self-conception because it allows us to see both the beauty and ugliness of our past as it was. It allows us the possibility of forging ahead in new and creative yet traditional ways that are bounded by our capabilities and reinforced by our culture and habits. The right sort of education allows for this possibility. It does not guarantee it. Whether the twilight we currently live in precedes a new dawn or a final dusk is up to us.

A tradition is not an account, a verbal entity. It is primarily a lived, practiced thing. For a tradition truly to be such, it must be lived from the inside out. Voting, loving, persuading, compromising, negotiating, picketing, dealing, and working with a traditionally American, nonimperial cast of mind will necessarily precede the lived manifestation of a nonimperial American politics. The hard work of persuading each other and embodying this new tradition will take generations and, if it occurs, be subject to halting progress and regress. There is no other possible point of origin for a tradition truly so called.

A mere account of what is traditional can exist and even garner a large number of adherents. This account is what I have tried to provide in these pages. But today, after a long line of development over many centuries, such an account cannot become livable until it is made thinkable. And so, while this book cannot guarantee the realization or reinvigoration of a new American political tradition, and while it cannot but be partial, it is nonetheless a necessary precursor to the new view, the new lived tradition. Realizing the *modality* of a new way of living together—even if it is traditional—is necessarily the first step, not the last, in the reinvigoration of a future and adequate American political order.

Acknowledgments

I am grateful to the numerous organizations and many people who added to the completion of this book. First, some of my ideas found their first public forum in the *Journal of Church and State*; portions of this book appeared in an earlier edition in its pages and I am grateful for that opportunity and the permission to use some of that work here. Many other portions were vetted at various conferences and I am grateful for the stipends that let me attend those and the generosity and knowledge of the participants in our conversations. I am thankful for help from the staffs of Cravens Library and the Kentucky Library of Western Kentucky University. While I can never repay fully the sum of experiences, knowledge, cheer, and generosity he has paid to me, I must thank George Carey for enlightening me in the ways of academia and life. An academic always owes a great debt to his family—the encouragement, patience, and interest shown by mine have been the only lights during some dark nights. Finally, I thank Sarah for her indefatigable hope, which has always spurred me on to achieve more than I set out to do and more than I thought possible. On this sea I would be adrift without her guiding star.

Notes

Introduction

1. Though by no means the only three to treat the topic, three prominent articulations can be found in the work of political theorists Michael Oakeshott and Leo Strauss and historian Friedrich Meinecke. See Oakeshott, "Masses in Representative Democracy"; Strauss, "What Is Liberal Education?"; Meinecke, *German Catastrophe*.

1. The Problem of American Exceptionalism

1. Columnist David Lake marshals statistics to show that, though the reasons behind it vary widely, most Americans "believe" in American exceptionalism. Lake's aim of establishing consensus amid controversy is laudable, but his efforts fall very short of the mark because he takes for granted the impossibility of narrowing down the meaning of *American exceptionalism*. See Lake, "Is America Exceptional?"

John A. Gans Jr. observes that though many on the political right fault President Obama for his stance "against" American exceptionalism, he seems to discuss the idea and give credence to it extremely often. See Gans, "American Exceptionalism."

2. Obama answered,

> I believe in American exceptionalism, just as I suspect that the Brits believe in British exceptionalism and the Greeks believe in Greek exceptionalism. I'm enormously proud of my country and its role and history in the world. . . . And if you think of our current situation, the United States remains the largest economy in the world. We have unmatched military capability. And I think that we have a core set of values that are enshrined in our Constitution, in our body of law, in our democratic practices, in our belief in free speech and equality, that, though imperfect, are exceptional. . . . And so I see no contradiction between believing that America has a continued extraordinary role in leading the world towards peace and prosperity and recognizing that that leadership is incumbent, depends on, our ability to create partnerships."

See White House, Office of the Press Secretary, "News Conference by President Obama."

3. J. P. Diggins observes that some have used *American exceptionalism* as a blanket term for "the idea that America is and would continue to be distinct from Europe," rightly

noting the widely divergent meanings subsumed under the single term. But Diggins does not clearly delineate the various meanings, only cataloging them without much order. See Diggins, *On Hallowed Ground*, 102ff.

4. Hartz, *Liberal Tradition in America*. I will say more on Hartz's book later in connection with the theory of history implicit in it.

5. G. K. Chesterton, among others, argues that America is the only country ever to be founded on an idea. Chesterton, *What I Saw in America*. Daniel Boorstin argues that America is unique just because it never had a political philosophy. See Boorstin, *Genius of American Politics*.

6. Lipset, *American Exceptionalism*.

7. Krislov, "American Federalism as American Exceptionalism."

8. On the role of the frontier, see Turner, "Significance of the Frontier."

The whole genre of economic claims to American exceptionalism was sparked by Werner Sombart in his 1906 *Why Is There No Socialism in the United States?* For a discussion of this scholarship, see Gerber, "Shifting Perspectives on American Exceptionalism."

On the role of organized labor, see Voss, *Making of American Exceptionalism*. For alternate views, see Wilentz, "Against Exceptionalism"; and Foner, "Why Is There No Socialism?"

On the early advent of universal white manhood suffrage, see Katznelson, "Working-Class Formation and the State."

Joseph P. Ferrie notes that upward mobility formerly characterized the American economy but this trend seems to be closing. See Ferrie, "History Lessons."

On economic and natural resource abundance, see Potter, *People of Plenty*; and Gutfeld, *American Exceptionalism*.

9. See Kammen, "Problem of American Exceptionalism," 2. I want to address at the beginning that my use of the general term *social scientists* is decidedly not a straw man argument. I take up specific and representative arguments of social science. The general term is kept despite the danger of it turning into a straw man because my reasons for rejecting the most common approach of American exceptionalism have to do with the core assumptions of social science in general. Mine, therefore, is a genus-level critique that requires such a term.

Despite the terminological similarity, I am not following Dorothy Ross's arguments about social science and American exceptionalism, though I am aware of them. She first defines the term in this way:

> This vision of the unique place America occupied in history was the core of a set of ideas I will call American exceptionalism. Standing at the westernmost culmination of European history, the United States would not follow Europe into a historical future. American progress would be a quantitative multiplication and elaboration of its founding institutions, not a process of qualitative change. Still prehistoricist, tied to God's eternal plan outside of history, American ex-

ceptionalism prevented Americans from developing a fully historicist account of their own history through much of the nineteenth century and limited the extent to which they could absorb European historicism. (Ross, *Origins of American Social Science*, 26)

Thus Ross sees American exceptionalism primarily as a way to talk about Americans' views of their place in history. She continues later,

American exceptionalism was thus a connected body of interwoven ideas—indeed other dimensions, like America's mission to the world, could be plotted—and one whose scope has been difficult to specify. Fundamentally, American exceptionalism was a nationalist ideology, an idea of America in a country whose national self-conception had to be intellectually formed from the experience of gaining national independence. Explicitly argued at times of national and political crises during the late eighteenth and early nineteenth century, it quickly entered into popular literary, religious, and political discourse, and was so widely diffused that its premises often went unstated and its conclusions were often merely celebrated. (28).

Ian Tyrrell is perhaps foremost among historians who deny that America is exceptional, arguing for a new approach to the study of history that would show the chimerical nature of American exceptionalism and numerous other concepts of dubious coherence. See Tyrrell, "American Exceptionalism." In a volume full of scholars arguing for American exceptionalism, Andrew Greeley is unique in arguing against it. See his chapter in Shafer, *Is America Different?*

10. See Diggins, *On Hallowed Ground*, 104–5. The *Oxford English Dictionary*, for one, does not observe a use of *exceptionalism* until a *Communist* newspaper article—a firsthand, verbatim report of a speech at a New York City "membership meeting" on October 2, 1928—by Jay Lovestone. Though it should be noted that the *OED*'s reference, like Seymour Martin Lipset's discussion of Alexis de Tocqueville (discussed later in this chapter), is not to the two-word term, this is of little consequence since Lovestone's and Tocqueville's meanings are, given the surrounding texts, considerably different. The "peculiar specific conditions" Lovestone mentions are twofold: "the labor movement as a whole is very weak and, especially, politically backward." See Lovestone, "Sixth World Congress," 660. The Marxist theory of history requires an accounting for why the United States did not seem to follow the general pattern. Thus the note of comparison of a mental "control group" and an "experimental group" is present from the inception of the term in American Marxist usage, though not in Tocqueville's passage. Harvey Klehr noted the Marxist origins of the term *American exceptionalism*; Klehr argues that Marx and Engels cannot themselves rightly be called American exceptionalists, although he grants that their explicit thoughts on the matter are relatively few and meager. See Klehr, "Marxist Theory in Search of America."

11. Daniel Bell notes that the problem with Sombart's writing is that, as with "every good academic, theory triumphed over existent reality—it is the heritage of Hegel." See

Bell, "Hegelian Secret," 52–54. Sombart's book was also published in German, under the title *Warum gibt es in den Vereinigten Staaten keinen Sozialismus?* (Tübingen: J. C. B. Mohr, 1906), and had its roots in a series of articles written for the *Archiv für Sozialwissenschaft und Sozialpolitik* (vol. 21, 1905), the periodical led by both himself and Max Weber and in which Weber's noted essay "The Protestant Ethic and the Spirit of Capitalism" was first published in two parts (1904 and 1905). Weber and Sombart both wrote their now-famous monographs in the wake of a visit to America for the 1904 World's Fair in St. Louis, Missouri. For more on the link between Sombart and Weber, see Tiryakian, "American Religious Exceptionalism."

12. One can see at least the shadow of a Marxist theory of history in how Hartz takes Europe as the historical norm from which America deviates. For Hartz, America was unique in the world because its own particular liberalism was not born out of a struggle against aristocracy or a traditional way of societal life. Because America had no feudal past, it could have no radical future. There was no need to pull down the existing edifice, as there was in Europe, because the status quo in America already complied with liberal demands. Hartz argues that, thus, liberalism arose on American shores undisputed, so that it had neither the radical policies nor the often-violent tendencies of its Continental counterparts. Hartz, among others, argues that Marxist theory works very well for Europe, but not elsewhere. Even scholars like Hartz who were not devoted to a Marxist theory of history find themselves responding to it nonetheless. See Hartz, *Liberal Tradition in America*, 9.

13. I will argue later that this is the case, especially in reference to the role of religious thought in America generally and the case of the idea of American exceptionalism more specifically.

14. Parts of this argument, this chapter, and the next chapter first appeared in Litke, "Varieties of American Exceptionalism."

15. Historian Ernest R. May outlines the degree to which political actors in the twentieth century use history as a predictor in politics. See May, *"Lessons" of the Past*, ix–xiv. He then argues that "previous centuries" cannot be treated similarly, presumably because before the twentieth century a great amount of political reasoning and prediction was tied up with religious thought.

16. As they are used today, *imperial* and *empire* suggest a certain value judgment, i.e., a rejection of the thing, activity, people, or regime that is called such. I have selected the words, however, in a spirit similar to Nexon and Wright, seeking to identify a certain sort of phenomenon as distinct from others. Those authors, and Michael Doyle before them, distinguished between *empire* on the one hand and *hegemony, unipolarity,* or *dependent states* on the other. The sorts of phenomena these authors attribute to "empires"—e.g., directly placing a third party into power, whether recruited from the core's or the periphery's elites—were exhibited by the United States in its annexation and control of the Philippines around the turn of the twentieth century. On these authors' criteria it does not seem that other so-called imperial actions (e.g., westward

expansion under "manifest destiny") fit the same bill. See Nexon and Wright, "What's at Stake"; Doyle, *Empires* 12–13ff.

Hardt and Negri argue for a different view of "Empire," which I do not follow and which they usually capitalize to emphasize their particular meaning, "a new global form of sovereignty." See Hardt and Negri, *Empire*, quote on xii.

17. Historian H. W. Brands has noticed that Americans traditionally have been divided between two foreign policy camps. In *What America Owes the World*, Brands distinguishes between what he calls the "exemplarists" and the "vindicators":

> On one side have been those who hold that the United States owes the world merely the example of a humane, democratic, and prosperous society. These exemplarists, as they might be called, have argued that perfecting American institutions and practices at home is a full-time job. To try for more, as by meddling in the affairs of other nations, would not only not do much good for the nations meddled in, since societies have to solve their problems themselves, but could jeopardize American values at the source. In attempting to save the world, and probably failing, America would risk losing its democratic soul. On the other side of the debate have been those who contend that America must move beyond example and undertake active measures to vindicate the right. In a nasty world, these vindicators say, the sword of wrath must complement the lantern of virtue. Evil goes armed, and so must good. Human nature is too recalcitrant for mere example to have much lasting effect, and until human nature changes—a development most vindicators anticipate about the time of the Second Coming—military might, even if it doesn't necessarily make right, certainly can restrain wrong. (vii–viii)

Brands's distinction provides a helpful starting point for answering the question of the origin of American exceptionalism because it points out that two varieties of argument might be equally "exceptionalist" without coming to the same practical conclusions. Each side sees America as unique in the world; each sees the consequences of this uniqueness as demanding a different foreign policy. It is my argument, however, that Brands does not go far enough in illustrating how deeply divergent these two groups have been in American history. Though Brands discusses the differences between what precisely these two groups believe America to "owe the world," their differences penetrate to the heart of what each account holds as specifically and truly American.

18. See Lipset, *American Exceptionalism*, 18. Lipset has made the claim in numerous other places, e.g. Lipset and Marks, *It Didn't Happen Here*, 15. While I concede that "exceptionalism" necessarily has reference to other things, the lack of nuance leads to errors in analysis, which could have been prevented with a better framework, like the one provided earlier in this chapter.

19. Indeed, elsewhere Lipset writes that that American exceptionalism is "obviously" a comparative term. See Lipset, review of *American Exceptionalism*.

20. For the purposes of this chapter, I will argue explicitly and at length with Lipset.

The same critiques could just as well apply, however, to many scholars who write on the topic of American exceptionalism, which as indicated previously has long been the almost-exclusive province of social scientists. Michael Kammen has noted the degree to which few historians have continued to pursue the subject and many social scientists have taken it up. See Kammen, "Problem of American Exceptionalism." It should be noted that although Kammen rightly picks up the distinction between a "cultural" basis for exceptionalism in the original American settlers and a "comparative" basis in social science literature, he does not suggest a way forward that might reconcile and make sense of his two categories. Though Kammen's article is helpful in its effort to be an exhaustive accounting of the scholarship up to 1993, he seems to have missed the fact that did not escape Byron Shafer in 1991, i.e., that with social science the scale of inquiry greatly influences the degree to which the claim to exceptionalism is confirmed or denied. A change in scope results also in a change in the study's conclusions. See Shafer, *Is America Different?* I examine Shafer's framework later in the chapter.

21. Tocqueville, *Democracy in America*, ed. Reeve, 2:36–37. See also Tocqueville, *Democracy in America*, ed. Mayer, 455–56; Tocqueville, *Democracy in America*, ed. Mansfield and Winthrop, 430.

22. See Tocqueville, *De la démocratie en Amérique*, 2:42.

23. Tocqueville, *Democracy in America*, ed. Reeve, 2:36–37.

24. It might be said that this particular comment by Tocqueville is aimed at those, like John Locke, who suppose that America presents a picture of the civilized world at its embryonic stage. But Tocqueville argues against this view in this passage and elsewhere in *Democracy in America*, suggesting instead that the country is worthy of study in its own right.

25. At least two authors have taken up the methodological implications of *Democracy in America* at length. John C. Koritansky argues that Tocqueville's book was not supposed to be a grand statement on politics in general but a statement that America's unique background was necessary to its unique flowering; i.e., Koritansky, too, believes that Tocqueville is pointing out America's uniqueness or idiosyncrasy. Tocqueville is not a political scientist formulating general laws of politics but an author defining the nature of political and cultural institutions in terms of their origins. See Koritansky, *Alexis de Tocqueville and the New Science of Politics*.

Saguiv A. Hadari concurs with John Stuart Mill that the greatest significance of Tocqueville's work is not in its substantive findings but in its new approach to the subject, blending various approaches to social science. Tocqueville, Hadari thinks, successfully defends three moments in conducting social science: formal modeling, hermeneutics, and a normative stand. Concentration on any substantive claim, like that of an empirical basis of American exceptionalism, would thereby miss, for Hadari, the main profit of Tocqueville's work. See Hadari, *Theory in Practice*, 4ff.

The section in which Lipset's reference occurs is titled "The Example of the Americans Does Not Prove That a Democratic People Can Have No Aptitude and No Taste for

Science, Literature, or Art." Tocqueville's point, even in the title of the section to which Lipset refers, is that it is possible to have a democratic people who do not wallow in ignorance and poverty. Or to put it more positively, as Tocqueville himself does on a subsequent page: it is possible to have a democratic people who are "enlightened" and so are less susceptible to the ambitions of despots. Tocqueville, *Democracy in America*, ed. Reeve, 2:38. But when it is recalled that Tocqueville cautions against making broad, law-like statements, it appears that he is more true to a scientific mindset than was first supposed: he is loath to draw a broad causal conclusion from what would today be called a "small-n study." He refuses to make a generalization based on a limited set of data. Rather, he is making a modal claim about democracies and despotism. It is thus clear that Tocqueville's passage is a warning against scientific generalization rather than something that, as Lipset argues, "could only have arisen by comparing this country with other societies." Lipset, review of *American Exceptionalism.* The comparisons are made not in order to achieve the result but in order to make his observations clearer.

Might there be another reason, then, that Lipset suggests Tocqueville as the origi-nator of the term? If Tocqueville coined the term, and if it can be convincingly argued that Tocqueville is the first comparative social scientist, then Lipset has shown his own preferred methodology to be adequate to the topic—a burden every scholar strives to bear. Without the premises that (1) Tocqueville was the first to make a claim to American exceptionalism and (2) Tocqueville made the claim in the idiom of comparative political science, the preparatory remarks for his book would need to include a justification of his method. Making this particular argument at the outset is a matter of covering all of the bases of his subsequent arguments; with this bald reading of Tocqueville's words, Lipset seems to have provided a firm foundation for his own book. In short, asserting that Tocqueville coined the term in this way saves Lipset some work. He has a real interest, then, in the oversimplification of the matter. In order to show that thinking on American exceptionalism has taken place squarely in the field of comparative political science, Lipset must claim that the idea has no antecedent in American history prior to Tocqueville. This is a task neither Lipset nor anyone else could actually perform, however, since the idea actually has several antecedents.

26. Indeed, as at least one reviewer has noted, Lipset's *American Exceptionalism* contains little that was not previously recorded in his *The First New Nation* or *Conti-nental Divide.* See Nelles, "American Exceptionalism." It should be noted that although I am criticizing the extent to which Lipset partakes of the scientific approach, some, like Nelles, have noted the "pseudo-scientific" nature of Lipset's work (755). This is due to the extent that he attributes America's exceptional character to his five very intangible traits and, in the preface, even the "hand of Providence." With this critique duly noted, however, it should be noted also that for the purposes of this chapter all that is needed is an example of the comparative view—and Lipset is certainly this, even if his conclu-sions are rejected by some who share his comparative method.

27. In a widely cited journal article, historian Ian Tyrrell argues for a new, "trans-

national history" in which parochial national biases are done away with. These narrow viewpoints are to blame for erroneous claims to American exceptionalism, Tyrrell claims, essentially arguing that the persistence of claims to American exceptionalism is the result of either bad or ideological history. Instead of narratives focused on nation-states, which are increasingly unimportant as historical forces, Tyrrell suggests that a more adequate perspective would take a much wider view. See Tyrrell, "American Exceptionalism."

28. Science requires an experimental group and a control group, which are established inductively in biology or physics but only with difficulty in the social sciences. When Lipset argues in his book that "to know one country" is to "know no country," he is repeating the basic scientific orthodoxy that one cannot see the significance of a particular phenomenon except in contrasting it with other controlled instances. While this method is effective for claims to significance in the natural sciences—with their phenomena and data so far removed from everyday life and the consequent lack of context to render the data intelligible, and unburdened by unpredictability of conscious actors—the same cannot be said for the social sciences, which take the occurrences of everyday life to be the phenomena explained and data interpreted. The very data considered in the social sciences are simultaneously created in their consideration. In trying to interpret human action, in other words, the interpretation becomes a new ground for subsequent human action. The "laboratory" of the social sciences is not sealed and pure; the scientific method cannot apply directly, then, but only analogously.

In her review of Lipset's *American Exceptionalism*, Mary Nolan notes the degree to which Lipset cites, unproblematically, similar answers given by respondents from different countries. Noting that "the answers elicited are not easily comparable" because of their "distinctive political and discursive contexts," Nolan doubts that there can be an adequate measure—especially across different cultures—of amorphous phenomena like "patriotism." Lipset does not apparently see a problem with this. See Nolan, "Against Exceptionalisms."

29. Shafer's schema muddles the key theoretical differences between Winthrop and Marxism, a difference my own schema can account for. Further, Shafer seems to place Winthrop in the camp of empirically comparative American exceptionalism, which I will show in chapter 2 is simply incorrect.

30. They are mutually reinforcing. But here there occurs a further problem, because for Marxists there can be no lasting deviation from the pattern. Seeming contradictions to the trajectory of history, like that of America, will always be dismissed or explained away as only apparent problems or delays in the manifestation of the true pattern. This is what Sombart argued. The logic of history is taken as a given, not introduced as one datum among many; thus, even though historically the term *American exceptionalism* has its roots in Marxist-style theories of history, the claim is not ultimately tenable in the context of social science. This quality—taking the theory for granted and dismissing counterexamples—is what leads many to dismiss Marxist history as ideological and therefore incompatible with science (the claims of which should, by definition, be

falsifiable). Note the similarity on this point to what Daniel Bell calls the "heritage of Hegel" in "The 'Hegelian Secret.'"

31. NB: The idea that many nations now exhibit the characteristics of eighteenth-century America is a direct departure from Tocqueville's passage cited by Lipset. But Shafer is not arguing against Tocqueville so much as missing Tocqueville's point. Tocqueville is taking seriously the factors he names, among which are America's "Puritan origins," never possibly reproduced. Note also the degree to which Shafer has muddied the important difference between the comparative and unique senses of American exceptionalism.

32. Lipset and others have long operated as if this were not the case. They have continued to explore Sombart's main thought ever since its debut. See, for example, Perlman, *Theory of the Labor Movement*; Heffer and Rovet, *Why Is There No Socialism*; and Lipset and Marks, *It Didn't Happen Here*.

33. Note the term *isolated* and its connotations of scientific method and finality.

34. All quotations are taken from Shafer's very brief introduction. See Shafer, *Is America Different?*, v–xi.

It should perhaps be noted that, though Lipset contributes a long essay to Shafer's volume, the same essay was updated later and serves as the first two chapters of his own *American Exceptionalism*. The latter version has, therefore, been used in the analysis of this chapter.

In an earlier article, Shafer essentially repeats his apology for a new, albeit still comparative, perspective; see Shafer, "'Exceptionalism' in American Politics?"

35. Witness Andrew Greeley's extended apology for the methods of social science and his contention that the null hypothesis cannot be rejected. Greeley, "American Exceptionalism: The Religious Phenomenon," in Shafer, *Is America Different?*, 95–102. Greeley should be praised for his methodological self-awareness and rigor, but his own exhibition of these makes all the more glaring the lack of it in the other authors, like Lipset.

36. Lipset notes that any claim to American exceptionalism "only has meaning in a comparative context" and that within that context there have been three main "traditions" of interpretation. The first, that to which Deborah Madsen's book belongs, is mainly followed by students of history or literature and "deals with the founding myth of the United States as a society." The second is "Tocquevillian"; it looks at the practices of various countries and sees the United States as "sociologically unique." This is Lipset's chosen tradition. The third, Lipset says, is mainly covered in the socialist and communist literature. It follows Sombart and has mainly to do with the failure or success of labor parties in the United States. Though Lipset introduces his own threefold distinction of the possible methods or meanings of the term *American exceptionalism*, all of them are comparative to the core. Even with the first of the three, which seems the least scientific, the fundamental presumption is that examination of data—in this case the various national "myths of origin"—will yield a pattern from which the U.S. deviates. See Lipset, review of *American Exceptionalism*. The notion that comparisons

of this kind are fruitful is at the heart of the method of the social sciences, as has been alluded to previously when defining the various senses of American exceptionalism.

37. Kendall and Carey, *Basic Symbols*, 21.

38. Kendall and Carey write, "Unless we can see a *correspondence* between the symbols we have in hand and the people's action in history, the symbols we have in hand do not in fact represent that people, and we must look a second time for the symbols that do in fact represent them." Ibid., 26 (emphasis in original).

39. Ibid.

40. Kendall and Carey tackle just this when they write that Voegelin's method does not come to them with an explicit "set of rules" for determining which are the foundational symbols of a political tradition. They infer two rules, therefore, from Voegelin's practice in his own work. First, one should "begin at the beginning," though they find that this is no easy task. Contrast this with Robert Bellah's seemingly effortless choice of the signing of the Declaration of Independence as the true beginning of the United States as a nation, which accordingly emphasized its first several clauses at the expense of the colonial tradition. See Bellah, *Broken Covenant*. The second rule, which they take to be implicit in Voegelin, concerns the correspondence between action and history already noted. Further, the authors add two strictures of their own: first, they will "keep to this side of the Atlantic," since they are looking for the basic symbols of the American political tradition; second, they will keep to the "same literary category," focusing on "public documents of self-interpretation." Kendall and Carey, *Basic Symbols*, 30.

41. Whereas Kendall and Carey use only documents that seem to be, in a word, self-consciously "symbolic," I will examine a few documents and speeches they do not, so as to allow for the possibility that something might become a symbol without being first intended that way. This is how I will treat Lincoln's Gettysburg Address in chapter 4. Weber makes a very similar distinction in *The Protestant Ethic and the Spirit of Capitalism*. Notice the difference between treating historical phenomena in themselves and as historically significant:

> Judgments of the importance of a historical phenomenon may be judgments of value or faith, namely, when they refer to what is alone interesting, or alone in the long run valuable in it. Or, on the other hand, they may refer to its influence on other historical processes as a causal factor. Then we are concerned with judgments of historical imputation. If now we start, as we must do here, from the latter standpoint and inquire into the significance which is to be attributed to that dogma [i.e., predestination in Calvinism] by virtue of its cultural and historical consequences, it must certainly be rated very highly. (Weber, *Protestant Ethic*, 98–99)

In chapter 4, this shows up as the difference between what Lincoln was trying to do and what he actually did in his recasting of the founding.

42. See Kendall and Carey, *Basic Symbols*, 24. The distinction between differentiation and derailment is not dissimilar to Bernard Bailyn's between "manifest" and "latent"

history, though there does not seem to be a one-to-one correspondence between the two. Bailyn's terms are, of course, drawn from Freudianism. See Bailyn, "Challenge of Modern Historiography."

43. On "compactness" and "differentiation," see Kendall and Carey, *Basic Symbols*, 24.

44. See Gamble, *In Search of the City on a Hill*, 15 and passim.

45. Recall, again, that today's "differentiated" categories of political, social, and religious thought are distinct, whereas the old Puritan mind's compact version contained each of these without distinction. Though without using this terminology, Perry Miller notes this phenomenon in "The Puritan State and Puritan Society," in *Errand into the Wilderness*, 142.

46. One contemporary scholar of Jewish political thought thoroughly explores the background of the Puritan understanding of societal order. Though Joshua A. Berman does not write with the Puritans in mind, the similarity is evident with even a cursory comparison. Recall also that both groups use the same text as the foundation of their thinking. See Berman, "God's Alliance with Man."

47. By way of introducing what he calls the "ambiguities of chosenness," Bellah writes,

> An extreme example will put the issue sharply. Senator Albert J. Beveridge delivered a speech on the floor of the United States Senate shortly after his return from a tour of the Philippines in January 1900. He referred to the wealth of the islands and their importance to the United States, to the indolence of the natives and their incapacity for self-government, and to the war of subjugation which the United States Army was then waging against the Filipino independence movement. The American opposition to that war, he said, in terms we have become familiar with in late years, was "the chief factor in prolonging it." Warming to his subject he laid down the justification for annexation in the following words: "God has not been preparing the English-speaking and Teutonic peoples for a thousand years for nothing but vain and idle self-contemplation and self-admiration. No. He made us master organizers of the world to establish system where chaos reigned. He has given us the spirit of progress to overwhelm the forces of reaction throughout the earth. He has made us adept in government that we may administer government among savage and senile peoples. Were it not for such a force as this the world would relapse into barbarism and night. And of all our race He has marked the American people as his chosen nation to finally lead in the redemption of the world."
>
> Even though the biblical imagery has been muddied over with 19th-century racism, a subject to which we will return, we can see in grotesquely heightened form precisely the arguments used to justify American treatment of Indians and blacks from the very beginning. (Bellah, *Broken Covenant*, 37–38)

Beveridge's contribution to the idea of imperial American exceptionalism will be explored more fully in chapter 5.

48. I am here following Bellah's analysis, though I disagree that a "synthesis" was effected in the Declaration of Independence. "Balance" is the better word. See Bellah, *Broken Covenant*, 27.

49. Kendall and Carey, *Basic Symbols*, ix.

50. Bellah, *Broken Covenant*, 179.

51. Indeed, this may be part of what makes Lincoln for Bellah the "greatest" civil theologian, since a civil theology is particular rather than general. He seems to follow the lead of society rather than vice versa, though the relation is admittedly a two-way one. These themes will be taken up in chapter 4.

2. John Winthrop: A Divinely Sanctioned, Practically Circumscribed Colony

1. A recent and typical example is sufficient. In *Americanism: The Fourth Great Western Religion*, David Gelernter unproblematically asserts that Winthrop "foresaw" the city on a hill that America would become (17), which is obviously chronologically problematic. Gelernter says that Winthrop sensed he was "onto something big" (23) and that Winthrop was the first to begin "weaving the American creed," though it was the "revolutionary generation that finished it" (40). In the concluding pages of the book, Gelernter makes plain the chief source of his interpretation: "In one of his favorite, best-remembered phrases, [President Ronald Reagan] told the world that America was and must always be the 'shining city upon a hill.' 'The phrase comes from John Winthrop,' he explained, 'who wrote it to describe the America he imagined'" (201). Offered virtually without comment, these statements leave the reader to conclude that Gelernter is following Reagan's interpretation of Winthrop's words. Yet as will be shown, Reagan's common understanding of the phrase is distant even from a plain reading of the document from which it is drawn.

2. Robert Kagan is one among many who seek to make this link between late American imperialism and early Puritan designs, a claim that I reject. See Litke "Varieties of American Exceptionalism."

3. Kendall and Carey, *Basic Symbols*, 31–32.

4. Voegelin notes that the logic of representation reaches its limit in Lincoln's "masterful, dialectical concentration" in the Gettysburg Address. See Voegelin, *New Science of Politics*, 40. But a people so heterogeneous creates problems for governing. If a people is not to be torn apart by the contentions of everyday politics, distinctions will need to be made—both in institutions and in the people's self-conception. This is just what happens in America. See chapter 3.

5. In 1633 there was a revolt in favor of wider suffrage in the colony, which has been pointed to as a precursor of the later American emphasis on popular rule. Of course, unanimity and consensus are related to the idea of self-rule, and so there are examples of this in the tradition even before Winthrop in the Mayflower Compact. But self-rule and a "deliberate assembly" are different things.

6. Voegelin, *New Science of Politics*, 41.

7. Ibid., 1.

8. Kendall and Carey, *Basic Symbols*, 26.

9. Voegelin, *New Science of Politics*, 82.

10. These are Voegelin's words, not Winthrop's. See ibid., 1.

11. Though both groups are "Puritans," the conventional name given to the settlers at Plymouth helps reduce the awkwardness of writing about them. I will use the terms in this way throughout.

12. Kendall and Carey argue that the Mayflower Compact connotes no notion of "chosenness," indicating a great difference from Winthrop's writings. Unlike with the Puritans, with the Pilgrims there is not even an inkling that they are the vanguard of human history. See Kendall and Carey, *Basic Symbols*, 40–41.

13. See "Reasons," no. 2, in Winthrop et al., *Winthrop Papers*, 2:138–39. See also "Humble Request," in which the Puritans of the *Arbella* fleet affirm their conviction to remain Nonseparatist; Winthrop et al., *Winthrop Papers*, 2:231–33.

14. Kendall and Carey, *Basic Symbols*, 36. Note the Pilgrims' frequent generic claims to "justice" as opposed to the peculiarly Christian charity of Winthrop. See Kendall and Carey, *Basic Symbols*, 38ff.

15. This notion appears to have come down from the English Puritan William Ames. See P. Miller, "The Marrow of Puritan Divinity," in *Errand into the Wilderness*, 68–69.

16. It could be argued that the Christian impulse here is peculiarly English. Christians do not exist in a vacuum and their national cultures play an important part in forming their religious practices and beliefs. English colonial expansionism, then, combined with Christian universalism, could be uniquely responsible for the practical historical result. Deborah Madsen argues along these lines in *American Exceptionalism*. Yet it is important to recall that the symbols we seek are the self-articulations of a people. If actors in history could not have taken a perspective at the time of their action, that perspective could not possibly have been a part of the action itself. Thus we should take the Puritans' word that theirs was a Christian mission and action and not an imperial one.

17. See Winthrop et al., *Winthrop Papers*, 2:106–45. On this logic, it might be tempting to read the "Common Grievances" (ca. 1624) similarly as an early or inchoate symbol. But note that it cannot qualify as a symbol on Voegelinian grounds because it was not associated with any political action.

18. P. Miller, "Thomas Hooker and the Democracy of Connecticut," in *Errand into the Wilderness*, 37.

19. Winthrop et al., *Winthrop Papers*, 2:138. The text of the document is clearly divided by sections and numbers. Unless I am directly quoting the material, I will provide these numbers as an indirect reference to the text.

20. Baritz, *City on a Hill*, 6. Summerfield Baldwin also picks up on the parallel between the Massachusetts Puritans and the Jesuits. See Baldwin, "God and the Secular Power," 35–36.

21. Robert Kagan misunderstands Perry Miller when he quotes him as evidence that the Puritans of Massachusetts Bay were performing a "flank attack" on pernicious forces. The military metaphors are significantly overshadowed by the very unmilitaristic "tactics" deployed: living excellent lives of Christian virtue. When he calls the 1630 Puritans the "first imperialists," claiming they were "global revolutionaries," Kagan misunderstands their mission. Rather than seeking to "establish a base from which to launch a counteroffensive across the Atlantic," their aims, as I will show, were far from imperialistic. As they understood themselves, their project was, in fact, exemplary, which Kagan explicitly, though inexplicably, denies. See Kagan, *Dangerous Nation*, 8.

22. As Bercovitch has noted, "For Winthrop and Mather, the progress of the American theocracy, church, and commonwealth together, is part of ecclesiastical history." Bercovitch, *Puritan Origins*, 73.

23. Hugh Dawson has suggested that the explicit absence of calls to evangelization in the "Model" means that it is not a concern for the colony. To the contrary, Winthrop mentions the "increase of the Body of Christ," which, while surely suggesting in part the education of Puritan children, cannot but mean conversion of the native Americans as well, especially given the prominence in the "Reasons," in the charter, and in the call to evangelization at the heart of Christianity. See Winthrop et al., *Winthrop Papers*, 2:293. See also Dawson, "'Christian Charitie' as Colonial Discourse."

24. Winthrop et al., *Winthrop Papers*, 2:139.

25. See a seminal article by Thomas M. Davis, "The Exegetical Traditions of Puritan Typology." Madsen also uses the term. See Madsen, *American Exceptionalism*, 4–6ff.

26. As Perry Miller notes, the "federal theologians," so important to Winthrop and many Puritans, could not say that the natural law was "immutable and eternal," though they could say it was "generally reliable." See P. Miller, "The Marrow of Puritan Divinity," in *Errand into the Wilderness*, 94. In fairness it should be noted against Miller's fairly simplistic view of natural law thinking that even Aquinas allows for a flexibility of the natural law according to developments in understanding. See *Summa Theologiae* Ia-IIae, Q. 94, a. 5, especially ad. 3.

27. While Calvinism's "total depravity" is sometimes taken to mean that man can do nothing in this life but for the grace of God, it is also taken to mean that *all* of man's faculties—including his reason—partake of the fall from grace. This means that none of man's natural faculties are at all a help in attaining salvation. Such an understanding opens the door to doctrines of natural law but does not go as far as implying or requiring it.

28. NB: "Reasons" 3, 4, 5, 6, and 9 all contain hints of this inchoate theory of history.

29. Bercovitch, *Puritan Origins*, 109ff.

30. See ibid., 108. Recall Voegelin's observations about "representation" and truth.

31. The corruption of this idea will be discussed in chapter 5, especially. Loren Baritz says that the early Puritan view was that all of history was converging on the "cosmic climax of Boston's founding." See Baritz, *City on a Hill*, 31.

32. Winthrop's implicit theory of property here might bring to mind John Locke's

arguments in his *Second Treatise on Government*, yet Winthrop's work precedes Locke's by sixty years. This says as much about Locke as Winthrop, since Winthrop's source in a certain interpretation of scripture is an element shared with Locke's account, though this is only infrequently recalled. Many prefer to place Locke in a firmly naturalistic pose.

33. Winthrop et al., *Winthrop Papers*, 2:140–41.

34. Ibid., 2:141. Cf. Bercovitch, *Puritan Origins*, 99–103. This differs significantly from the imperialism around the turn of the twentieth century, which gives as its justification mainly U.S. economic gain, a theory of Anglo-Saxon racial superiority, and an amorphous sense of transcendent purpose. Much more will be said on this in chapter 5.

35. Interestingly, this point seems to push back against the idea that—as far as churches go—this one in New England is particularly special. In this "reason" Winthrop suggests to the contrary that the colony's church will *not* be different and special.

36. Ivy Schweitzer has argued that in the "Model" discourse, "Winthrop outlines his rationale for translating the original royal charter of the Company of the Massachusetts Bay, a commercial enterprise, into a theologically based social, economic, and political program for the new commonwealth in New England." Schweitzer, "John Winthrop's 'Model' of American Affiliation," 445. And again, "Subtly, through the strategic repetition of the first-person plural pronoun and verbs enacting connection ('knits,' 'bonds'), the elite stockholding 'company' dissolves into a diverse but now unified spiritual state" (451). Though she notes that the "import of this crucial vision" is "still under debate," it is not clear that Winthrop ever saw the colony as anything but a religious mission. In the two major documents under consideration here, Winthrop is unequivocal that the colony is explicitly and primarily a religious venture. It is religious; it is political. These are not in conflict with each other for the Puritans, even if they are for many contemporary readers.

37. Winthrop et al., *Winthrop Papers*, 2:143.

38. It should be highlighted, however, that Winthrop does not believe that the proper structure of government is the sole problem to be overcome. The virtue of the citizenry will have to remain extremely firm, lest the colony become an example of failure for all nations and ages. See discussion of the last part of "Model," later in the chapter.

39. Some have suggested that this point, in particular, accounts later for the loss of Puritan faith and the subsequent breaking of the original covenant. See Boorstin, *Genius of American Politics*, 36–40, 52–55. Nevertheless, it is enough at this point to notice the notion itself. It will be important in subsequent chapters.

40. The group of prominent Puritans who joined the company at the same time as Winthrop made two demands: that the actual charter accompany them to the new colony and that the day-to-day governance be transferred there as well. Though he was the sitting governor, Craddock had no intention to emigrate, which led him to resign that post in order to guarantee keeping the new members.

41. There has been a controversy about the moment of delivery of the "Model," which should be noted at the outset of its treatment here. There is no reason to doubt

Winthrop was its author—this seems never to have been in dispute. But Hugh Dawson contends that the text itself suggests it was not, as it is purported, written "on board the *Arbella*." The title and date were later inscribed on the oldest surviving copy of the "Model" discourse in a different hand. Dawson argues forcefully that the sermon was likely not delivered on the *Arbella*, since it was only one of a great many ships making the journey and the text of the sermon seems to be addressed to all the colonists. Dawson is convinced that the sermon was delivered *before* departure, which means it was addressed both to the colonists and to all who were gathered in Southampton to see the colonists off. With various textual observations like this one, Dawson seeks to effect a reinterpretation of a great many lines in the famous sermon. Yet for the purposes of this chapter and this project, the controversy is of little consequence. For reasons already discussed, it is enough that Winthrop penned the words and preached them to the whole body of the colonists. Even if only some of them heard it initially, it is clear that copies of it were made and circulated both in England and New England; the oldest manuscript in existence appears to be one of these copies. If Winthrop set out this vision for the new colony in public, which no one disputes, it can easily be considered an overt political act and thus qualify as a symbol. In any event, Dawson's own refrain about the ambiguity of Winthrop's language is more than enough ammunition for Dawson's critics. See Dawson, "'Christian Charitie' as Colonial Discourse."

42. This is Kendall and Carey's omission.

43. See Morgan, "John Winthrop's 'Modell of Christian Charity.'"

44. The idea that the Puritan political order was a strict Christian theocracy is made more important, ironically, by those who argue for fairly strict versions of the secularization thesis. To advance this thesis, there has to be a noticeably linear decline in Christian belief and practice, which means that the theory requires both the absence of Christian belief and practice today (or at least a low ebb of it) and the ubiquity of it at some point in the past. Without this, the theory loses traction. Thus there is an interest in making Winthrop look like a religious fanatic. And though by today's standards he probably would be one, several scholars have remarked about the surprisingly separated character of the institutions of church and state in the early days at Massachusetts Bay. See, for example, Hoskins, "Original Separation of Church and State." It ought to be kept in mind that Winthrop's ideas may have lagged behind some of his contemporaries' in regard to the proper balance of church and state, but even granting this, there would not be a substantial number in the colony who disagreed with him for a few generations.

45. Winthrop et al., *Winthrop Papers*, 2:290.

46. E. Clinton Gardner, for one, has noted the extent to which the "Model" discourse itself is intended and seen as a covenant. See Gardner, "Justice in the Puritan Covenantal Tradition."

47. Winthrop et al., *Winthrop Papers*, 2:282.

48. "The third consideration is concerning the exercise of this love, which is two-

fold, inward and outward, the outward hath been handled in the former preface of this discourse." See Ibid., 2:290.

49. Ibid., 2:286.

50. Ibid., 2:285–86.

51. Ibid., 2:287.

52. See "Reasons," Objections 5–9, ibid., 143–44.

53. Winthrop et al., *Winthrop Papers*, 2:290.

54. Ibid., 2:288.

55. Early in "Model," Winthrop introduces a contradiction between the "Law of Nature" and the "Law of the Gospel," affirming the former as the "golden rule" that tends toward unity and the latter as fundamentally divisive because of its insistence on loving enemies (since to be an enemy is to be radically divided from another). The rest of the discourse, however, speaks of the unifying nature of God's love, the church, the covenant, etc. And, further, Bercovitch has noted that most Calvinists conceived of grace as unifying and nature as dividing. See Bercovitch, *Puritan Origins*, 14. So, while noting the point in passing, I will take the greater thrust of the discourse, and the authority of the secondary literature, as the guide for my interpretation.

56. Kendall and Carey, *Basic Symbols*, 32.

57. Winthrop et al., *Winthrop Papers*, 2:292.

58. It might be said that Kendall and Carey's method would demand that colonial charters be used in making this kind of claim. I submit that, counterintuitively, the various charters are not central to the colonists' way of life. Winthrop and others disparaged the colony of Virginia as a primarily commercial colony, but one of the first lines of its charter then in effect said that the propagation of the Christian faith was that colony's purpose. Charters, as Ronald Dale Karr has pointed out in a different context, were written in fairly standard forms and language. Explanation of the difference in colonial practice, then, should be sought in terms of the colonists' different articulated thoughts and actions; in the case of the Massachusetts Bay Colony, this means turning to Winthrop. See Karr, "Missing Clause."

59. Winthrop et al., *Winthrop Papers*, 2:292.

60. Ibid., 2:293.

61. Ibid. The good of the whole cannot be achieved at the expense of the part, he seems to say; they are inseparable, they are one.

62. One can, perhaps, already anticipate the protests of Roger Williams.

63. Winthrop et al., *Winthrop Papers*, 2:293.

64. Ibid. (emphasis added).

65. Ibid.

66. Ibid. In the reference to failure, Winthrop refers perhaps to the "calamity" mentioned in the "Reasons" and its being brought on by figures perhaps like Charles I and William Laud.

"The elect," writes Bercovitch, "must repay God in time . . . for what he granted them from eternity, by making palpable the fruits of their calling." They were obligated to do service to God, even though it could not possibly *achieve* their salvation. Again, "[g]radually, they rewelded the sundered bonds of grace and works, though the notion of mutual obligation." Bercovitch, *Puritan Origins*, 80.

67. Winthrop et al., *Winthrop Papers*, 2:294.

68. Perry Miller elucidates the meaning of Winthrop's "the Lord hath given us leave to draw our own articles": God "left the particular form to be determined by circumstance—this was one important human art on which the Puritans said the Bible was *not* an absolute and imperious lawgiver—but He enacted that all men should be under some sort of corporate rule, that they should all submit to the sway of their superiors, that no man should live apart from his fellows, that the government should have full power to enforce obedience and to inflict every punishment that the crimes of men deserved." See P. Miller, "The Puritan State and Puritan Society," in *Errand into the Wilderness*, 142–43.

69. See Berman, "God's Alliance with Man," 93 and note 56, in which the author points to Deuteronomy 4:26, 30:19, 32:1; Isaiah 1:2; and Micah 6:1–2. Each of these passages speaks with the voice of God calling natural forces as passive hearers of a threat or promise by God. Winthrop's usage differs in that he speaks of events in history—that is, a disastrously tumultuous journey across the ocean or a calm one—as confirming or denying God's involvement in certain actions. By calling concrete events as *active* witnesses to the covenant, Winthrop has done something entirely different from these biblical passages, and this makes a very great difference in the attendant theory of history. He has given the covenant, in yet another way, a uniquely historical character, which is also borne out in the next part, the series of blessings and curses.

70. Winthrop et al., *Winthrop Papers*, 2:294.

71. Ibid.

72. Ibid., 2:294–95.

73. Ibid., 2:295.

74. Others, too, see the ambiguity. See Madsen, *American Exceptionalism*, 18–20. See also Baritz, *City on a Hill*, 16–17.

75. Winthrop et al., *Winthrop Papers*, 2:295.

76. See "Reasons," 3, 4, 5, 6, and 9, in ibid., 2:141.

77. Bercovitch, *Puritan Origins*, 62.

78. Perry Miller has suggested that many of the Puritan theologians were "dangerously close" to Arminianism, though they did not see this. See P. Miller, "The Marrow of Puritan Divinity," in *Errand into the Wilderness*, 78.

79. Cited in Bercovitch, *American Jeremiad*, 12.

80. Matthew 5:11–16, in *Geneva Bible* (emphasis in original). In the 1560 version, the Geneva Bible offers this commentary on the imagery of salt and light: "Your office is to season men with the salt of heavenly doctrine" and "Because you are seen far off, give good example of life." In the 1602 version, the Geneva Bible's commentary is similar but different. Regarding salt: "The ministers of the word especially . . . must needs lead

other [*sic*] both by word and deed to this greatest joy and felicity. Your doctrine must be very sound and good, for if it be not so, it shall be naught set by, and cast away as a thing unsavory and vain. What shall you have to salt withal? And so are fools in the Latin tongue called saltless, as you would say, men that have no salt, or savor and taste in them." Regarding light: "You shine and give light, by being made partakers in the true light."

81. NB: Winthrop has reversed himself from the "Reasons," where he was trying to persuade prominent Puritans and ministers to accompany him. There he says that failure will bring no shame on the ministers, but here he warns that it will. One can account for the discrepancy when the difference in aim is noted. In the "Reasons" Winthrop was recruiting. He needed to make it easier to *join* the venture, and so he played down the possible risks. Here he is guiding his colonists, trying to persuade them to work tirelessly for the colony's success, thus making it easier to succeed.

82. Dawson points up the distinctively nonutopian character of Winthrop's thought in other documents. See Dawson, "'Christian Charitie' as Colonial Discourse," 137, especially note 22.

83. Note the references to this Bible passage by the imperial exceptionalists at the turn of the twentieth century. Whether used in argument against imperial policies or rejected by those arguing for imperialism, the discourse was still shot through with Christian reflection, which gives further evidence for the persistence of the theme throughout the American political tradition.

84. Winthrop mentions the limitedness of our perspective in the context of admitting the possibility that the apparently wayward colony of Virginia may serve some good purpose one day. See Winthrop et al., *Winthrop Papers*, 2:142–43.

85. James Ceaser recognizes this when he notes that the Puritans were "concerned with achieving sanctity and not worldly power." Ceaser, *Nature and History*, 17.

86. See P. Miller, "The Puritan State and Puritan Society, in *Errand into the Wilderness*, 147. The issue of compliance of church members was wholly different, as Miller notes, "To allow no dissent from the truth was exactly the reason they had come to America." They would have done the same thing in England, "could they have secured the power" (145).

3. The Founders: A Providentially Guided, Temporally Bound Country

1. Niall Ferguson writes, "There were no more self-confident imperialists than the Founding Fathers." Ferguson, *Colossus*, 33.

2. See, for example, Ferguson, *Colossus*, 34, and Kagan, *Dangerous Nation*, 38. It should be pointed out that this argument is not, however, original to contemporary scholars. In the contentious Senate debates on the invasion of the Philippines, which will be discussed more in chapter 5, Senator Donelson Caffery of Louisiana argues that the Supreme Court's use of the word *empire* amounts to that body's sanction of imperial policy. See *Congressional Record* 33 (February 5, 1900): 1495. Kagan, Ferguson, and Caf-

fery alike put too much weight on the word and too little weight on its meaning in the context of the actions and documents they examine. *Empire* in the founding period is used synonymously with *large republic*, *extended republic*, and numerous other blanket terms—sometimes even *confederacy*, although the authors of the *Federalist* famously use that term in a particular way. And, it should be noted, the matter of whether a large country could exist with a participatory core had yet to be settled.

3. Forrest McDonald has pointed out the perils of basing historical arguments on specific words. See F. McDonald, *Novus Ordo Seclorum*, x–xi.

4. Thomas Jefferson and Benjamin Franklin—perhaps the two most prominent Americans associated with the radical French Enlightenment—wished the Great Seal of the United States to depict the scene from Exodus when Israel crossed the Red Sea. The not-so-implicit claim would have been the marking of a great transition from the old world to the new, from metaphorical slavery to real and lasting freedom. Despite their desire to so prominently use a biblical image, it would be difficult to substantiate the claim that these two men saw history, religion, and politics in the manner of the Puritans, who might have been *expected* to use such a scene to show what their political community was about. Jefferson and Franklin, then, wished to use the image more metaphorically, which illustrates something of the shift that had occurred by their time.

5. To do this, Kendall and Carey's *Basic Symbols* will again serve as a guide. After a brief recapitulation of Kendall and Carey's account of three founding documents between the Mayflower Compact and the Declaration of Independence, I will offer my own brief examination of the Declaration, the Articles of Confederation, the Constitution, and the *Federalist*. It might be asked why the famous words of Thomas Paine or J. Hector St. John de Crèvecœur do not form part of the inquiry here. While each of these authors is often cited in considerations of the question of American exceptionalism, they have little to do with the actual self-conception of the American people during the founding period. The number of discrete observations from this period of the difference between America and other countries—or its idiosyncratic uniqueness over the course of its history—could be multiplied nearly endlessly. That today we know the names of these two authors does not make them necessarily significant for discovering the operative American political theory at the time of their writing. And indeed, if we look for the operationally significant symbols, we find them in the usual places—some named by Kendall and Carey and some overlooked—but none terribly surprising.

6. Kendall and Carey, *Basic Symbols*, 43–44.

7. Ibid. To be sure, its very implications allow later for its misinterpretation and revision. But at this stage, the documents show, the understanding remains even without the previous language.

8. Ibid., 45.

9. This, again, had much to do with the divergent conceptions of government (and universality) held by the Puritans and the Pilgrims. We must wait as long as possible to take up the issue of differentiation, because the differences and similarities between the

Puritans and the founders will help illustrate the difference before we discuss it openly. Put another way, we may be able to grasp the difference between differentiation, change, and derailment intuitively and implicitly *before* it is lined out explicitly and rigorously *if* we first explain what the founding generation thought and then what the differences between the Puritans and the founders were.

10. Kendall and Carey, *Basic Symbols*, 46.

11. It is far from clear in the text, as noted by Kendall and Carey, that the particular notion of chosenness belongs to the people of Connecticut exclusively.

12. Kendall and Carey, *Basic Symbols*, 46–48.

13. Ibid., 53.

14. Ibid.

15. Ibid., 56.

16. Ibid., 57–58.

17. Even political thinkers in the *medieval* period, for example, emphasized the principle that all good government is aimed at the good of the people, and this in a period stereotyped as anything but republican.

18. Kendall and Carey, *Basic Symbols*, 72.

19. Ibid., 73.

20. Ibid., 74. See also Buckley, "Use and Abuse of Jefferson's Statute." Buckley argues that the Virginia separation was not characteristic but unique at the time, even trend-setting in light of the *Everson* case and the twentieth-century balance it effected (43). Interestingly, however, Buckley agrees that the separation in Virginia between church and state was promoted, widened, and exacerbated by religious, not political, figures. Certain Baptist ministers, especially, wanted to eliminate the competitive advantage that the established Anglican (later Episcopal) Church had over their potential flock (54). Nevertheless, even the strictest of separationists thought that the "welfare of the commonwealth" in fact "depended upon religion" (55).

Robert Kagan has also argued that the Virginia and New England cultures were more different than similar and that it was the former, and not the latter, that was more influential and ascendant. Virginia's tendency toward individualism and acquisitiveness is tantamount, for Kagan, to imperialism, or at least its necessary precursor. See Kagan, *Dangerous Nation*, 10–11.

21. NB: I am not here addressing the voluminous literature on the separation of church and state, which treats the matter as largely legal in character. My point is that the proper relationship between politics and religion had changed by the time of the founding from what it was in the Massachusetts Bay Colony. Noting this change and its consequences will eventually shed light on the question of American exceptionalism.

Though Jefferson's famous metaphor has become the main standard of interpretation on questions of religion and politics today, and though his conception takes a primarily political tack, we know that from the beginning the most ardent separationists were religious figures like Roger Williams. Williams seems to have been the first to coin the phrase for which Jefferson is so famous. See Driesbach, "Thomas Jefferson, a Mammoth Cheese, and the 'Wall of Separation,'" 84–85.

22. Hutson, "Future State of Rewards."

23. The point is not missed by Kendall and Carey. See *Basic Symbols*, 45–47, 55–57.

24. For an extended treatment of the former view and how it came about, see Maier, *American Scripture*, chapter 4. A good example of the former view in the scholarly literature is David Armitage's *The Declaration of Independence: A Global History*. Armitage's account goes on to trace the historical influence of the Declaration on other, similar documents around the world. Though I do not deny that this account of its influence is much as Jefferson ultimately intended, I do deny that this is a sufficient understanding of the document's meaning. Its main role in the articulation of America's self-conception will be taken up immediately.

Philip F. Detweiler has written that the view of the Declaration as a charter of universal human freedom was decidedly not the original one:

> In its earliest years, however, the Declaration was not honored as political scripture. In the 1780's, for example, Jefferson's language in the preamble was not remarked for its peculiar grace or distinction, and few Americans seemed aware that the Declaration would come to be "the charter of American democracy." In the 1790's, when its reputation was taking shape, politics made it impossible for men of opposing political views to share the same opinion of the Declaration.
>
> The changing reputation of the Declaration in the early years of the American republic is of more than antiquarian interest. It is—or should be—of continuing interest to the numerous historians and politicians who confidently paraphrase or interpret the preamble. Customarily we are told what the Founding Fathers meant by a particular phrase. But the Fathers, although they did not ignore the phrases of the preamble, viewed the Declaration principally as a proclamation of independence. Americans of 1776 were not arguing about the meaning of the preamble in the fashion in which they argued some ten years later about the meaning of the Constitution. This fact explains why we have no contemporary commentary, such as *The Federalist Papers* afford for many clauses of the Constitution, to determine the meaning or application of the preamble of the Declaration. Rather we must base much of our understanding of the specific language of the preamble on the whole body of Revolutionary writing. (Detweiler, "Changing Reputation," 557–58)

Detweiler's article is an effort to begin to understand the Declaration in this manner.

25. Maier, *American Scripture*, 149, xvii.

26. For more details on how the Declaration was drafted and its truly corporate nature, see ibid., 143–53. Robert M. S. McDonald has noted, in an article that in part evaluates Maier's book, that John Adams resented the reputation Jefferson came to possess as the Declaration's sole author:

> Adams's resentment resulted from confusion as much as jealousy. When he was

young, an author was an authorizer, and Congress, not Jefferson, had authorized the Declaration. Few people had known that Jefferson drafted the document, and even fewer people cared. Now, however, the meaning of authorship was shifting in ways that Adams did not yet grasp. For increasing numbers of Americans, authorship was an individual act of creation and, since the 1790s, Jeffersonian Republicans had told them that Jefferson did more than any other individual to create the Declaration. Adams still thought of him as the Declaration's penman, but they had come to exalt him as its author. (R. McDonald, "Thomas Jefferson's Changing Reputation," 170)

27. The text of the Declaration, the Articles of Confederation, and the Constitution are widely available and do not vary from edition to edition. In lieu of citing page numbers from any particular edition—which would impede reading unnecessarily—I have indicated in the text the precise place from which I draw quotations by reference to their internal structures.

28. Kendall and Carey, *Basic Symbols*, 79–80.

29. The document was not approved, signed, and promulgated on the same day. Though adopted by Congress on July 4, 1776, the heading "The unanimous Declaration of the thirteen united States of America" was added only when word reached the Second Continental Congress that New York State had approved of the Declaration—the last state to do so. See Maier, *American Scripture*, 151. This being said, one of the recurrent themes in Maier's book is the degree to which most of America was already convinced that separation from Great Britain was necessary. Many states and localities had undertaken or were undertaking similar declarations of their own—which shows once more the degree to which the Declaration is "representative" in both the Voegelinian and more colloquial senses.

30. Recall the four-part division of documents in the American political tradition. See Kendall and Carey, *Basic Symbols*, 32.

31. It is puzzling that Kendall and Carey do not treat the Articles of Confederation in *Basic Symbols*, since it clearly meets each of their criteria for the kinds of documents they wish to consider. The omission is remedied here and helps to paint an even clearer picture of American self-conception during this period.

32. Now, to be sure, even in acting to raise up a new general government, the American people does not—in the Constitution or at any time since—truly act as a unit. Participation in federal action is still mediated through the several states. But the action undertaken is *federal* action as opposed to state action, and this is new. Even members of the House of Representatives, tied primarily to a locality and not a state, still have roles to play as delegates from particular states on certain occasions. See Article I, sections 2.3, 2.4, 4.4; and Article II, section 1.3, for example.

33. Recall Voegelin's discussion of this point in *New Science of Politics*, 40.

34. This is, of course, not an uncontroversial argument. The arguments between the "consensus" and "democratic" historians are well documented. See Jensen, "American

People and the American Revolution," especially notes 11 and 12. Jensen, for one, has taken issue with the idea that there even *was* an American people at the time of the Constitution:

> [T]he assumption that there was an entity that can be called the "American people" is as unproved and unprovable as assumptions that there was a consciousness of "American nationality" or that there was a distinctive "American character." One must generalize, of course, as the Founding Fathers did, but one must not forget, as they did not, that the American people were divided among thirteen states whose interests often clashed, and whose citizens were far more concerned with the affairs of their own states than with that distant and amorphous entity, based on hope and faith, the United States of America. Furthermore, the people in any given state were divided by religion, economic interests, political ideas, and ambitions, and differing combinations thereof (9–10).

Jensen goes on to relate what he suggests *was* the "role of the people in the American Revolution," but there is a problem with his approach. Criticizing much of the history and many views of the Revolution as "elitist," he does concede that it was often only the elites who left good records of their thoughts. Having no other material to work with, Jensen and other historians are forced to revert to often-anonymous newspaper diatribes and complaints—pieces even he admits are not wed to a strict view of "truth in reporting." Jensen's more "popular" history, then, is problematic for reasons opposite to the so-called elite histories: though the former's "representativeness" of the people might be questioned, we can say that they were the definite views of certain people, and people, furthermore, who often had some kind of public endorsement or sanction through elected office. Except on very circumscribed points, it is unclear *who* thought *what* about the topics Jensen covers; the problem Jensen set out to address with his new method—sorting out who represents whom in history—persists when following his approach. Yet it is *this* problem that may be alleviated by looking for symbols in the usual manner.

35. These and other problems are discussed throughout the *Federalist*, especially in Nos. 1–20.

36. Note the change this undergoes with Woodrow Wilson's recasting of the United States' role in world politics, which is touched on in chapter 5.

37. George W. Carey, "Editor's Introduction," in *Federalist*, xlvi–xlvii.

38. *Federalist*, No. 1, 1.

39. Hodgson, *Myth of American Exceptionalism*, 35.

40. Ibid., 20.

41. *Federalist*, No. 1, 4.

42. Kendall and Carey, *Basic Symbols*, 97–98.

43. Ibid., 98–99.

44. Ibid., 98.

45. *Federalist*, No. 1, 1 (emphasis added).

46. *Federalist*, No. 2, 6.

47. Ibid. (ellipses in original).

48. Ibid.

49. Ibid., No. 2, 6–7.

50. Scholarship on theories of history that were current at the time of the founding does not address precisely these questions. Rutherford Delmage and Stow Persons, for example, authored widely cited articles on conceptions of progress and the cyclicality of history. Neither of these articles, however, looks at these principal documents of the American political tradition. They base their arguments on gleanings from sermons and philosophers. This is not to say that their work is not important or not true but that the extent to which it is true need not affect what has been said. See Delmage, "American Idea of Progress"; and Persons, "Cyclical Theory of History."

51. This, of course, frames the question more sociologically than theologically, which is not the way the Puritans saw it themselves.

52. *Federalist*, No. 2, 6.

53. Recall that Kendall and Carey divided the spheres into "political" and "social" rather than "political" and "religious."

54. This, indeed, seems to have been the true meaning and purpose of Jefferson's famous thought that there should be a "wall of separation" in matters of religion. The wall divides not the church from the state but the federal authority on religion (that is to say, no authority) from state authority (where churches could be and still were established, even under Jefferson's famous "Statute of Religious Freedom"), later interpretations of Jefferson and the First Amendment notwithstanding. See Driesbach, "Thomas Jefferson, a Mammoth Cheese, and the 'Wall of Separation,'" 75.

55. See Carey, "Constitution and Community."

56. Washington, *Writings*, 971. One recalls here also the arguments of Benjamin Rush.

57. The distinction is an old one. Aristotle distinguished between the good man and the good citizen in *Politics* III. But the distinction seems to have lost currency in Winthrop's community, which did not understand man's moral existence as distinct from his political existence.

58. Butler, "Why Revolutionary America Wasn't a 'Christian Nation,'" 189.

59. Shain, "Revolutionary-Era Americans," 276.

60. James Hutson illustrates the notable difference on the question of religion between Washington and Adams, on the one hand, and Madison and Jefferson, on the other, by labeling them, respectively, "cooperationists" and "separationists" on the question of religion and politics. Hutson, "Future State of Rewards."

61. This is a marked difference from Abraham Lincoln's second inaugural address, discussed in chapter 4, which speaks of the utter inscrutability of God's plan.

62. Whether or not this change has its roots in the history of theology is not my main concern. Whether the separation of the spheres was justified on largely theological, philosophical, or political grounds is irrelevant to the important facts that, first,

the separation was widely held to be proper and, second, the separation was enacted in America's fundamental federal law. For a further discussion of the theological aspects of the question and a critique of the prevailing Weberian views on politics and religion, see Mitchell, "Protestant Thought and Republican Spirit."

63. This is markedly different from the Progressive Era, when government is once again invested with universal significance, though the task is more profane than sacred at that point. See chapter 5.

4. Abraham Lincoln: An Ideally United, Potentially Unbound Union

1. Though unity of the Puritans was not achieved for long, its early place in the history of political entities on these shores has given it a special place in the imagination of anyone who ponders the history of American political thought. This point is made very famously by Tocqueville but has been echoed by many others.

2. Though I concluded in chapter 3 that the expansionism of which the founders are often accused is often mistakenly brought as evidence of their supposed imperial exceptionalism, my primary focus was the possible role they will play in the future conception of imperial American exceptionalism. To argue they were not, then, imperialists is not the same as arguing that their words cannot, centuries later, be used as grounds for the imperialism of others.

3. The Progressive period could be called a high-water mark for Lincoln enthusiasm. The Lincoln penny and Lincoln Memorial were spearheaded and introduced in 1902 and 1904, respectively. Merrill D. Peterson has noted the links between Lincoln and figures in the Progressive Era. See Peterson, *Lincoln in American Memory*, 163–65, 186, 384–85. I do not intend to either directly add to or subtract from this interesting subject in the course of this project.

4. This view is widely held, but perhaps most famously by Harry V. Jaffa, along with scholars like John Patrick Diggins and Reinhold Niebuhr. Jaffa writes, "Lincoln's interpretation of [the phrase from the Declaration] 'all men are created equal' . . . transforms that proposition from a . . . norm which prescribes what civil society ought not to be, into a transcendental affirmation of what civil society ought to be." Jaffa, *Crisis of the House Divided*, 321. See Jaffa, *New Birth of Freedom*; Diggins, *Lost Soul of American Politics*; Niebuhr, "Religion of Abraham Lincoln."

5. Fletcher, *Our Secret Constitution*, 2. What Fletcher accounts for as the distinction and transition between the extant and "secret" constitutions I describe as a process of differentiation and derailment of the American political tradition. The importance of an initial deposit of one idea in terms that are later reread very differently is highlighted by both his book and the present work.

James M. McPherson, too, sees Abraham Lincoln as the pivot point for the interpretation of the Civil War and the American political tradition. See McPherson, "Abraham Lincoln and the Second American Revolution," 143.

Again, Glen E. Thurow sees Lincoln as thoroughly changing the meaning of the American political tradition. See Thurow, "Gettysburg Address and the Declaration of Independence," 56–57.

Once again, Allen C. Guelzo seems to agree with this assessment in a concluding assertion in *Abraham Lincoln*, 456.

6. Others have concurred in this view. See Bradford, "Heresy of Equality"; Kendall and Carey, *Basic Symbols*, 144–56. See also some newspaper commentary of the period, which makes clear that although Lincoln's view soon took hold it was not universally accepted at the time. See Donald, *Lincoln*, 465–66.

7. I should note here that Kendall and Carey did not neglect mentioning Lincoln's contribution to the basic symbols of the American tradition. They merely saw the symbols he introduced as an utter derailment of that tradition. It was not, in other words, a case of symbols arising from illegitimate sources or announced by the wrong person or body—which their methodological considerations may have led the reader to believe. Though in their view Congress is perhaps the only legitimate source of symbols in the American tradition, the nub of the matter is that the symbols Lincoln introduces— notably the high importance of equality for the American political tradition—are discontinuous from the previous tradition. The train of U.S. history would need to leave the track it had been running along in order to follow Lincoln's lead. Indeed, it did so: thus the "derailment." See, e.g., Kendall and Carey, *Basic Symbols*, 145.

8. Niebuhr, "Religion of Abraham Lincoln," 381.

9. See W. Miller, "Lincoln's Second Inaugural," 346. The Lincoln text can be found in Lincoln, *His Speeches and Writings*, 688.

10. Abraham Lincoln, "First Inaugural Address," in Lincoln, *His Speeches and Writings*, 582.

11. Ibid.

12. This is usually in reference to the famous saying of Alexander H. Stevens, who asserted that Lincoln invested the union with "the sublimity of religious mysticism." Quoted in Peterson, *Lincoln in American Memory*, 194.

13. In the Gettysburg Address Lincoln famously revises this position to the Declaration of Independence in 1776.

14. *Journals of Congress*, 32. All quotations from this source have been updated with modern spellings where appropriate.

15. Ibid., 31–32 (emphasis added).

16. Ibid., 34–35.

17. Lincoln, *His Speeches and Writings*, 584.

18. See Hamburger, "Natural Rights, Natural Law," 907–60. Publius's view on the lack of necessity for the Bill of Rights is also instructive on this point. See *Federalist*, No. 84.

19. Lincoln, *His Speeches and Writings*, 583.

20. Ibid., 586–87 (emphasis in original).

21. Ibid., 587. At the time Lincoln was being urged by some Northern radicals to broker conditions for Southern secession, by way of purging the Union of the moral pollution of slavery and slaveholders.

22. Ibid., 588. In an interesting reversal of *Federalist* No. 51's "If men were angels, no government would be necessary," Lincoln suggests that the problem the Union faces has its solution in the better part of our nature. This runs opposite to Publius's solution, which depends on the constancy of the worse parts of human nature, where "ambition must be made to counteract ambition."

See Weiner, "Madison's Metronome," which details the importance of delay in the political thought of James Madison. Delay has a salutary effect on deliberation, Madison thought, and this helped especially in the formation and success of salutary majorities. This seems to be part of Lincoln's point in the passage above. Yet Lincoln ends with a somewhat ambiguous appeal to the "better angels of our nature." While on the one hand this suggests the intervention of a source of guidance beyond our own character, on the other hand Lincoln could be supposed as speaking of strictly human possibilities. It may well be that Lincoln simply uses the phrase as a rhetorical flourish in an appeal to what is best in his fellow citizens.

23. William Wolf writes of Lincoln's views in the first inaugural, "Vox populi, vox dei meant for Lincoln that, if not thwarted by man's rebellion, God so guided the consciences of men in history that the people's verdict was properly their response to His guidance." Wolf, *Almost Chosen People*, 116. Wolf's interpretation, while based firmly on the text of the first inaugural, seems to be overstated. Lincoln's point is not as well developed as Wolf claims, even if the thrust of its logic would seem to move in the direction he indicates.

24. Jayne, *Lincoln and the American Manifesto*.

25. See Kendall and Carey, *Basic Symbols*, appendix 1, 156.

26. Willmoore Kendall writes,

> The proposition "all men are created equal" is so ambiguous as to merit classification as, for all practical purposes, meaningless and therefore useless—especially if, in reading it, we take into account the time at which it was written. The phrase "all men," to begin with, is by no means so simple and unambiguous as (for reasons too complicated to go into on this occasion) it is likely to seem to the unsuspecting undergraduate in 1967. The Declaration's Framers might have written, but chose not to write, "each man is created equal to every other man," and they might have added, but did not add, "and therefore ought to be treated, for governmental purposes, as the equal of every other man." Much has been made, as some of you know, even or perhaps especially by the glorifiers of the Declaration, of the fact that the assembly that approved the Declaration suppressed the passionate denunciation of slavery that Jefferson wrote into the original draft (how could they, critics ask, have been so "inconsistent," or, variously, how could they have been so "hypocritical"—is it not obvious that if you believe that "all men are created equal" you have got to denounce slavery?).

Either the one, or the other: they were poor logicians, or they were hypocrites, that is, vicious men paying the vicious man's normal tribute to virtue. . . . There is, in other words, a third possible explanation for the suppression of Jefferson's denunciation of slavery, namely, that the men who approved the Declaration did not mean by "all men" what their critics mean by "all men," but rather, like the Levellers, something more like "all men that count." (Kendall, "Equality," 69–70)

27. See the Republican Party Platform of 1856, which gestures in this direction, even if it does not exactly spell out Lincoln's thought:

Resolved: That the maintenance of the principles promulgated in the Declaration of Independence, and embodied in the Federal Constitution are essential to the preservation of our Republican institutions, and that the Federal Constitution, the rights of the States, and the union of the States, must and shall be preserved.

Resolved: That, with our Republican fathers, we hold it to be a self-evident truth, that all men are endowed with the inalienable right to life, liberty, and the pursuit of happiness, and that the primary object and ulterior design of our Federal Government were to secure these rights to all persons under its exclusive jurisdiction; that, as our Republican fathers, when they had abolished Slavery in all our National Territory, ordained that no person shall be deprived of life, liberty, or property, without due process of law, it becomes our duty to maintain this provision of the Constitution against all attempts to violate it for the purpose of establishing Slavery in the Territories of the United States by positive legislation, prohibiting its existence or extension therein. That we deny the authority of Congress, of a Territorial Legislation, of any individual, or association of individuals, to give legal existence to Slavery in any Territory of the United States, while the present Constitution shall be maintained.

28. Even those who share our English political heritage—and who should, consequently, be able to see the error involved—have unproblematically accepted Lincoln's views on the nature of the American political tradition. See, for example, Chesterton, *What I Saw in America*, 6.

29. Garry Wills, for one, asserts this interpretation is deliberate on Lincoln's part. It was, Wills says, "one of the most daring acts of open-air sleight-of-hand ever witnessed by the unsuspecting. Everyone in that vast throng of thousands was having his or her intellectual pocket picked." Wills, *Lincoln at Gettysburg*, 38. Deliberate or not, my main concern is its error.

30. While I do not seek to deny entirely the influence of John Locke on the American founding, I do deny that understanding his thought is sufficient for understanding the American political tradition. This is something often denied implicitly in both scholarly and popular circles by the distinct absence of understanding of the lived American tradition in self-government from the colonies onward. As I have emphasized and Kendall and Carey and others have long argued, the American political tradition is intelligible

as an organic growth from the lived tradition of British-inspired constitutionalism.

31. Kendall and Carey, *Basic Symbols*, 21, 25 (emphasis in original).

32. Glen Thurow argues that this move was necessary in order for Lincoln to achieve his practical political end of perpetuating the Union. See Thurow, "Gettysburg Address and the Declaration of Independence," 68–70.

33. Wilbur F. Storey of the *Chicago Times*, quoted in Donald, *Lincoln*, 466.

34. William Wolf has noted that "[t]he conflicting evidence on Lincoln's religion is incredibly complex. One could 'prove' about anything by selecting what he wanted from the sources. The fair-minded investigator must finally admit that the only really reliable testimony, with few exceptions, must be gleaned from Lincoln's own speeches and letters." Wolf, *Almost Chosen People*, 26. Wolf's book is an attempt to operate along these lines; my work is similar, though with a different set of aims and concerns.

35. Historian Sarah Vowell writes, in the midst of a discussion of belief in America's chosenness and its terrible mistakes, particularly the 2005 prisoner abuse scandal at Iraq's Abu Ghraib prison: "I hate to admit it, but I still believe that, too. Because even though my head tells me that the idea that America was chosen by God as his righteous city on a hill is ridiculous, my heart still buys into it. And I don't even believe in God! Why is America the last best hope of Earth? What if it's Liechtenstein? Or, worse, Canada?" Vowell, *Wordy Shipmates*, 71.

36. It is once again tempting to multiply citations to various speeches and letters in which Lincoln repeats or reiterates his attachment to the founders' abstract "philosophy." The nature of the present inquiry, however, both obviates and precludes such multiplication. Because I am seeking the operative symbols of the American political tradition, however, and because none are perhaps more operative or potent than the various phrases in the Gettysburg Address, this is unnecessary. Further, insofar as symbols become operative in their constant repetition, it is the Gettysburg Address and Lincoln's inaugurals, and neither his more obscure speeches nor his completely obscure personal letters, that give symbols their meaning and force. This is the case, but it need not have been so. A letter by Thomas Jefferson is the source of his now very famous and ostensibly authoritative statement that there should be a "wall of separation" between politics and religion for the federal government. The prominence of the phrase and letter was achieved by the U.S. Supreme Court's *Everson v. Board of Education* ruling in 1947. Just as that phrase and letter became a pretext for certain political action in regard to religion, so also have these three speeches become an authority on the nature and scope of America. Thus I confine myself to these three addresses.

37. W. Miller, "Lincoln's Second Inaugural," 349. Though Miller's article was originally published in 1980, one can imagine the events of the twenty-first century that might fall to this same criticism. John Patrick Diggins comments, too, on this point; in discussing his own work as a historian and his aim to interpret American history, Diggins notes that though he seeks consensus, "consensus hardly implies uniformity, nor does exceptionalism imply superiority." Diggins, *On Hallowed Ground*, 124. Both consensus and exceptionalism, then, can be signposts or tools for the historian, but they are not necessities.

38. Lincoln himself helps raise such a question, for, as he says in the opening paragraphs of his first inaugural, "the intention of the law-giver is the law." Lincoln, *His Speeches and Writings*, 581.

39. Thurow, "Gettysburg Address and the Declaration of Independence," 73.

40. Glen Thurow, who has given one of the most complete analyses of the Gettysburg Address and the second inaugural address side by side, argues that the two speeches purposefully contradict each other. See Thurow, *Abraham Lincoln and American Civil Religion*, 108–19.

41. Lincoln, *His Speeches and Writings*, 792.

42. Ibid., 793.

43. Ibid. This is perhaps what Lincoln had in mind in the famous line from his 1861 address to the New Jersey Senate, just before his presidential inauguration: "I shall be most happy indeed if I shall be an humble instrument in the hands of the Almighty, and of this, his almost chosen people, for perpetuating the object of that great struggle [the American Revolution]." Ibid., 575.

44. Stewart Winger has argued that a strained, lifelong examination of the issues both within and without the Christian tradition eventually led Lincoln back to the bosom of biblical faith, whence his more universal yet still Christian standpoint in the second inaugural. Winger, *Lincoln, Religion, and Romantic Cultural Politics*, 208.

45. Grant N. Havers has written about the place of charity in politics and political theory, with Lincoln as its organizing touchstone. Havers, *Lincoln and the Politics of Christian Love*.

46. Dealing with historical judgments means we are not dealing with Lincoln's thought as such but largely its reception and effect.

47. Lincoln, *His Speeches and Writings*, 586. In using Lincoln to make what I take to be a very "un-Lincolnian" point, I am not trying to point up an inconsistency in the man. I am showing merely that the historical record of his thought and action is broader than the traditional and politically operative view of him, even as the latter view is the one I mainly deal with.

48. Ibid., 585.

49. Kendall and Carey, *Basic Symbols*, 35.

50. Ibid., 98.

51. This is echoed by Pauline Maier in the introduction to *American Scripture*, though she believes the change Lincoln effects to be legitimate and salutary. Maier, *American Scripture*, xx. I disagree.

52. This has been noted by many, but two examples link the phenomenon with Lincoln. Don E. Fehrenbacher argues for its advent in Lincoln's time, noting Clinton Rossiter's agreement. Fehrenbacher, "Lincoln and the Constitution," 119. Later in the same essay Fehrenbacher more delicately echoes the point: "It is accordingly possible to conclude that Lincoln's use of executive power was wise and appropriate in its context, but not an unmixed blessing as a presidential tradition" (122).

5. Albert Beveridge: A Racially Defined, Imperially Aimed Nation

1. *Congressional Record* 31 (April 19, 1898): 4066.

2. As David H. Burton has written, "When the fuse of war was lighted by the loss of the *Maine*, more and more did the mood of the nation come to resemble that of Theodore Roosevelt. The American Republic was ready to take the plunge. It was the right and duty of a great nation to expand; the responsibility that expansion entailed . . . could not and should not be avoided." Burton, *Theodore Roosevelt*, 56.

3. *Congressional Record* 31 (April 18, 1898): 4062. The "Teller amendment" that is incorporated as the fourth resolve of Congress's resolution was added just before the declaration of war was approved. It states that the United States' only purpose in Cuba was to settle the dispute between Spain and Cuba and then to leave the island to its own self-government, prohibiting annexation. It has been argued that Senator Henry M. Teller of Colorado mainly wanted to protect his state's sugar beet industry from the potential flood of cheap sugarcane from Cuba. Whatever the reason, the U.S. government abided by the letter of the resolution, intervening only when the government of Cuba later collapsed in 1902. A similar amendment never passed in regard to the Philippines.

4. For the resolution, which passed nearly unanimously, and direct comparisons of the Cuban situation to the achievement of American independence, see *Congressional Record* 31 (April 20, 1898): 4100ff.

5. Hofstadter, "Cuba, the Philippines, and Manifest Destiny," 172.

6. See "Treaty of Peace between the United States and Spain," Article 3.

7. Hofstadter, "Cuba, the Philippines, and Manifest Destiny," 168.

8. Beveridge, "Our Philippine Policy," 58. The text of the speech in the book is identical to the official version in the *Congressional Record*, except in being truncated near the middle, where Beveridge reads several redundant letters from figures knowledgeable about the Philippines, and except for the floor speech's conclusion. The full text may be found at *Congressional Record* 33 (January 9, 1900): 704–12.

9. Beveridge, "Our Philippine Policy," 58–59.

10. Ibid, 59, 60.

11. Ibid., 61–62. In responding immediately to this particular charge, Senator George F. Hoar of Massachusetts remarks that in scriptures it was Satan himself who offered worldly luxury and wealth to Christ, though at the price of Christ denying who he was.

12. See Hardt and Negri, *Empire*, xii: "The boundaries defined by the modern system of nation-states were fundamental to European colonialism and economic expansion: the territorial boundaries of the nation delimited the center of power from which rule was exerted over external foreign territories through a system of channels and barriers that alternately facilitated and obstructed the flows of production and circulation. Imperialism was really an extension of the sovereignty of the European nation-states beyond their own boundaries."

13. Beveridge, "Our Philippine Policy," 63.

14. See Ross, *Origins of American Social Science*, 24–25.

15. Beveridge, "Our Philippine Policy," 65, 68. Beveridge does not personify *civilization* like this elsewhere in his speech, and the reader is left to conclude from the context that this is simply an alternative reference to the Anglo-Saxon race.

16. Ibid., 71 (emphasis in original).

17. Ibid., 72, 73. It should be noted here that the view that self-government takes time to learn is not an idea necessarily connected with imperialism. This notion becomes imperial only when the task of raising the world to self-government is taken on by a single people as a mission that allows or even requires the violation of the sovereignty of other peoples. The difference, pointed out by Beveridge's opponents at the time, is the same as that between raising a child and keeping a slave—though even this supposes that, as with children, the United States had some sort of obligation to rear the world's other countries.

18. Ibid., 76. Richard M. Gamble has noted the degree to which a kind of Darwinized theory of salvation took hold during this period, making such utterances not uncommon. See Gamble, *War for Righteousness*, 30.

19. Beveridge, "Our Philippine Policy," 79, 84. While it must be conceded that questions of race *are* raised by the Constitution's provisions regarding slavery, it must also be admitted that such questions are there not essentially but accidentally racial. It certainly happened that the slaves in question were of a different race from the drafters and ratifiers of the Constitution, but this is not the sense in which the slaves are treated in that document. Beveridge is here arguing that which particular race *wrote* the U.S. Constitution affects the *meaning* of the words on the page, which is a very different claim from merely recognizing that the Constitution raises questions about race.

20. Ibid., 84–85.

21. Ibid., 59, 60.

22. Ibid., 63.

23. From among a great number, I will cite one work aimed against Beveridge's arguments on taking, possessing, or retaining the Philippines. Moorfield Storey and Marcial P. Lichauco, prominent lawyers from the American Bar Association and Harvard Law School, echo these points against Beveridge's "Christian imperialism" and argue forcefully that the chief and nearly only reason for the entire Philippine venture and its persistence was that a few in America stood to make a profit. I cite it not so much for the compelling evidence they marshal, though it is compelling, but to further reinforce a point I will address more thoroughly—namely that even at a time very close to Beveridge's there were broad-based and full-blown contradictory accounts. The American political tradition is, again, derailed, unraveled. There are now only "consensuses." See Storey and Lichauco, *Conquest of the Philippines*.

24. Beveridge, "Our Philippine Policy," 77–78.

25. Senator Hoar disagrees with this, agreeing, notably, with Kendall and Carey's argument in chapter 5 of *Basic Symbols*. On April 17, 1900, Hoar says,

The confusion of the argument of our friends on the other side comes from confounding the statement in the Declaration of the rights of individuals with the statement of the rights of nations, or peoples, in dealing with one another. The whole Declaration is a statement of political rights and political relations and political duties. First. Every man is equal in political rights, including the right to life, liberty, and the pursuit of happiness, to every other. Second. No people can come under the government of any other people, or of any ruler, without its consent. The law of nature and of nature's God entitle every people to its separate and equal station among the powers of the earth. Our fathers were not dealing in this clause with the doctrine of the social compact; they were not considering the rights of minorities; they used the word "people" as equivalent to "nation," or "state," as an organized political being, and not as a mere aggregate of persons not collected or associated. They were not thinking of Robinson Crusoe in his desolate island, or of scattered settlers, still less of predatory bands roaming over vast regions they could neither own nor occupy. They were affirming the right of each of the thirteen colonies separately or of them all together to throw off the yoke of George III and to separate itself or themselves from Great Britain. Now, you must either admit that what they said was true, or you must affirm the contrary. (*Congressional Record* 33 [April 18, 1900]: 4384–85)

26. Beveridge, "Our Philippine Policy," 78.

27. Beveridge reiterates just this point, in fact, directly after the section on Declaration of Independence. See ibid., 79.

28. Ibid., 82 (emphasis in original).

29. Ibid., 86.

30. Ibid., 85. Now, the Christian belief in Providence might be said to lend itself to such a view. But this is not necessarily so. In the Christian tradition, generally speaking, man sees Providence at work retroactively. Here Beveridge not only argues this but also goes further to suggest that he sees where it is going. The hubris of such a suggestion is obvious and butts up against traditional Christian self-estimations, which are always to be governed by a great degree of humility.

31. See Dobson, *Reticent Expansionism*, 121.

32. Alfonso, *Theodore Roosevelt and the Philippines*, 28–30. David H. Burton further notes, "Roosevelt's imperialistic rationale, insofar as it had become explicit when he took over direction of affairs in 1901, was compounded of a sense of the superiority of the white race (especially the Anglo-Saxon Americans) and the persuasions of democracy, of western man's urge to dominate and his wish, often more than a pious one, to be the preceptor of less able people and less fortunate human beings." Burton goes on to note that Roosevelt, like many of the period, saw no contradiction between race superiority and democracy, between domination and protection. Burton, *Theodore Roosevelt*, 61–62.

33. Dobson, *Reticent Expansionism*, 101.

34. Alfonso, *Theodore Roosevelt and the Philippines*, 212–13. David H. Burton wonders whether Teddy Roosevelt can be considered "representative," but he closes the question as soon as he raises it, writing, "[t]o such questions perhaps no certain answers can be given." Burton, *Theodore Roosevelt*, viii.

35. Dobson, *Reticent Expansionism*, 110–11, 114–15.

36. It may be lost on some that Roosevelt and other figures of this period do not use the word *nation* in the general sense in which it is used today. He intends usually the more technical and narrow sense, which is tied to biology and has a strong racial tone. Roosevelt, "First Annual Message to Congress," in *Works of Theodore Roosevelt*, 15:111.

37. Ibid., 15:111, 115, 116.

38. Roosevelt, "Fourth Annual Message to Congress," in *Works of Theodore Roosevelt*, 15:257.

39. Ibid., 15:258.

40. Ibid., 15:263, 264.

41. See *Congressional Record* 33 (April 17, 1900): 4281.

42. Roosevelt, "Inaugural Address," in *Works of Theodore Roosevelt*, 15:267. Alexis de Tocqueville seems to articulate something very similar in the introduction to his *Democracy in America*, though with a different aim: "A new political science is needed for a world itself quite new. But it is just that to which we give least attention. Carried away by a rapid current, we obstinately keep our eyes fixed on the ruins still in sight on the bank, while the stream whirls us backward—facing toward the abyss." Tocqueville, *Democracy in America*, ed. Mayer, 12–13. Neither Roosevelt nor Tocqueville believes we can understand American politics unless we understand the sense in which it has been cut off from previous political ways. I would add, and this is perhaps more important than in Tocqueville's time, that it is just as important to recognize how connected and beholden we still are to the past.

43. Roosevelt, "Inaugural Address," 15:268, 269 (emphasis added).

44. Roosevelt, "Fifth Annual Message to Congress," in *Works of Theodore Roosevelt*, 15:300, 302.

45. In regard to the second takeover of Cuba, see Roosevelt, "Sixth Annual Message to Congress," in *Works of Theodore Roosevelt*, 15:389. The same subject is treated again in the "Seventh Annual Message to Congress." See the "Eighth Annual Message to Congress," where Roosevelt reasserts the Golden Rule (15:535) but still denies—now in 1909—that the Filipinos should govern themselves (15:538–39).

46. Woodrow Wilson, "First Inaugural Address," in *Political Thought of Woodrow Wilson*, 198, 200.

47. Wilson, "Second Inaugural Address," in *Political Thought of Woodrow Wilson*, 308.

48. Ibid., 308–9. Note the more contemporary and less racial connotation of Wilson's use of the term *nation*.

49. Wilson, "Address to Congress, April 2nd, 1917," in *Political Thought of Woodrow Wilson*, 340.

50. Ibid., 346. Now having heard a litany of similar expressions, one is left with the suspicion that these figures doth protest too much.

51. Ibid., 348.

52. As Richard M. Gamble has noted,

> While progressive Christianity's skill at reconstructing institutions would become clear as it tackled first the church, then American society, and ultimately international affairs, its theology was grounded in a few elemental assumptions about the way the world worked. First among these assumptions was a belief in inherent, inevitable spiritual progress, in the gradual tendency of the physical universe and of human history toward the good, a process that determined the manner in which God achieved His will. For the progressives, the world was in motion. *But this was not a random or inscrutable movement. Creation, humanity, and history were not merely changing; they were changing in a clear direction, toward a knowable goal, toward nothing less than the kingdom of God on earth.* This idea of purposeful, teleological change dominated the intellectual world of the late nineteenth century. The law of evolution that was thought to control the natural world was presumed to direct the spiritual world as well. (Gamble, *War for Righteousness*, 30–31; emphasis added)

53. Robert Nisbet seems to make just the same point, though from the middle of the twentieth century:

> The single most powerful cause of the present size and the world-wide deployment of the military establishment is the moralization of foreign policy and military ventures that has been deeply ingrained, especially in the minds of presidents, for a long time. Although it was Woodrow Wilson who, by virtue of a charismatic presence and a boundless moral fervor, gave firm and lasting foundation to American moralism, it was not unknown earlier in our history. The staying power of the Puritan image of America as a "city upon a hill" was considerable throughout the eighteenth and nineteenth centuries. America the Redeemer Nation was very much a presence in the minds of a great many Americans. American "exceptionalism" began in the conviction that God had created one truly free and democratic nation on earth and that it was to the best interests of all other nations to study America and learn from her.

He goes on, a little later, "Ever since Wilson, with only rarest exceptions, American foreign policy has been tuned not to national interest but to national morality." Nisbet, *Present Age*, 29–30.

54. Woodrow Wilson, quoted in Steel, *Pax Americana*, 3.

55. Ibid., 308. Steel believes this transition happened finally with the massive industrialization and mobilization associated with the Second World War. But there is room for doubt that Steel is right about its timing; I have already shown that the theoretical differences between the traditional American understanding and an imperial one are palpable in the wake of the Spanish-American War.

Godfrey Hodgson puts it this way, though he too puts the transition later than I have: "It was not until the twentieth century that this combination of exceptionalism with at least a theoretical universalism—a belief, that is, that the United States has a special destiny to bring freedom to the Americas, brought to bear on the idea that the United States could be an example of freedom to the world—began to take the characteristics of a program." Hodgson, *Myth of American Exceptionalism*, 182.

56. Just as with Lincoln, the theological roots of these claims, while interesting and important, are not directly relevant to the point being made here. Thus I only acknowledge, while passing over it, that this aspect of my account could bear more detail, though as part of a decidedly different project.

57. David H. Burton argues that "[i]n matters of state his mind simply did not operate on a theoretical plane." Burton, *Theodore Roosevelt*, 62.

58. *Congressional Record* 33 (January 15, 1900): 806.

59. John Quincy Adams, address in Washington, D.C., July 4, 1821, quoted in Steel, *Pax Americana*, xi.

60. *Congressional Record* 33 (February 20, 1900): 1971.

Conclusion: The Possibility of a New and Traditional American Political Order

1. Beveridge, "Our Philippine Policy," 72.

2. Dobson, *Reticent Expansionism*, 110–11.

3. Roosevelt, "First Annual Message," 15:111.

4. Tocqueville, *Democracy in America*, ed. Nolla, 2:490, 493–94.

5. Tate, "Remarks on the Southern Religion," 155–75. I have in mind here just the sort of damaging undertaking Tate indicates, admonishing Southerners both to avoid it and to do it. They should avoid it, he seems to say, because this sort of explication and exploration kills traditions. And if the "Southern tradition" still lives at all, then this sort of nontraditional traditionalism would kill it. But if the tradition is already dead, Tate seems to say near the end of the essay, the only available means for its preservation seems to be "boring from without," recovery by "violence."

Alasdair MacIntyre makes a similar point about traditions in speaking about Edmund Burke: "Traditions, when vital, embody continuities of conflict. Indeed when a tradition becomes Burkean, it is always dying or dead." MacIntyre, *After Virtue*, 222.

BIBLIOGRAPHY

Alfonso, Oscar M. *Theodore Roosevelt and the Philippines, 1897–1909*. Quezon City: University of the Philippines Press, 1970.

Allen, Barbara. *Tocqueville, Covenant, and the Democratic Revolution: Harmonizing Earth with Heaven*. Lanham, Md.: Lexington Books, 2005.

Aristotle. *Metaphysics*. Translated by W. D. Ross. In *The Basic Works of Aristotle*, edited by Richard McKeon, 681–926. New York: Random House, 1941.

———. *Politics*. Translated by Benjamin Jowett. In *The Basic Works of Aristotle*, edited by Richard McKeon, 1113–316. New York: Random House, 1941.

Armitage, David. *The Declaration of Independence: A Global History*. Cambridge, Mass.: Harvard University Press, 2007.

Bacevich, A. J. *The Limits of Power: The End of American Exceptionalism*. New York: Metropolitan Books, 2008.

Bailyn, Bernard. "The Challenge of Modern Historiography." *American Historical Review* 87, no. 1 (February 1982): 1–24.

———. *The Ideological Origins of the American Revolution*. Cambridge, Mass.: Harvard University Press, 1967.

Baker, Jean H. "Lincoln's Narrative of American Exceptionalism." In *"We Cannot Escape History": Lincoln and the Last Best Hope of Earth*, edited by James M. McPherson, 33–44. Urbana: University of Illinois Press, 1995.

Baldwin, Summerfield. "God and the Secular Power." In *Essays in History and Political Theory: In Honor of Charles Howard McIlwain*, 3–36. New York: Russell and Russell, 1936.

Baritz, Loren. *City on a Hill: A History of Ideas and Myths in America*. New York: John Wiley and Sons, 1964.

Becker, Carl. *The Declaration of Independence: A Study in the History of Political Ideas*. New York: Harcourt Brace, 1922. Reprint, New York: Vintage Books, 1970.

Bellah, Robert Neely. *The Broken Covenant: American Civil Religion in a Time of Trial*. 2nd ed. Chicago: University of Chicago Press, 1992.

———. "Civil Religion in America." In *The Robert Bellah Reader*, edited by Robert N. Bellah and Steven M. Tipton, 225–45. Durham, N.C.: Duke University Press, 2006.

———. "Religious Evolution." *American Sociological Review* 29, no. 3 (June 1964): 358–74.

Bell, Daniel. "The 'Hegelian Secret.'" In *Is America Different? A New Look at American Exceptionalism*, edited by Byron E. Shafer, 46–70. Oxford: Oxford University Press, 1991.

Bercovitch, Sacvan. *The American Jeremiad*. Madison: University of Wisconsin Press, 1978.

———. *The Puritan Origins of the American Self*. New Haven, Conn.: Yale University Press, 1975.

Berman, Joshua A. "God's Alliance with Man." *Azure*, no. 25 (Summer 5766 / 2006): 79–113.

Berry, Wendell. "Nature as Measure." In *What Are People For?*, 204–10. New York: North Point Press, 1990.

Beveridge, Albert J. "Our Philippine Policy." In *The Meaning of the Times*, 58–88. Indianapolis: Bobbs-Merrill, 1908.

Boorstin, Daniel. *The Genius of American Politics*. Chicago: University of Chicago Press, 1953.

Bowers, Claude. *Beveridge and the Progressive Era*. Boston: Houghton-Mifflin, 1932.

Bradford, M. E. *A Better Guide than Reason: Studies in the American Revolution*. La Salle, Ill.: Sherwood Sugden, 1979.

———. "The Heresy of Equality: A Reply to Harry Jaffa." In *Lincoln's American Dream: Clashing Political Perspectives*, edited by Kenneth L. Deutsch and Joseph Fornieri, 98–115. Washington, D.C.: Potomac Books, 2005.

———. *Original Intentions: On the Making and Ratification of the United States Constitution*. Athens: University of Georgia Press, 1993.

Brands, H. W. *Bound to Empire: The United States and the Philippines*. Oxford: Oxford University Press, 1992.

———. *What America Owes the World: The Struggle for the Soul of Foreign Policy*. Cambridge: Cambridge University Press, 1998.

Bremer, Francis J. *John Winthrop: America's Forgotten Founding Father*. Oxford: Oxford University Press, 2003.

———. *The Puritan Experiment: New England Society from Bradford to Edwards*. Hanover, N.H.: University Press of New England, 1995.

Bremer, Francis J., and Lynn A. Botelho, eds. *The World of John Winthrop: Essays on England and New England, 1588–1649*. Boston: Massachusetts Historical Society, 2005.

Buckley, Thomas E., S.J. "The Use and Abuse of Jefferson's Statute: Separating Church and State in Nineteenth Century Virginia." In *Religion and the New Republic*, edited by James H. Hutson, 41–63. Lanham, Md.: Rowman and Littlefield, 2000.

Burton, David H. *Theodore Roosevelt: Confident Imperialist*. Philadelphia: University of Pennsylvania Press, 1969.

Butler, Jon. "Why Revolutionary America Wasn't a 'Christian Nation.'" In *Religion and the New Republic*, edited by James H. Hutson, 187–202. Lanham, Md.: Rowman and Littlefield, 2000.

Carey, George W. "The Constitution and Community." In *Community and Tradition: Conservative Perspectives on the American Experience*, edited by George W. Carey and Bruce Frohnen, 63–84. Lanham, Md.: Rowman and Littlefield, 1998.

Ceaser, James. *Nature and History in American Political Development: A Debate.* Cambridge, Mass.: Harvard University Press, 2006.

Chesterton, G. K. *What I Saw in America.* London: Hodder and Stoughton, 1922.

Colburn, H. Trevor. *The Lamp of Experience: Whig History and the Intellectual Origins of the American Revolution.* Chapel Hill: University of North Carolina Press, 1965.

Croly, Herbert David. *The Promise of American Life.* Cambridge, Mass.: Belknap Press of Harvard University Press, 1965.

Davis, Thomas M. "The Exegetical Traditions of Puritan Typology." *Early American Literature* 5, no. 1 (Spring 1970): 11–50.

Dawson, Hugh J. "'Christian Charitie' as Colonial Discourse: Rereading Winthrop's Sermon in Its English Context." *Early American Literature* 33, no. 2 (1998): 117–48.

Deglar, Carl. "In Pursuit of an American History." *American Historical Review* 92, no. 1 (February 1987): 1–12.

Delmage, Rutherford E. "The American Idea of Progress, 1750–1800." *Proceedings of the American Philosophical Society* 91, no. 4 (October 24, 1947): 307–14.

Detweiler, Philip F. "The Changing Reputation of the Declaration of Independence: The First Fifty Years." *William and Mary Quarterly*, 3rd ser. 19, no. 4 (October 1962): 557–74.

———. Review of *The Basic Symbols of the American Political Tradition*, by Willmoore Kendall and George W. Carey. *Journal of Southern History* 37, no. 2 (May 1971): 283–84.

Diamond, Martin. *As Far as Republican Principles Will Admit.* Edited by William A. Schambra. Washington, D.C.: AEI Press, 1992.

Diggins, John Patrick. *The Lost Soul of American Politics: Virtue, Self-Interest, and the Foundations of Liberalism.* Chicago: University of Chicago Press, 1984.

———. *On Hallowed Ground: Abraham Lincoln and the Foundations of American History.* New Haven, Conn.: Yale University Press, 2000.

DiLorenzo, Thomas J. *The Real Lincoln: A New Look at Abraham Lincoln, His Agenda, and an Unnecessary War.* Roseville, Calif.: Prima, 2002.

Dobson, John M. *Reticent Expansionism: The Foreign Policy of William McKinley.* Pittsburgh: Duquesne University Press, 1988.

Donald, David Herbert. *Lincoln.* New York: Touchstone Books, 1995.

Doyle, Michael W. *Empires.* Ithaca, N.Y.: Cornell University Press, 1986.

Driesbach, Daniel. "Thomas Jefferson, a Mammoth Cheese, and the 'Wall of Separation between Church and State.'" In *Religion and the New Republic*, edited by James H. Hutson, 65–114. Lanham, Md.: Rowman and Littlefield, 2000.

Engeman, Thomas, and Michael Zuckert, eds. *Protestantism and the American Founding.* South Bend, Ind.: University of Notre Dame Press, 2004.

The Federalist. Indianapolis: Liberty Fund, 2002.

Fehrenbacher, Don E. "Lincoln and the Constitution." In *Lincoln in Text and Context*, 113–28. Stanford, Calif.: Stanford University Press, 1987.

Ferguson, Niall. *Colossus: The Price of America's Empire*. New York: Penguin Press, 2004.

Ferrie, Joseph P. "History Lessons: The End of American Exceptionalism? Mobility in the United States since 1850." *Journal of Economic Perspectives* 19, no. 3 (Summer 2005): 199–215.

Fletcher, George D. *Our Secret Constitution: How Lincoln Redefined American Democracy*. Oxford: Oxford University Press, 2001.

Foner, Eric. "Why Is There No Socialism in the United States?" *History Workshop* 17 (Spring 1984): 57–80.

Fukuyama, Francis. *America at the Crossroads: Democracy, Power, and the Neoconservative Legacy*. New Haven, Conn.: Yale University Press, 2007.

Gamble, Richard M. *In Search of the City on a Hill: The Making and Unmaking of an American Myth*. London: Continuum Books, 2012.

———. *The War for Righteousness: Progressive Christianity, the Great War, and the Rise of the Messianic Nation*. Wilmington, Del.: ISI Books, 2003.

Gans, John A., Jr. "American Exceptionalism and the Politics of Foreign Policy." *Atlantic Online*. November 21, 2011. Accessed January 6, 2012. http://www.theatlantic.com/international/archive/2011/11/american-exceptionalism-and-the-politics-of-foreign-policy/248779/.

Gardner, E. Clinton. "Justice in the Puritan Covenantal Tradition." *Journal of Law and Religion* 6, no. 1 (1988): 39–60.

Gelernter, David. *Americanism: The Fourth Great Western Religion*. New York: Doubleday, 2007.

The Geneva Bible: A Facsimile of the 1560 Edition. With an Introduction by Lloyd E. Berry. Madison: University of Wisconsin Press, 1969.

Gerber, Larry G. "Shifting Perspectives on American Exceptionalism: Recent Literature on American Labor Relations and Labor Politics." *Journal of American Studies* 31, no. 2 (August 1997): 253–74.

Glaser, Elisabeth, and Hermann Wellenreuther, eds. *Bridging the Atlantic: The Question of American Exceptionalism in Perspective*. Washington, D.C.: German Historical Institute; Cambridge: Cambridge University Press, 2002.

Guelzo, Allen C. *Abraham Lincoln: Redeemer President*. Grand Rapids, Mich.: William B. Eerdmans, 1999.

Guétin, Nicole. *Religious Ideology in American Politics: A History*. Jefferson, N.C.: McFarland, 2009.

Gutfeld, Arnon. *American Exceptionalism: The Effects of Plenty on the American Experience*. Brighton, U.K.: Sussex Academic Press, 2002.

Hadari, Saguiv A. *Theory in Practice: Tocqueville's New Science of Politics*. Stanford, Calif.: Stanford University Press, 1989.

Halpern, Rick, and Jonathan Morris, eds. *American Exceptionalism?: U.S. Working-Class Formation in an International Context*. New York: St. Martin's Press, 1997.

Hamburger, Philip A. "Natural Rights, Natural Law, and American Constitutions." *Yale Law Journal* 102, no. 4 (January 1993): 907–60.

Hardt, Michael, and Antonio Negri. *Empire*. Cambridge, Mass.: Harvard University Press, 2000.

Hartz, Louis. *The Liberal Tradition in America*. New York: Harcourt Brace, 1955.

Havers, Grant N. *Lincoln and the Politics of Christian Love*. Columbia: University of Missouri Press, 2009.

Heffer, Jean, and Jeanine Rovet, eds. *Why Is There No Socialism in the United States?* Paris: L'École des Hautes Études en Sciences Sociales, 1988.

Heimert, Alan. *Religion and the American Mind from the Great Awakening to the Revolution*. Cambridge, Mass.: Harvard University Press, 1966.

Hietala, Thomas R. *Manifest Design: American Exceptionalism and Empire*. Ithaca, N.Y.: Cornell University Press, 2003.

Hodgson, Godfrey. *The Myth of American Exceptionalism*. New Haven, Conn.: Yale University Press, 2009.

Hofstadter, Richard. "Cuba, the Philippines, and Manifest Destiny." In *The Paranoid Style in American Politics and Other Essays*, 145–87. New York: Alfred A. Knopf, 1965.

Hoskins, Richard J. "The Original Separation of Church and State in America." *Journal of Law and Religion* 2, no. 2 (1984): 221–39.

Huntington, Samuel. *American Politics: The Promise of Disharmony*. Cambridge, Mass.: Harvard University Press, 1981.

Hutson, James H. "'A Future State of Rewards and Punishment': The Founders' Formula for the Social and Political Utility of Religion." In *Forgotten Features of the Founding*, edited by James H. Hutson, 1–44. Lanham, Md.: Lexington Books, 2003.

Hyneman, Charles S., and Donald S. Lutz, eds. *American Political Writing during the Founding Era, 1760–1805*. 2 vols. Indianapolis: Liberty Fund, 1983.

Jaffa, Harry V. *Crisis of the House Divided: An Interpretation of the Lincoln-Douglas Debates*. 50th Anniversary ed. Chicago: University of Chicago Press, 2009.

———. *A New Birth of Freedom: Abraham Lincoln and the Coming of the Civil War*. Lanham, Md.: Rowman and Littlefield, 2000.

Jayne, Allen. *Lincoln and the American Manifesto*. Amherst, N.Y.: Prometheus Books, 2007.

Jensen, Merrill. "The American People and the American Revolution." *Journal of American History* 57, no. 1 (June 1970): 5–35.

Journals of Congress: Containing their Proceedings from September 5, 1774, to January 1, 1776. Philadelphia: Folwell's Press, 1800.

Kagan, Robert. *Dangerous Nation: America's Place in the World from Its Earliest Days to the Dawn of the 20th Century*. New York: Alfred A. Knopf, 2006.

———. *Of Paradise and Power: America and Europe in the New World Order*. New York: Vintage Books, 2004.

Kammen, Michael. "The Problem of American Exceptionalism: A Reconsideration." *American Quarterly* 45, no. 1 (March 1993): 1–43.

Karr, Ronald Dale. "The Missing Clause: Myth and the Massachusetts Bay Charter of 1629." *New England Quarterly* 77, no. 1 (March 2004): 89–107.

Katznelson, Ira. "Working-Class Formation and the State: Nineteenth-Century England in American Perspective." In *Bringing the State Back In*, edited by Peter B. Evans, Dietrich Rueschemeyer, and Theda Skocpol, 257–84. New York: Cambridge University Press, 1985.

Kendall, Willmoore. "Equality: Commitment or Ideal." In *Lincoln's American Dream: Clashing Political Perspectives*, edited by Kenneth L. Deutsch and Joseph Fornieri, 60–71. Washington, D.C.: Potomac Books, 2005.

Kendall, Willmoore, and George Carey. *The Basic Symbols of the American Political Tradition*. Washington, D.C.: Catholic University of America Press, 1995.

Kirk, Russell. *The Roots of American Order*. La Salle, Ill.: Open Court, 1974.

Klehr, Harvey. "Marxist Theory in Search of America." *Journal of Politics* 35, no. 2 (May 1973): 311–31.

Kohut, Andrew. *America against the World: How We Are Different and Why We Are Disliked*. New York: Times Books, 2006.

Koritansky, John C. *Alexis de Tocqueville and the New Science of Politics: An Interpretation of Democracy in America*. Durham, N.C.: Carolina Academic Press, 1986.

Krislov, Samuel. "American Federalism as American Exceptionalism." *Publius* 31, no. 1 (Winter 2001): 9–26.

Lake, David. "Is America Exceptional? Liberals, Conservatives Agree—and Disagree." CNN Online. December 2, 2011. Accessed January 6, 2012. http://www.cnn.com/2011/12/02/opinion/lake-america-exceptional/?hpt=hp_c3.

Levinson, Sanford. *Constitutional Faith*. Princeton, N.J.: Princeton University Press, 1988.

Lincoln, Abraham. *His Speeches and Writings*. Edited by Roy P. Basler. Cleveland: World, 1946.

Linn, Brian McAllister. *The Philippine War, 1899–1902*. Lawrence: University Press of Kansas, 2000.

Lipset, Seymour Martin. *American Exceptionalism: A Double-Edged Sword*. New York: W. W. Norton, 1997.

———. Review of *American Exceptionalism*, by Deborah L. Madsen. *Journal of American History* 87, no. 3 (December 2000): 1019.

Lipset, Seymour Martin, and Gary Marks. *It Didn't Happen Here: Why Socialism Failed in the United States*. New York: W. W. Norton, 2001.

Litke, Justin B. "Varieties of American Exceptionalism: Why John Winthrop Is No Imperialist." *Journal of Church and State* 54, no. 2 (Spring 2012): 197–213.

Lockhart, Charles. *The Roots of American Exceptionalism: History, Institutions and Culture*. New York: Palgrave Macmillan, 2003.

Lodge, Henry Cabot. *The Senate of the United States, and Other Essays and Addresses Historical and Literary*. New York: Charles Scribner's Sons, 1925.

Lovestone, Jay. "The Sixth World Congress of the Communist International." *Communist* 3, no. 11 (November 1928): 659–75.

Lutz, Donald. *The Origins of American Constitutionalism*. Baton Rouge: Louisiana State University Press, 1988.

MacIntyre, Alasdair. *After Virtue: A Study in Moral Theory*. 3rd ed. Notre Dame, Ind.: University of Notre Dame Press, 2007.

Madsen, Deborah. *American Exceptionalism*. Jackson: University Press of Mississippi, 1998.

Maier, Pauline. *American Scripture*. New York: Alfred A. Knopf, 1997.

May, Ernest R. *"Lessons" of the Past: The Use and Misuse of History in American Foreign Policy*. London: Oxford University Press, 1973.

McClellan, James. *Liberty, Order, and Justice*. Washington, D.C.: Center for Judicial Studies, 1989.

McDonald, Forrest. *Novus Ordo Seclorum: The Economic Origins of the Constitution*. Lawrence: University Press of Kansas, 1985.

McDonald, Robert M. S. "Thomas Jefferson's Changing Reputation as Author of the Declaration of Independence: The First Fifty Years." *Journal of the Early Republic* 19, no. 2 (Summer 1999): 169–95.

McDougall, Walter A. *Promised Land, Crusader State: The American Encounter with the World since 1776*. New York: Houghton Mifflin Harcourt, 1998.

McEvoy-Levy, Siobhan. *American Exceptionalism and U.S. Foreign Policy: Public Diplomacy at the End of the Cold War*. New York: Palgrave, 2001.

McPherson, James M. "Abraham Lincoln and the Second American Revolution." In *Abraham Lincoln and the American Political Tradition*, edited by John L. Thomas, 142–60. Amherst: University of Massachusetts Press, 1986.

Meinecke, Friedrich. *The German Catastrophe*. Translated by Sidney B. Fay. 1950. Reprint, Boston: Beacon Press, 1963.

Merk, Frederick. *Manifest Destiny and Mission in American History: A Reinterpretation*. New York: Alfred A Knopf, 1963.

Miller, Perry. *Errand into the Wilderness*. Cambridge, Mass.: Belknap Press of Harvard University Press, 1956.

Miller, Perry, and Thomas H. Johnson, eds. *The Puritans*. New York: American Book, 1938.

Miller, William Lee. "Lincoln's Second Inaugural: The Zenith of Statecraft." In *Lincoln's American Dream: Clashing Political Perspectives*, edited by Kenneth L. Deutsch and Joseph Fornieri, 333–50. Washington, D.C.: Potomac Books, 2005.

Mitchell, Joshua. "Protestant Thought and Republican Spirit: How Luther Enchanted the World." *American Political Science Review* 86, no. 3 (September 1992): 688–95.

Morgan, Edmund. "John Winthrop's 'Modell of Christian Charity' in a Wider Context." *Huntington Library Quarterly* 50, no. 2 (Spring 1987): 145–51.

Morone, James A. *Hellfire Nation: The Politics of Sin in American History*. New Haven, Conn.: Yale University Press, 2003.

Nelles, H. V. "American Exceptionalism: A Double-Edged Sword" (review essay). *American Historical Review* 102, no. 3 (June 1997): 749–57.

Nexon, Daniel H., and Thomas Wright. "What's at Stake in the American Empire Debate." *American Political Science Review* 101, no. 2 (May 2007): 253–71.

Niebuhr, Reinhold. *The Irony of American History*. Chicago: University of Chicago Press, 2008.

———. "The Religion of Abraham Lincoln." In *Lincoln's American Dream: Clashing Political Perspectives*, edited by Kenneth L. Deutsch and Joseph Fornieri, 378–85. Washington, D.C.: Potomac Books, 2005.

Nietzsche, Friedrich. *On the Advantage and Disadvantage of History for Life*. Translated by Peter Preuss. Indianapolis: Hackett, 1980.

Nisbet, Robert. *The Present Age: Progress and Anarchy in Modern America*. Indianapolis: Liberty Fund, 1988.

Nolan, Mary. "Against Exceptionalisms." *American Historical Review* 102, no. 3 (June 1997): 769–74.

Noll, Mark A. *America's God: From Jonathan Edwards to Abraham Lincoln*. New York: Oxford University Press, 2002.

Oakeshott, Michael. "The Masses in Representative Democracy." In *Rationalism in Politics and Other Essays*, 363–83. New and expanded ed. Indianapolis: Liberty Fund, 1991.

Pease, Donald E. *The New American Exceptionalism*. Minneapolis: University of Minnesota Press, 2009.

Pelikan, Jaroslav. *The Vindication of Tradition*. New Haven, Conn.: Yale University Press, 1984.

Perlman, Selig. *A Theory of the Labor Movement*. New York: Macmillan, 1928.

Persons, Stow. "The Cyclical Theory of History in Eighteenth-Century America." *American Quarterly* 6, no. 2 (Summer 1954): 147–63.

Peterson, Merrill D. *Lincoln in American Memory*. Oxford: Oxford University Press, 1995.

Potter, David M. *People of Plenty: Economic Abundance and the American Character*. Chicago: University of Chicago Press, 1954.

"Republican Party Platform of 1856." June 18, 1856. In Gerhard Peters and John T. Woolley, *The American Presidency Project*. Accessed January 28, 2013. http://www.presidency.ucsb.edu/ws/?pid=29619.

Roosevelt, Theodore. *Works of Theodore Roosevelt*. 20 vols. National ed. New York: Scribner's Sons, 1926.

Rorty, Richard. *Achieving Our Country: Leftist Thought in Twentieth-Century America*. Cambridge, Mass.: Harvard University Press, 1998.

Ross, Dorothy. *The Origins of American Social Science*. New York: Cambridge University Press, 1991.

Sandel, Michael. *Democracy's Discontent: America in Search of a Public Philosophy*. Cambridge, Mass.: Harvard University Press, 1996.

Sandoz, Ellis. *A Government of Laws: Political Theory, Religion, and the Founding*. Baton Rouge: Louisiana State University Press, 1990.

———, ed. *Political Sermons of the Founding Era: 1730–1805*. Indianapolis: Liberty Fund, 1991.

Schuck, Peter H., and James Q. Wilson. *Understanding America: The Anatomy of an Exceptional Nation*. New York: Public Affairs, 2008.

Schweitzer, Ivy. "John Winthrop's 'Model' of American Affiliation." *Early American Literature* 40, no. 3 (2005): 441–69.

Shafer, Byron E. "'Exceptionalism' in American Politics?" *PS: Political Science and Politics* 22, no. 3 (September 1989): 588–94.

———, ed. *Is America Different? A New Look at American Exceptionalism*. Oxford: Oxford University Press, 1991.

Shain, Barry Alan. "Revolutionary-Era Americans: Were They Enlightened or Protestant? Does It Matter?" In *The Founders on God and Government*, ed. Daniel L. Driesbach, Mark D. Hall, and Jeffry H. Morrison, 273–98. Lanham, Md.: Rowman and Littlefield, 2004.

Sombart, Werner. *Why Is There No Socialism in the United States?* Edited with an introductory essay by C. T. Husbands. Translated by Patricia M. Hocking and C. T. Husbands. Foreword by Michael Harrington. White Plains, N.Y.: International Arts and Sciences Press, 1976.

Spanos, William V. *American Exceptionalism in the Age of Globalization: The Specter of Vietnam*. Albany: State University of New York Press, 2008.

Steel, Ronald. *Pax Americana*. New, rev. ed. New York: Viking Press, 1970.

Stoner, James Reist. *Common Law and Liberal Theory: Coke, Hobbes, and the Origins of American Constitutionalism*. Lawrence: University Press of Kansas, 1992.

———. "Is There a Political Philosophy in the Declaration of Independence?" *Intercollegiate Review* 40, no. 2 (Fall/Winter 2005): 3–11.

Storey, Moorfield, and Marcial P. Lichauco. *The Conquest of the Philippines by the United States, 1898–1925*. New York: G. P. Putnam's Sons, 1926.

Strauss, Leo. "What Is Liberal Education?" In *Liberalism Ancient and Modern*, 3–8. New York: Basic Books, 1968.

Tate, Allan. "Remarks on the Southern Religion." In *I'll Take My Stand*, 155–75. 75th Anniversary ed. Baton Rouge: Louisiana State University Press, 2006.

Thurow, Glen E. *Abraham Lincoln and American Civil Religion*. Albany: State University of New York Press, 1976.

———. "The Gettysburg Address and the Declaration of Independence." In *Abraham Lincoln, the Gettysburg Address, and American Constitutionalism*, edited by Leo Paul S. de Alvarez, 55–76. Irving, Tex.: University of Dallas Press, 1976.

Tiryakian, Edward A. "American Religious Exceptionalism: A Reconsideration." *Annals of the American Academy of Political and Social Science* 527 (May 1993): 40–54.

Tocqueville, Alexis de. *De la démocratie en Amérique*. Paris: Gallimard, 1951.

———. *Democracy in America*. 2 vols. Edited by Henry Reeve. New York: Alfred A. Knopf, 1945.

———. *Democracy in America*. Edited by J.P Mayer. Translated by George Lawrence. New York: HarperCollins, 1969.

———. *Democracy in America*. Edited and translated by Harvey C. Mansfield and Delba Winthrop. Chicago: University of Chicago Press, 2000.

———. *Democracy in America*. Edited by Eduardo Nolla. Translated by James T. Schleifer. Bilingual French-English ed. 4 vols. Indianapolis: Liberty Fund, 2009.

"Treaty of Peace between the United States and Spain; December 10, 1898." Avalon Project. Yale University. Accessed March 29, 2010. http://avalon.law.yale.edu/19th_century/sp1898.asp.

Turner, Frederick Jackson. "The Significance of the Frontier in American History" [1893]. In *The Frontier in American History*, 1–38. New York: Dover, 2010.

Tuveson, Ernest Lee. *Redeemer Nation: The Idea of America's Millennial Role*. Chicago: University of Chicago Press, 1980.

Tyrrell, Ian. "American Exceptionalism in an Age of International History." *American Historical Review* 96 (October 1991): 1031–72.

Voegelin, Eric. *The New Science of Politics: An Introduction*. Chicago: University of Chicago Press, 1987.

———. *Order and History*. Vol. 1, *Israel and Revelation*. Baton Rouge: Louisiana State University Press, 1956.

Voss, Kim. *The Making of American Exceptionalism: The Knights of Labor and Class Formation in the Nineteenth Century*. Ithaca, N.Y.: Cornell University Press, 1993.

Vowell, Sarah. *The Wordy Shipmates*. New York: Riverhead Books, 2008.

Washington, George. *Writings*. New York: Library of America, 1997.

Weber, Max. *The Protestant Ethic and the Spirit of Capitalism*. Translated by Talcott Parsons. Mineola, N.Y.: Dover, 2003.

Weiner, Gregory. "Madison's Metronome: The Constitution and the Tempo of American Politics." PhD diss., Georgetown University, 2010.

Wettergreen, John A. Review of *The Basic Symbols of the American Political Tradition*, by Willmoore Kendall and George W. Carey. *American Political Science Review* 66, no. 2 (June 1972): 617–18.

White House, Office of the Press Secretary. "News Conference by President Obama, Palaiz de la Musique et Des Congres, Strasbourg, France." Press release, April 4, 2009. Accessed April 28, 2009. http://www.whitehouse.gov/the_press_office/News-Conference-By-President-Obama-4-04-2009/.

Wilentz, Sean. "Against Exceptionalism: Class Consciousness and the American Labor Movement, 1790–1920." *International Labor and Working Class History* 26 (Fall 1984): 1–24.

Wills, Garry. *Lincoln at Gettysburg: The Words that Remade America*. New York: Simon and Schuster, 1992.

Wilson, Woodrow. *The Political Thought of Woodrow Wilson.* Edited by E. David Cronon. Indianapolis: Bobbs-Merrill, 1965.

Winger, Stewart. *Lincoln, Religion, and Romantic Cultural Politics.* DeKalb: Northern Illinois University Press, 2003.

Winthrop, John. *The Journal of John Winthrop, 1630–1649.* Edited by Richard Dunn and Laetitia Yaendle. Cambridge, Mass.: Belknap Press of Harvard University Press, 1996.

Winthrop, John, et al. *Winthrop Papers.* 6 vols. Edited by Worthington C. Ford, Stewart Mitchell, Allyn Bailey Forbes, and Malcolm Freiberg. Boston: Massachusetts Historical Society, 1929–92.

Wolf, William. *The Almost Chosen People: A Study of the Religion of Abraham Lincoln.* Garden City, N.Y.: Doubleday and Company, Inc., 1959.

Wrobel, David M. *The End of American Exceptionalism: Frontier Anxiety from the Old West to the New Deal.* Lawrence: University Press of Kansas, 1993.

Zuckert, Michael P. "Natural Rights and Protestant Politics." In *Protestantism and the American Founding,* edited by Thomas S. Engeman and Michael P. Zuckert, 21–75. Notre Dame, Ind.: University of Notre Dame Press, 2004.

———. "Self-Evident Truth and the Declaration of Independence." *Review of Politics* 49, no. 3 (Summer 1987): 319–39.

Index

Abraham (Old Testament patriarch), 45
Adams, John, 59
Adams, John Quincy, 139–40
Aguinaldo, Emilio, 121
America: as an idea, 102–3, 113, 136–37, 140–41; as "last best hope of earth," 90
American exceptionalism. *See* exceptionalism, American
American Exceptionalism: A Double-Edged Sword (Lipset), 10, 12
American order: framers' conception of, 54
American political tradition: the founders and, 142–43, 149; God's role in political order, 151; history's role in, 151–52; Jefferson and, 150; Lincoln and, 87–88, 142–43, 150; new and old political orders combined, 145–54; the Puritans and, 142–43; universality's role in, 152; usual account of, 150–51; Voegelin on, 151
Americans: as liberators, 147
annexation of the Philippines: economic arguments for, 123–24. *See also* Philippines, imperialism in
Arbella fleet, 29, 35
Aristotle, 112
Articles of Association (1774), 91–92, 94–95

Articles of Confederation and Perpetual Union (Articles of Confederation), 64–68, 74, 91–92, 95–96

Baritz, Loren, 28
Bellah, Robert, 46, 152
Bercovitch, Sacvan, 23, 30–31, 47
Beveridge, Albert, 115–43; on the Declaration of Independence, 126, 129; exceptionalism today, 141–43; the founders' relationship to, 139–41; imperialism and the Philippines, 122–32 (*see also* Philippines, imperialism in); joint resolution, purpose of, 122–23; McKinley's relationship to, 132; plurality in tradition, 117–18; the Puritans' relationship to, 137–39; Roosevelt's relationship to, 115, 131–35; separation of church and state, 140; Spanish-American War, 119–22; symbols of self-conception, 118; theoretical problem of derailed tradition, 115–19; unraveling of tradition, 116–18, 131, 141–43
Butler, Jon, 80

Calvin, John, 29
Carey, George: on the American tradition, 101–2; disregard of Winthrop, 25–26; on the *Federalist*, 69, 71–72; on the Fundamental Orders of

Carey, George *(cont.)*
Connecticut, 55–56; interpretive method of, 24; on the Massachusetts Body of Liberties, 56–58; on the Mayflower Compact, 112; on political philosophy, 15, 113; on political tradition, 88; on structure of documents, 40–44; on symbols generally, 15, 68, 116
chosenness: ambiguity of, 19, 46, 55, 107, 152
Christian truth: propagation of, 28–29
city on a hill, 23–24, 46–49
colonial period: political characterization of, 57
comparative exceptionalism, 8–13, 48
Congress, U.S., 119–22, 131–32
Constitution, U.S.: adoption of, 66–67; Beveridge on, 122–23, 126–27, 129–30, 140; the Declaration of Independence, relationship to, 59, 66; the *Federalist,* relationship to, 71–72, 74, 119; God's role/will in political order and, 69; historical context and significance, 69–70; interpretation of, 66; Lincoln on, 91, 93–94, 97, 111–13; overview, 66–69; positivistic interpretation of, 97; scope of, 67–69; self-conception in American political tradition, 15–17; separation of church and state, 57–58; symbols in, 67–68; unification of Americans and, 77; unity and, 67, 88. *See also* founders
Continental Congress, 65, 94–95. *See also* First Continental Congress; Second Continental Congress
covenant between God and man, 37–46; blessings and curses

of, 43–46, 48, 49; chosenness and, 19; parties to, 40–41, 54; purpose of, 41–42. *See also* "A Model of Christian Charity" (Winthrop)
covenant of political order, 54–55
Craddock, Matthew, 35
cultural exceptionalism, 9

Danforth, Samuel, 48
Declaration of Independence: as a distorted symbol, 117; Beveridge on, 126, 129; claims of, 62–63; the Constitution, relationship to, 59, 66; features of, 59–60; the *Federalist* on, 74, 119; Lincoln and, 87–88, 91–92, 95–97, 100–101, 113; as nonimperial, 148; origin/intention of, 59; overview, 58–64; on the right to revolution, 96–97; principles/interpretation of, 60–62; self-conception in the American political tradition and, 15–17; theory of history, 63–64; universalization of, 121
democracy: promotion as a symbol, 148
Democracy in America (Tocqueville), 9, 10–11
Democratic Party, 145
derailed tradition: defined, 16; vs. differentiation, 55–58, 80–82; the Gettysburg Address and conception of America as, 72, 99–105, 112; Lincoln's conception of America as, 87, 108–13, 119, 126; theoretical problem of, 115–19
differentiation, 55–57, 62, 72
Dobson, John M., 132

education, 148–49, 153
exceptionalism, American: causes underlying, 5–6; city on a hill and, 23–24, 46–49; comparative sense of, 8–12, 13; elements of, 18–21; the *Federalist* on, 9, 70–72; the founders and, 82–83; Lincoln and, 85–90; Marxist theories of history and, 7–8, 47; opponents of/contrasting views of, 5; political theory and, 14–18; religious ties to, 9, 18–20; scholarship on, 6, 7, 13–14; Shafer on, 12–14; social science on, 12–14; term usage, 5–8, 10–14; theories of history, relationship to, 7–8, 46–47; today, 141–43; "unique" sense of, 9–13; Winthrop as father of, 9, 85–86
exemplary exceptionalism, 9, 18–20, 23–24, 49–51, 53–54, 118, 141
expansionism: vs. imperialism, 138–39

Farewell Address (Washington), 79
Federalist (Federalist Papers), 69–75; on the Articles of Confederation, 74; the Constitution, relationship to, 71–72, 74, 119; exceptionalism and, 9, 70–72; on the Declaration of Independence, 74, 119; God's role/will in political order and, 73–75; Lincoln and, 102–3; persuasion in, 71; possibilities in politics and, 72–73; symbol in American tradition, 71–72, 113; unification of Americans and, 76–78
Federalist-Constitution, 113
Ferguson, Niall, 126
First Continental Congress, 92. *See also* Continental Congress

Fletcher, George D., 87
founders: Articles of the Confederation, 64–68; characterization of, 82–83; conception of American order, 54; the Constitution and, 66–69; covenant of political order, 54–55; the Declaration of Independence and, 58–64, 66; derailment vs. differentiation, 55–58, 80–82; exceptionalism and, 82–83; Fundamental Orders of Connecticut, 57, 62; God's role/will in political order, 54, 56, 81; later claims of exceptionalism and, 82–83; Massachusetts Body of Liberties, 55–56, 57, 58, 62; Mayflower Compact, 55–56, 60, 62; political characterization of colonial period, 57; political tradition analysis, 142–43, 149; relationship to Beveridge, 139–41; scholarship on, 53; self-conception of American people, 75–76; separation of church and state, 78–80, 108–9; symbols of, 55–56, 57; unity of representative assembly, 57, 86; universality in politics, 78–79
Fourth of July oration (Adams), 139–40
Foxe, John, 30
framers. *See* founders
Franklin, Benjamin, 59
Fundamental Orders of Connecticut (1639), 25, 27, 35, 54–57, 62

Geneva Bible, 49
Gettysburg Address (Lincoln), 72, 99–105, 108

God's role/will in political order:
Beveridge on, 127–28, 130–31,
137–39; the Constitution on, 69;
the Declaration of Independence
and, 64; exceptionalism and,
19–20; the *Federalist* on, 73–75;
the founders and, 54, 56, 81;
Lincoln and, 20, 99, 103–4, 106–
10; political tradition analysis,
151; the Puritans and, 26–27, 76;
Winthrop and, 32–33, 39–40, 55,
80, 108
Goethe, 149
Golden Rule, 134
Great Society, 145

Hamburger, Philip, 97
Hamilton, Alexander, 69
Hartz, Louis, 7
Hearst, William Randolph, 120
historical judgment, 16
history, theories of: Beveridge on, 127–
31; the Constitution and, 69–70;
Declaration of Independence,
63–64; judgments of history, 16;
Lincoln and, 109–10; Marxist
theories, 7–8, 47; role in political
tradition, 151–52; Winthrop and,
46–47, 69, 108–9
Hodgson, Godfrey, 70
Hutson, James, 58

imperial exceptionalism, 10, 20–21, 36,
81–83, 113, 118–19, 141, 146
imperialism: in presidency as
well as Congress, 131–35; vs.
expansionism, 138–39. *See also*
Philippines, imperialism in
Intolerable Acts, 94
Iraq War, 146–48
Is America Different?: A New Look at

American Exceptionalism (Shafer,
ed.), 12–14

Jefferson, Thomas, 59, 94, 101, 150
Jesus, 48–49
judgment, historical, 16

Kendall, Willmoore: on the
American tradition, 101–2;
disregard of Winthrop, 25–26;
on the *Federalist*, 71–72; on
the Fundamental Orders of
Connecticut, 55–56; interpretive
method of, 24; on the
Massachusetts Body of Liberties,
56–58; on the Mayflower
Compact signers, 112; on
political philosophy, 15, 113; on
political tradition, 88; structure of
documents, 40–44; on symbols,
15, 68, 116
Kenney, Richard, 142, 145

Lee, Robert E., 89
legislative supremacy: in the
Massachusetts Body of Liberties,
55–56
liberal education, 153
Lincoln, Abraham, 85–113;
American exceptionalism and,
85–90; conception of America as
derailment, 87, 108–13, 119, 126;
conception of America as an idea,
113, 140–41; the Constitution and,
91, 93–94, 97, 111–12, 113; the
Declaration of Independence and,
87–88, 91–92, 95–97, 100–101,
113, 117, 121; the *Federalist* and,
102–3; first inaugural address,
90–99, 111, 112; the Gettysburg
Address, 72, 99–105, 108; God's

role/will in political order, 20, 99, 103–4, 108–10; political aims, 89; in political tradition, 87–88, 142–43, 150; positivistic interpretation of the Constitution, 97; on reconciliation of North and South, 106–7; Roosevelt on, 134; secession and, 91–98, 100, 112; second inaugural address, 105–8, 151; symbols in American tradition and, 102, 112, 131, 140; the Union's relationship to the government and, 91–95, 97–98; unity and, 102; universality of, 99, 104–5; use of "United States" as a singular noun, 104
Lipset, Seymour Martin, 10–12, 14
Locke, John, 15, 101
Luther, Martin, 29, 30

Maier, Pauline, 59
Maine, USS, 119
Mao Zedong, 151
Marxist theories of history, 7–8, 47
Massachusetts Bay Colony. *See* Puritans
Massachusetts Body of Liberties (1641), 25, 27, 35–36, 55–58, 62
Mather, Cotton, 30
Matthew (New Testament), 48
Mayflower Compact (1620): continuity between Fundamental Orders of Connecticut and, 35; derailment vs. differentiation, 55–56; differentiation and, 17, 62; purpose/reflection of, 27; symbol in American tradition, 15, 24; as a uniting document, 60
McKinley, William, 120, 131–32, 135
Micah (Old Testament), 43–44
Miller, Perry, 28, 50–51

Miller, William Lee, 90, 105
Milton, John, 30
"Model of Christian Charity, A" (Winthrop), 35–47; application of principles and arguments of, 40–46; covenant between God and man, 37–46, 54 (*see also* covenant between God and man); God's role/will in political order, 39–40, 55; imperial exceptionalism, 36; love relationship in, 39–40, 39–43, 42, 43; mercy in, 37–38, 43; objections to, 37–38; Progressive Era, 36; on the purpose of leaving England, 41; Shafer on, 13; support of the government, 40–41, 40–42; as a symbol in political order, 18, 24; unity in, 36–40, 42–44, 55, 60, 62, 76–78
Monroe Doctrine, 133–35
Montesquieu (Charles-Louis de Sacondat, Baron de La Brède et de Montesquieu), 15
myth and political theory, 15, 18

Nehemiah (Old Testament figure), 38–39
neoconservatives, 146, 148, 152–53
New Deal, 145
New Science of Politics, The (Voegelin), 25
Niebuhr, Reinhold, 89
Nonseparatism, 26, 30

Obama, Barack, 5
Old Testament, 38–39, 43, 45
Our Secret Constitution (Fletcher), 87

Paine, Thomas, 58, 81
Parsons, Theophilus, 58, 81
Pettigrew, Richard F., 138–39

Philippines, imperialism in, 122–32; economic arguments for annexation of, 123–24; God's role/will in political order, 127–28, 130–31, 137–39; purpose of joint resolution, 122–23; racial arguments/theories, 124–30, 136; self-conception of American people and, 115, 118–19, 121–22, 124, 131; self-government of Filipinos, 125–26, 128–29, 134, 138, 146–48

Pilgrims, 26–27

plurality: in the wake of the American political tradition, 117–18

political philosophy, development of, 15

political theory: and exceptionalism, 14–18

political tradition. *See* American political tradition

presidential office: as a facilitator, 82; imperial mindset in, 131–35; relationship with the Constitution, 89. *See also specific presidents*

Progressive Era, 19–20, 36, 87, 118, 145, 148, 150. *See also* Beveridge, Albert

Publius. See *Federalist* (Federalist Papers)

Pulitzer, Joseph, II, 120

Puritans: characteristics of political order, 75–76, 82–83; emigration justification, 28–35; expansionism vs. imperialism, 138–39; God's role/will in political order, 26–27, 76; ideas as a precursor to exceptionalism, 18–20; mission of, 27, 29; as Nonseparatist, 26, 30; political tradition and , 142–43; propagation of Christian truth,

28–29; Reformation, comparison to, 38; relationship to Beveridge, 137–39; worldview, 17. *See also* Winthrop, John

racial arguments/theories: Beveridge and, 124–30, 136; Roosevelt and, 132–35

Reagan, Ronald, 36

realpolitik, 118

"Reasons to Be Considered, and Objections with Answers" (Winthrop), 27–35; church construction, 32; corruption of European churches, 29–30, 41–42; corruption of seminaries and schools, 32; emigration of prominent citizens, 32; land use, 31–32; objections, 31–34; population surplus, 30–31; reasons, 28–33; self-improvement and salvation of the Puritans, 29–30, 41–42; spread of the Gospel, 28–29, 41; as a symbol in American tradition, 24; temptations in England, 32; will of God, 32–33

Reformation, 29, 35, 38, 41

Reformers, 29

religion: ties to exceptionalism, 9, 18–20. *See also* God's role/will in political order

representation: development of concept, 57

Republican Party, 100

revolution, right to, 96–97

Roosevelt, Theodore: Americans as liberators, 147; Beveridge and, 115, 131–35; distinction between inward and outward focus of mission, 138; "Fifth

Annual Message to Congress," 134–35; "First Annual Message to Congress," 132–33; idea of America, 141; inaugural address, 134; on intervention in other countries, 133–34; on Lincoln, 134; racial arguments/theories, 132–35; Wilson and, 135, 137; on Washington, 134
Ross, Dorothy, 124–25

Schuck, Peter H., 8
secession, 91–98, 100, 112
Second Continental Congress, 59, 61, 64. *See also* Continental Congress
self-conception, American: Beveridge on, 115, 118–19, 121–22, 124, 131; change of, 121; the Constitution and, 15–17; the Declaration of Independence, 15–17; education, 153; the founders and, 75–76; the Gettysburg Address, 99–105; patriotism, 137; political tradition, 152; during the Progressive Era, 145; as reflected in Roosevelt's policy toward the Philippines, 135; today, 145–46; Winthrop and, 24, 27
self-government: in the colonial period, 70; Filipinos and, 125–26, 128–29, 132–35, 138, 146–48; the founders and, 82; history's importance to, 4; and imperialism abroad, 3; question of, 147; secessionists and, 112; symbols of, 59, 77, 103; Wilson on, 137
separation of church and state: Beveridge on, 140; the Constitution and, 57–58; the founders and, 78–80, 108–9; Massachusetts Body of Liberties, 58
Shafer, Byron, 12–14

Shain, Barry, 80
simple distinctiveness: as one sense of American exceptionalism, 12–13
social science: on exceptionalism, 12–14
Sombart, Werner, 7
Spanish-American War, 119–22
Stalin, Joseph, 151
symbolism in American tradition: Beveridge and, 118, 131; the Constitution as, 67–68; Declaration of Independence, 60, 117; the *Federalist* as, 71–72, 113; the founders and, 55–57; Fundamental Orders of Connecticut as, 55–56; the Gettysburg Address as, 72, 110, 112–13; global politics as, 148; Kendall and Carey on, 15, 68, 116; Lincoln and, 102, 107–8, 112, 131, 140; "A Model of Christian Charity" as, 18, 24; new ideas of, 148; political theory and, 14–18; of self-government, 59, 77, 103; Winthrop and, 24–25, 54–55. *See also specific documents*

Tate, Allan, 149
theories of history. *See* history, theories of
Thurow, Glen, 105, 108, 110
Tocqueville, Alexis de, 9, 10–12, 36, 148–49, 153
tradition: plurality in, 117–18; theoretical problem of derailed tradition, 115–19; unraveling of, 116–18, 131, 141–43

Understanding America: The Anatomy of an Exceptional Nation (Schuck and Wilson), 8

Union: relationship to the government, 91–95, 97–98
uniting documents, 60
unity: the Constitution and, 67, 77, 88; the *Federalist* and, 76–78; Lincoln and, 102; in "A Model of Christian Charity," 36–40, 42–44, 55, 60, 62, 76–78; of a representative assembly, 57, 86
universality, 78–79, 99, 104–5, 109, 121, 128, 152
U.S. Congress. *See* Congress, U.S.
U.S. Constitution. *See* Constitution, U.S.
USS *Maine*. See *Maine*, USS

Virginia Declaration of Rights, 57–58, 62
Voegelin, Eric, 15–16, 24–27, 36, 55, 101, 110, 151

Washington, George, 79–80, 134
Why Is There No Socialism in the United States (Sombart), 7
Williams, Roger, 75
Wills, Gary, 103
Wilson, James Q., 8

Wilson, Woodrow, 115, 135–37, 141
Winthrop, John, 23–51; city on a hill, 23–24, 46–49; comparative exceptionalism and, 13, 48; end of the Massachusetts Bay Colony, 49–51, 57; exemplary exceptionalism of, 23–24, 49–51, 53–54; as the father of American exceptionalism, 9, 85–86; God's role/will in political order, 32–33, 39–40, 55, 80, 108; identity of the American people, 27; on love and political community, 39–43; "A Model of Christian Charity," 13, 18, 24, 28, 35–47 (*see also* "Model of Christian Charity, A"); political theory of American people, 24, 27; "Reasons to Be Considered, and Objections with Answers," 27–35 (*see also* "Reasons to Be Considered, and Objections with Answers"); the Reformation and, 29, 35, 38, 41; representation of people, 25; symbols in political tradition, 24–25, 54–55; theories of history and, 46–47, 69, 108–9. *See also* Puritans

CPSIA information can be obtained at www.ICGtesting.com
Printed in the USA
BVOW03*2154210713

325830BV00001B/1/P